Penguin Education

Organization Theory
Edited by D. S. Pugh

Penguin Modern Management Readings

General Editor
D. S. Pugh

Advisory Board
H. C. Edey
R. L. Edgerton
T. Kempner
T. Lupton
B. J. McCormick
P. G. Moore
R. W. Revans
F. J. Willett

Organization Theory

Selected Readings

Edited by D. S. Pugh

Penguin Books

Penguin Books Ltd,
Harmondsworth, Middlesex, England
Penguin Books, 625 Madison Avenue,
New York, New York 10022, U.S.A.
Penguin Books Australia Ltd,
Ringwood, Victoria, Australia
Penguin Books Canada Ltd, 2801 John Street,
Markham, Ontario, Canada L3R 1B4
Penguin Books (N.Z.) Ltd
182-190 Wairau Road, Auckland 10, New Zealand

First published 1971
Reprinted 1973, 1974, 1975, 1976, 1977, 1978, 1979

Copyright acknowledgements for items in this volume
will be found on page 373

Made and printed in Great Britain by
Cox & Wyman Ltd.
London, Reading and Fakenham
Set in Monotype Times

For my children, Helena, Jonathan and Rosalind,
who already spend most of their waking lives
in formal organizations

Contents

Part Three Behaviour in Organizations 213

Introduction

Organization theory is the body of thinking and writing which addresses itself to the problem of how to organize. The subject matter is very wide, and many other volumes in the Penguin Modern Management Readings cover particular aspects in considerable detail. The basis of selection for this wide-ranging volume has been to include those writers whose work has had a clear impact on subsequent thinking, practice and research in the subject. They have all stimulated work by others, some of it in support of their theories, some of it highly critical. Their views are the subject of much current debate. In every case (except one, which will be explained later) the readings are primary sources, so that the reader may be in a position to sample the direct impact of the writer and his work.

More specifically organization theory can be defined as the study of the structure, functioning and performance of organizations and the behaviour of groups and individuals within them. The subject has a long history which can be traced back, for example, to the Old Testament when decentralization through the appointment of judges was undertaken to relieve the load on the chief executive. The first English textbooks appeared in the thirteenth century[1]. It is, however, in the present century that the administrative, as distinct from the political, aspects have come to the fore. It is also in this century that the impact of social science thinking has built up until it has become a major force. It is still, though, a heterogeneous study, with the systematic analysis of sociologists, psychologists and economists mingling with distilled practical experience of managers, administrators and consultants.

These writers have attempted to draw together information and distil theories of how organizations function and how they should be managed. Their writings have been theoretical in the sense that they have tried to discover generalizations applicable to all organizations. Every act of a manager rests on assumptions about

1. e.g. Robert Grosseteste, *The Rules of Saint Robert*: cf. Keil (1965).

what has happened and conjectures about what will happen; that is to say it rests on theory. Theory and practice are inseparable. As a cynic once put it: when someone says he is a practical man, what he means is that he is using old-fashioned theories! All the writers on this subject, who include many busy chief executives, believe that there is a necessity continually to examine, criticize and up-date thinking about the organization and how it functions if it is to develop and not to decay.

The concept of organizational behaviour is basic to this field. From this point of view the task of management can be considered as the organization of individuals' behaviour in relation to the physical means and resources to achieve the desired goal. The basic problem in this subject to which all writing may be related is: '*How much* organization and control of behaviour is necessary for efficient functioning?' It is in the implied answer to this question on the control of organizational behaviour that two sides of a continuing debate may be usefully distinguished. On the one hand there are those who may be called the 'organizers' who maintain that more and better control is necessary for efficiency. They point to the advantage of specialization and clear job definitions, standard routines and clear lines of authority. On the other hand there are those who, in this context, may be called the 'behaviouralists' who maintain that the continuing attempt to increase control over behaviour is self-defeating; that the inevitable rigidity in functioning, apathy in performance, and counter-control through informal relationships, means that increased efficiency does not necessarily occur with increased control. Even when it does it is only in the short term and at the cost of internal conflict and greatly reducing the organization's ability to cope with the inevitable environmental changes which take place in the long term.

It is around this continuing dilemma that the study of organization theory takes place. It is a dilemma because, of course, both sides of the discussion are right. It is not possible to opt for one view *to the exclusion of* the other, and it is one of the basic tasks of management to determine the optimum degree of control necessary to operate efficiently. This must be affected by many factors, such as the size of the organization, the training and experience of its members and the techniques used in the manufacture of the product or the carrying out of the service. It is through a study of the constraints in relation to the objectives that the most efficient organizational control systems can be established.

This volume has been arranged, inevitably somewhat arbitrarily, in three separate but highly inter-related sections. In Part One the selection focuses on the structure of organizations, examining the workings of the authority, task allocation and communication systems. Part Two is concerned with the management of organizations, the functions and the processes which it involves. Part Three on behaviour in organizations presents the work of those who have studied the effects of the form of organization and management on the behaviour of its members.

I am grateful to Iain Rangeley who compiled the Index and to Sue Taylor for secretarial assistance.

Reference

KEIL, I. (1965), 'Advice to the magnates: management education in the 13th century', *Bulletin of the Association of Teachers of Management*, no. 17, March, pp. 2–8.

Part One The Structure of Organizations

All organizations have to make provision for continuing
activities directed toward the achievement of given aims.
Regularities in activities such as task allocation, coordination and
supervision are established which constitute the organization's
structure. The contributors to this section examine in a systematic
way, comparatively across numbers of organizations, the causes
and the results of structural forms encountered.

Weber (Reading 1) analysed three general types of organization
stemming from the bases of wielding authority, and drew
attention to the fact that in modern society the bureaucratic type
has become dominant because, he considered, of its greater
technical efficiency. In doing so he formed the starting point of a
series of sociological studies designed to examine the nature and
functioning of bureaucracy, and particularly to draw attention to
the disfunctions of this structural form which were left out of the
original analysis. The contribution of March and Simon
(Reading 2) is the only one in this volume which is not a primary
source, and it is included because it cogently and creatively
summarizes many studies which have been undertaken with this
'bureaucratic disfunction' approach. They show that the
inadequacies of bureaucracy may, paradoxically, be just as great
a cause for its perpetuation as its efficiencies. Burns (Reading 3)
forms one culmination of this approach when he contrasts, on the
basis of studies of firms in stable and changing environmental
conditions, bureaucratic with organismic structures. In the latter,
authority, task allocation and communication are extremely
flexible, in contrast to the rigid rules and procedures of
bureaucracy.

Woodward (Reading 4) presented results to suggest that the structure of manufacturing concerns is strongly related to the technology of production and thus opened a debate on whether it is possible to conceive of basic principles of structure which are appropriate to all organizations. The paper by Leavitt (Reading 5) is the best known of a large series of laboratory studies of 'organizations' where the relationship of authority and communication networks to the achievement of the participants is explored.

1 M. Weber

Legitimate Authority and Bureaucracy

From M. Weber, *The Theory of Social and Economic Organisation*, Free Press, 1947, translated and edited by A. M. Henderson and T. Parsons, pp. 328–40. (Footnotes as in the original).

The three pure types of legitimate authority

There are three pure types of legitimate authority. The validity of their claims to legitimacy may be based on:

1. Rational grounds – resting on a belief in the 'legality' of patterns of normative rules and the right of those elevated to authority under such rules to issue commands (legal authority).

2. Traditional grounds – resting on an established belief in the sanctity of immemorial traditions and the legitimacy of the status of those exercising authority under them (traditional authority); or finally,

3. Charismatic grounds – resting on devotion to the specific and exceptional sanctity, heroism or exemplary character of an individual person, and of the normative patterns or order revealed or ordained by him (charismatic authority).

In the case of legal authority, obedience is owed to the legally established impersonal order. It extends to the persons exercising the authority of office under it only by virtue of the formal legality of their commands and only within the scope of authority of the office. In the case of traditional authority, obedience is owed to the *person* of the chief who occupies the traditionally sanctioned position of authority and who is (within its sphere) bound by tradition. But here the obligation of obedience is not based on the impersonal order, but is a matter of personal loyalty within the area of accustomed obligations. In the case of charismatic author-ity, it is the charismatically qualified leader as such who is obeyed by virtue of personal trust in him and his revelation, his heroism or his exemplary qualities so far as they fall within the scope of the individual's belief in his charisma.

1. The usefulness of the above classification can only be judged by its results in promoting systematic analysis. The concept of 'charisma' ('the gift of grace') is taken from the vocabulary of early Christianity. For the Christian religious organization Rudolf Sohm, in his *Kirchenrecht*, was the first to clarify the substance of the concept, even though he did not use the same terminology. Others (for instance, Hollin, *Enthusiasmus und Bussgewalt*) have clarified certain important consequences of it It is thus nothing new.

2. The fact that none of these three ideal types, the elucidation of which will occupy the following pages, is usually to be found in historical cases in 'pure' form, is naturally not a valid objection to attempting their conceptual formulation in the sharpest possible form. In this respect the present case is no different from many others. Later on the transformation of pure charisma by the process of routinization will be discussed and thereby the relevance of the concept to the understanding of empirical systems of authority considerably increased. But even so it may be said of every empirically historical phenomenon of authority that it is not likely to be 'as an open book'. Analysis in terms of sociological types has, after all, as compared with purely empirical historical investigation, certain advantages which should not be minimized. That is, it can in the particular case of a concrete form of authority determine what conforms to or approximates such types as 'charisma', 'hereditary charisma', 'the charisma of office', 'patriarchy', 'bureaucracy', the authority of status groups,[1] and in doing so it can work with relatively unambiguous concepts. But the idea that the whole of concrete historical reality can be exhausted in the conceptual scheme about to be developed is as far from the author's thoughts as anything could be.

1. *Ständische*. There is no really acceptable English rendering of this term. – Ed.

Legal authority with a bureaucratic administrative staff[2]

Legal authority: The pure type with employment of a
bureaucratic administrative staff

The effectiveness of legal authority rests on the acceptance of the validity of the following mutually inter-dependent ideas.

1. That any given legal norm may be established by agreement or by imposition, on grounds of expediency or rational values or both, with a claim to obedience at least on the part of the members of the corporate group. This is, however, usually extended to include all persons within the sphere of authority or of power in question – which in the case of territorial bodies is the territorial area – who stand in certain social relationships or carry out forms of social action which in the order governing the corporate group have been declared to be relevant.

2. That every body of law consists essentially in a consistent system of abstract rules which have normally been intentionally established. Furthermore, administration of law is held to consist in the application of these rules to particular cases; the administrative process in the rational pursuit of the interests which are specified in the order governing the corporate group within the limits laid down by legal precepts and following principles which are capable of generalized formulation and are approved in the order governing the group, or at least not disapproved in it.

3. That thus the typical person in authority occupies an 'office'. In the action associated with his status, including the commands he issues to others, he is subject to an impersonal order to which his actions are oriented. This is true not only for persons exercising legal authority who are in the usual sense 'officials', but, for instance, for the elected president of a state.

4. That the person who obeys authority does so, as it is usually stated, only in his capacity as a 'member' of the corporate group and what he obeys is only 'the law'. He may in this connection be the member of an association, of a territorial commune, of a church, or a citizen of a state.

2. The specifically modern type of administration has intentionally been taken as a point of departure in order to make it possible later to contrast the others with it.

5. In conformity with point 3, it is held that the members of the corporate group, in so far as they obey a person in authority, do not owe this obedience to him as an individual, but to the impersonal order. Hence, it follows that there is an obligation to obedience only within the sphere of the rationally delimited authority which, in terms of the order, has been conferred upon him.

The following may thus be said to be the fundamental categories of rational legal authority:

1. A continuous organization of official functions bound by rules.

2. A specified sphere of competence. This involves (a) a sphere of obligations to perform functions which has been marked off as part of a systematic division of labour. (b) The provision of the incumbent with the necessary authority to carry out these functions. (c) That the necessary means of compulsion are clearly defined and their use is subject to definite conditions. A unit exercising authority which is organized in this way will be called an 'administrative organ'.[3]

There are administrative organs in this sense in large-scale private organizations, in parties and armies, as well as in the state and the church. An elected president, a cabinet of ministers, or a body of elected representatives also in this sense constitute administrative organs. This is not, however, the place to discuss these concepts. Not every administrative organ is provided with compulsory powers. But this distinction is not important for present purposes.

3. The organization of offices follows the principle of hierarchy; that is, each lower office is under the control and supervision of a higher one. There is a right of appeal and of statement of grievances from the lower to the higher. Hierarchies differ in respect to whether and in what cases complaints can lead to a ruling from an authority at various points higher in the scale, and as to whether changes are imposed from higher up or the responsibility for such changes is left to the lower office, the conduct of which was the subject of complaint.

4. The rules which regulate the conduct of an office may be tech-

3. *Behörde.*

nical rules or norms.[4] In both cases, if their application is to be fully rational, specialized training is necessary. It is thus normally true that only a person who has demonstrated an adequate technical training is qualified to be a member of the administrative staff of such an organized group, and hence only such persons are eligible for appointment to official positions. The administrative staff of a rational corporate group thus typically consists of 'officials', whether the organization be devoted to political, religious, economic – in particular, capitalistic – or other ends.

5. In the rational type it is a matter of principle that the members of the administrative staff should be completely separated from ownership of the means of production or administration. Officials, employees and workers attached to the administrative staff do not themselves own the non-human means of production and administration. These are rather provided for their use in kind or in money, and the official is obligated to render an accounting of their use. There exists, furthermore, in principle complete separation of the property belonging to the organization, which is controlled within the sphere of office, and the personal property of the official, which is available for his own private uses. There is a corresponding separation of the place in which official functions are carried out, the 'office' in the sense of premises, from living quarters.

6. In the rational type case, there is also a complete absence of appropriation of his official position by the incumbent. Where 'rights' to an office exist, as in the case of judges, and recently of an increasing proportion of officials and even of workers, they do not normally serve the purpose of appropriation by the official, but of securing the purely objective and independent character of the conduct of the office so that it is oriented only to the relevant norms.

7. Administrative acts, decisions and rules are formulated and

4. Weber does not explain this distinction. By a 'technical rule' he probably means a prescribed course of action which is dictated primarily on grounds touching efficiency of the performance of the immediate functions, while by 'norms' he probably means rules which limit conduct on grounds other than those of efficiency. Of course, in one sense all rules are norms in that they are prescriptions for conduct, conformity with which is problematical. – Ed.

recorded in writing, even in cases where oral discussion is the rule or is even mandatory. This applies at least to preliminary discussions and proposals, to final decisions and to all sorts of orders and rules. The combination of written documents and a continuous organization of official functions constitutes the 'office' [5] which is the central focus of all types of modern corporate action.

8. Legal authority can be exercised in a wide variety of different forms which will be distinguished and discussed later. The following analysis will be deliberately confined for the most part to the aspect of imperative coordination in the structure of the administrative staff. It will consist in an analysis in terms of ideal types of officialdom or 'bureaucracy'.

In the above outline no mention has been made of the kind of supreme head appropriate to a system of legal authority. This is a consequence of certain considerations which can only be made entirely understandable at a later stage in the analysis. There are very important types of rational imperative coordination which, with respect to the ultimate source of authority, belong to other categories. This is true of the hereditary charismatic type, as illustrated by hereditary monarchy and of the pure charismatic type of a president chosen by plebiscite. Other cases involve rational elements at important points, but are made up of a combination of bureaucratic and charismatic components, as is true of the cabinet form of government. Still others are subject to the authority of the chief of other corporate groups, whether their character be charismatic or bureaucratic; thus the formal head of a government department under a parliamentary regime may be a minister who occupies his position because of his authority in a party. The type of rational, legal administrative staff is capable of application in

5. *Bureau*. It has seemed necessary to use the English word 'office' in three different meanings, which are distinguished in Weber's discussion by at least two terms. The first is *Amt*, which means 'office' in the sense of the institutionally defined status of a person. The second is the 'work premises' as in the expression 'he spent the afternoon in his office'. For this Weber uses *Bureau* as also for the third meaning which he has just defined, the 'organized work process of a group'. In this last sense an office is a particular type of 'organization', or *Betrieb* in Weber's sense. This use is established in English in such expressions as 'the District Attorney's Office has such and such functions.' Which of the three meanings is involved in a given case will generally be clear from the context. – Ed.

all kinds of situations and contexts. It is the most important mechanism for the administration of everyday profane affairs. For in that sphere, the exercise of authority and, more broadly, imperative coordination, consists precisely in administration.

The purest type of exercise of legal authority is that which employs a bureaucratic administrative staff. Only the supreme chief of the organization occupies his position of authority by virtue of appropriation, of election or of having been designated for the succession. But even *his* authority consists in a sphere of legal 'competence'. The whole administrative staff under the supreme authority then consists, in the purest type, of individual officials who are appointed and function according to the following criteria:[6]

1. They are personally free and subject to authority only with respect to their impersonal official obligations.

2. They are organized in a clearly defined hierarchy of offices.

3. Each office has a clearly defined sphere of competence in the legal sense.

4. The office is filled by a free contractual relationship. Thus, in principle, there is free selection.

5. Candidates are selected on the basis of technical qualifications. In the most rational case, this is tested by examination or guaranteed by diplomas certifying technical training, or both. They are *appointed*, not elected.

6. They are remunerated by fixed salaries in money, for the most part with a right to pensions. Only under certain circumstances does the employing authority, especially in private organizations, have a right to terminate the appointment, but the official is always free to resign. The salary scale is primarily graded according to rank in the hierarchy: but in addition to this criterion, the responsibility of the position and the requirements of the incumbent's social status may be taken into account.

7. The office is treated as the sole, or at least the primary, occupation of the incumbent.

6. This characterization applies to the 'monocratic' as opposed to the 'collegial' type, which will be discussed below [not included].

8. It constitutes a career. There is a system of 'promotion' according to seniority or to achievement, or both. Promotion is dependent on the judgment of superiors.

9. The official works entirely separated from ownership of the means of administration and without appropriation of his position.

10. He is subject to strict and systematic discipline and control in the conduct of the office.

This type of organization is in principle applicable with equal facility to a wide variety of different fields. It may be applied in profit-making business or in charitable organizations, or in any number of other types of private enterprises serving ideal or material ends. It is equally applicable to political and to religious organizations. With varying degrees of approximation to a pure type, its historical existence can be demonstrated in all these fields.

1. For example, this type of bureaucracy is found in private clinics, as well as in endowed hospitals or the hospitals maintained by religious orders. Bureaucratic organization has played a major role in the Catholic Church. It is well illustrated by the administrative role of the priesthood[7] in the modern church, which has expropriated almost all of the old church benefices, which were in former days to a large extent subject to private appropriation. It is also illustrated by the conception of the universal Episcopate, which is thought of as formally constituting a universal legal competence in religious matters. Similarly, the doctrine of Papal infallibility is thought of as in fact involving a universal competence, but only one which functions *ex cathedra* in the sphere of the office, thus implying the typical distinction between the sphere of office and that of the private affairs of the incumbent. The same phenomena are found in the large-scale capitalistic enterprise; and the larger it is, the greater their role. And this is not less true of political parties, which will be discussed separately. Finally, the modern army is essentially a bureaucratic organization administered by that peculiar type of military functionary, the 'officer'.

2. Bureaucratic authority is carried out in its purest form where it is most clearly dominated by the principle of appointment. There is no such thing as a hierarchy of elected officials in the same sense as

7. *Kaplanokratie.*

there is a hierarchical organization of appointed officials. In the first place, election makes it impossible to attain a stringency of discipline even approaching that in the appointed type. For it is open to a subordinate official to compete for elective honours on the same terms as his superiors, and his prospects are not dependent on the superior's judgment.[8]

3. Appointment by free contract, which makes free selection possible, is essential to modern bureaucracy. Where there is a hierarchical organization with impersonal spheres of competence, but occupied by unfree officials – like slaves or dependents, who, however, function in a formally bureaucratic manner – the term 'patrimonial bureaucracy' will be used.

4. The role of technical qualifications in bureaucratic organizations is continually increasing. Even an official in a party or a trade-union organization is in need of specialized knowledge, though it is usually of an empirical character, developed by experience, rather than by formal training. In the modern state, the only 'offices' for which no technical qualifications are required are those of ministers and presidents. This only goes to prove that they are 'officials' only in a formal sense, and not substantively, as is true of the managing director or president of a large business corporation. There is no question but that the 'position' of the capitalistic entrepreneur is as definitely appropriated as is that of a monarch. Thus at the top of a bureaucratic organization, there is necessarily an element which is at least not purely bureaucratic. The category of bureaucracy is one applying only to the exercise of control by means of a particular kind of administrative staff.

5. The bureaucratic official normally receives a fixed salary. By contrast, sources of income which are privately appropriated will be called 'benefices'.[9] Bureaucratic salaries are also normally paid in money. Though this is not essential to the concept of bureaucracy, it is the arrangement which best fits the pure type. Payments in kind are apt to have the character of benefices, and the receipt of a benefice normally implies the appropriation of opportunities for earnings and of positions. There are, however, gradual transitions in this field with many intermediate types. Appropriation by

8. On elective officials.
9. *Pfrüden.*

virtue of leasing or sale of offices or the pledge of income from office are phenomena foreign to the pure type of bureaucracy.

6. 'Offices' which do not constitute the incumbent's principal occupation, in particular 'honorary' offices, belong in other categories. The typical 'bureaucratic' official occupies the office as his principal occupation.

7. With respect to the separation of the official from ownership of the means of administration, the situation is essentially the same in the field of public administration and in private bureaucratic organizations, such as the large-scale capitalistic enterprise.

8. Collegial bodies will be discussed separately below [not included]. At the present time they are rapidly decreasing in importance in favour of types of organization which are in fact, and for the most part formally as well, subject to the authority of a single head. For instance, the collegial 'governments' in Prussia have long since given way to the monocratic 'district president'.[10] The decisive factor in this development has been the need for rapid, clear decisions, free of the necessity of compromise between different opinions and also free of shifting majorities.

9. The modern army officer is a type of appointed official who is clearly marked off by certain class distinctions. This will be discussed elsewhere [not included]. In this respect such officers differ radically from elected military leaders, from charismatic condottieri, from the type of officers who recruit and lead mercenary armies as a capitalistic enterprise, and, finally, from the incumbents of commissions which have been purchased. There may be gradual transitions between these types. The patrimonial 'retainer', who is separated from the means of carrying out his function, and the proprietor of a mercenary army for capitalistic purposes have, along with the private capitalistic entrepreneur, been pioneers in the organization of the modern type of bureaucracy. This will be discussed in detail below.[11]

10. *Regierungs präsident.*

11. The parts of Weber's work included in this translation contain only fragmentary discussions of military organization. It was a subject in which Weber was greatly interested and to which he attributed great importance for social phenomena generally. This factor is one on which, for the ancient world, he laid great stress in his important study, *Agrarverhältnisse im Altertum.* Though at various points in the rest of *Wirtschaft und Gesellschaft*

The monocratic type of bureaucratic administration

Experience tends universally to show that the purely bureaucratic type of administrative organization – that is, the monocratic variety of bureaucracy – is, from a purely technical point of view, capable of attaining the highest degree of efficiency and is in this sense formally the most rational known means of carrying out imperative control over human beings. It is superior to any other form in precision, in stability, in the stringency of its discipline, and in its reliability. It thus makes possible a particularly high degree of calculability of results for the heads of the organization and for those acting in relation to it. It is finally superior both in intensive efficiency and in the scope of its operations, and is formally capable of application to all kinds of administrative tasks.

The development of the modern form of the organization of corporate groups in all fields is nothing less than identical with the development and continual spread of bureaucratic administration. This is true of church and state, of armies, political parties, economic enterprises, organizations to promote all kinds of causes, private associations, clubs, and many others. Its development is, to take the most striking case, the most crucial phenomenon of the modern Western state. However many forms there may be which do not appear to fit this pattern, such as collegial representative bodies, parliamentary committees, soviets, honorary officers, lay judges, and what not, and however much people may complain about the 'evils of bureaucracy', it would be sheer illusion to think for a moment that continuous administrative work can be carried out in any field except by means of officials working in offices. The whole pattern of everyday life is cut to fit this framework. For bureaucratic administration is, other things being equal, always, from a formal, technical point of view, the most rational type. For the needs of mass administration today, it is completely indispensable. The choice is only that between bureaucracy and dilletantism in the field of administration.

The primary source of the superiority of bureaucratic administration lies in the role of technical knowledge which, through the development of modern technology and business methods in the

the subject comes up, it is probable that he intended to treat it systematically but that this was never done. – Ed.

production of goods, has become completely indispensable. In this respect, it makes no difference whether the economic system is organized on a capitalistic or a socialistic basis. Indeed, if in the latter case a comparable level of technical efficiency were to be achieved, it would mean a tremendous increase in the importance of specialized bureaucracy.

When those subject to bureaucratic control seek to escape the influence of the existing bureaucratic apparatus, this is normally possible only by creating an organization of their own which is equally subject to the process of bureaucratization. Similarly the existing bureaucratic apparatus is driven to continue functioning by the most powerful interests which are material and objective, but also ideal in character. Without it, a society like our own – with a separation of officials, employees, and workers from ownership of the means of administration, dependent on discipline and on technical training – could no longer function. The only exception would be those groups, such as the peasantry, who are still in possession of their own means of subsistence. Even in case of revolution by force or of occupation by an enemy, the bureaucratic machinery will normally continue to function just as it has for the previous legal government.

The question is always who controls the existing bureaucratic machinery. And such control is possible only in a very limited degree to persons who are not technical specialists. Generally speaking, the trained permanent official is more likely to get his way in the long run than his nominal superior, the Cabinet minister, who is not a specialist.

Though by no means alone, the capitalistic system has undeniably played a major role in the development of bureaucracy. Indeed, without it capitalistic production could not continue and any rational type of socialism would have simply to take it over and increase its importance. Its development, largely under capitalistic auspices, has created an urgent need for stable, strict, intensive, and calculable administration. It is this need which gives bureaucracy a crucial role in our society as the central element in any kind of large-scale administration. Only by reversion in every field – political, religious, economic, etc. – to small-scale organization would it be possible to any considerable extent to escape its influence. On the one hand, capitalism in its modern stages of development strongly tends to foster the development of bureaucracy, though both capitalism and bureaucracy have arisen from many different historical sources. Conversely, capitalism is the most rational economic basis for bureaucratic administration and enables it to develop in the most rational form, especially because, from a fiscal point of view, it supplies the necessary money resources.

Along with these fiscal conditions of efficient bureaucratic administration, there are certain extremely important conditions in the fields of communication and transportation. The precision of its functioning requires the services of the railway, the telegraph and the telephone, and becomes increasingly dependent on them. A socialistic form of organization would not alter this fact. It would be a question whether in a socialistic system it would be possible to provide conditions for carrying out as stringent bureaucratic organization as has been possible in a capitalistic order. For socialism would, in fact, require a still higher degree of formal bureaucratization than capitalism. If this should prove not to be possible, it would demonstrate the existence of another of those fundamental elements of irrationality in social systems – a conflict between formal and substantive rationality of the sort which sociology so often encounters.

Bureaucratic administration means fundamentally the exercise of control on the basis of knowledge. This is the feature of it which makes it specifically rational. This consists on the one hand in technical knowledge which, by itself, is sufficient to ensure it a position of extraordinary power. But in addition to this, bureaucratic organizations, or the holders of power who make use of them, have the tendency to increase their power still further by the knowledge growing out of experience in the service. For they acquire through the conduct of office a special knowledge of facts and have available a store of documentary material peculiar to themselves. While not peculiar to bureaucratic organizations, the concept of 'official secrets' is certainly typical of them. It stands in relation to technical knowledge in somewhat the same position as commercial secrets do to technological training. It is a product of the striving for power.

Bureaucracy is superior in knowledge, including both technical knowledge and knowledge of the concrete fact within its own sphere of interest, which is usually confined to the interests of a private business – a capitalistic enterprise. The capitalistic entrepreneur is, in our society, the only type who has been able to maintain at least relative immunity from subjection to the control of rational bureaucratic knowledge. All the rest of the population have tended to be organized in large-scale corporate groups which are inevitably subject to bureaucratic control. This is as inevitable as the dominance of precision machinery in the mass production of goods.

The following are the principal more general social consequences of bureaucratic control:

1. The tendency to 'levelling' in the interest of the broadest possible basis of recruitment in terms of technical competence.

2. The tendency to plutocracy growing out of the interest in the greatest possible length of technical training. Today this often lasts up to the age of thirty.

3. The dominance of a spirit of formalistic impersonality, *sine ira et studio*, without hatred or passion, and hence without affection or enthusiasm. The dominant norms are concepts of straightforward duty without regard to personal considerations. Everyone is subject to formal equality of treatment; that is, everyone in the same empirical situation. This is the spirit in which the ideal official conducts his office.

The development of bureaucracy greatly favours the levelling of social classes and this can be shown historically to be the normal tendency. Conversely, every process of social levelling creates a favourable situation for the development of bureaucracy; for it tends to eliminate class privileges, which include the appropriation of means of administration and the appropriation of authority as well as the occupation of offices on an honorary basis or as an avocation by virtue of wealth. This combination everywhere inevitably foreshadows the development of mass democracy, which will be discussed in another connection.

The 'spirit' of rational bureaucracy has normally the following general characteristics:

1. Formalism, which is promoted by all the interests which are concerned with the security of their own personal situation, whatever

this may consist in. Otherwise the door would be open to arbitrariness and hence formalism is the line of least resistance.

2. There is another tendency, which is apparently in contradiction to the above, a contradiction which is in part genuine. It is the tendency of officials to treat their official function from what is substantively a utilitarian point of view in the interest of the welfare of those under their authority. But this utilitarian tendency is generally expressed in the enactment of corresponding regulatory measures which themselves have a formal character and tend to be treated in a formalistic spirit. This tendency to substantive rationality is supported by all those subject to authority who are not included in the class mentioned above as interested in the security of advantages already controlled. The problems which open up at this point belong in the theory of 'democracy'.

2 J. G. March and H. A. Simon

The Dysfunctions of Bureaucracy

Extract from J. G. March and H. A. Simon, *Organizations*, Wiley, 1958, chapter 3, pp. 36–47.

Modern studies of 'bureaucracies' date from Weber (1946, 1947) as to both time and acknowledged intellectual debt. But, in a sense, Weber belongs more to the preceding chapter than he does to the present one. His major interests in the study of organizations appear to have been four: (1) to identify the characteristics of an entity he labelled 'bureaucracy'; (2) to describe its growth and the reasons for its growth; (3) to isolate the concomitant social changes; (4) to discover the consequences of bureaucratic organization for the achievement of bureaucratic goals (primarily the goals of a political authority). It is in the last-named interest that Weber most clearly differentiates himself from the other writers who will be considered here. Weber wishes to show to what extent bureaucratic organization is a rational solution to the complexities of modern problems. More specifically, he wishes to show in what ways bureaucratic organization overcomes the decision-making or 'computational' limits of individuals or alternative forms of organization (i.e., through specialization, division of labor, etc.).

Consequently, Weber appears to have more in common with Urwick, Gulick, and others than he does with those who regard themselves as his successors. To be sure, Weber goes beyond the 'machine' model in significant ways. In particular, he analyses in some detail the relation between an official and his office. But, in general, Weber perceives bureaucracy as an adaptive device for using specialized skills, and he is not exceptionally attentive to the character of the human organism.

When we turn from Weber to the more recent students of bureaucracy, however, we find them paying increasing attention to the 'un-anticipated' responses of the organization members (Merton, 1936; Gouldner, 1957). Without denying Weber's essential proposition that bureaucracies are more efficient (with respect to the goals of the formal hierarchy) than are alternative forms of organization, the research and analyses of Merton (1940), Selznick (1949) and Gouldner (1954) have suggested important dysfunctional consequences of bureaucratic organization. In addition – explicitly in the case of Gouldner and implicitly in the other two authors – they have hypothesized that the unintended consequences of treating individuals as machines actually encourage a continued use of the 'machine' model.

The general structure of the theoretical systems of all three writers is remarkably similar. They use as the basic independent variable some form of organization or organizational procedure designed to control the activities of the organization members. These procedures are based primarily on what we have called the 'machine' model of human behavior. They are shown to have the consequences anticipated by the organizational leaders, but also to have other, unanticipated consequences. In turn, these consequences reinforce the tendency to use the control device. Thus, the systems may be depicted as in Figure 1.

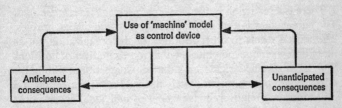

Figure 1 The general bureaucracy model

The several systems examined here posit different sets of variables and theoretical relations. However, their structures are sufficiently similar to suggest that these studies in 'bureaucracy' belong to a single class of theories.

The Merton model

Merton (1940) is concerned with dysfunctional organizational learning: organization members generalize a response from situations where the response is appropriate to similar situations where it results in consequences unanticipated and undesired by the organization. Merton asserts that changes in the personality of individual members of the organization stem from factors in the organizational structure. Here personality refers to any fairly reliable connection between certain stimuli and the characteristic responses to them. The label 'personality' is attached to such a response pattern when the pattern does not change easily or rapidly.

Merton's system of propositions begins with a *demand for control* made on the organization by the top hierarchy. This demand takes the form of an increased *emphasis on the reliability of behavior* within the organization. From the point of view of the top hierarchy, this represents a need for accountability and predictability of behavior. The techniques used to secure reliability draw upon what has been called here the 'machine' model of human behavior. Standard operating procedures are instituted, and control consists largely in checking to ensure that these procedures are, in fact, followed.

Three consequences follow from this emphasis on reliability in behavior and the techniques used to install it:

1. There is a reduction in the *amount of personalized relationships*. The bureaucracy is a set of relationships between offices, or roles. The official reacts to other members of the organization not as more or less unique individuals but as representatives of positions that have specified rights and duties. Competition within the organization occurs within closely defined limits; evaluation and promotion are relatively independent of individual achievement (e.g., promotion by seniority).

2. *Internalization of the rules of the organization* by the participants is increased. Rules originally devised to achieve organizational goals assume a positive value that is independent of the organizational goals. However, it is important to distinguish two phenomena, both of which have been called the 'displacement of goals'. In one case, a given stimulus evokes an activity perceived as leading to a preferred state of affairs. In a series of such situations, the repeated choice of the acceptable alternative causes a gradual transfer of the preference from the final state of affairs to the instrumental activity. In the other case, the choice of a desired alternative reveals additional desirable consequences not originally

anticipated. The instrumental activity has, therefore, positively valued consequences even when it does not have the originally anticipated outcomes. It is this latter phenomenon (secondary reinforcement) that is operating in the present situation: the organizational setting brings about new personal or subunit consequences through participation in organizationally motivated actions.

3. There is increased *use of categorization as a decision-making technique*. To be sure, categorizing is a basic part of thinking in any situation. The special feature involved here is a tendency to restrict the categories used to a relatively small number and to enforce the first formally applicable category rather than search for the possible categories that might be applied and choose among them. An increase in the use of categorization for decision making decreases the *amount of search for alternatives*.

The reduction in personalized relationships, the increased internalization of rules, and the decreased search for alternatives combine to make the behavior of members of the organization highly predictable; i.e., they result in an increase in the *rigidity of behavior* of participants. At the same time, the reduction in personalized relationships (particularly with respect to internal competition) facilitates the development of an *esprit de corps*, i.e., increases the *extent to which goals are perceived as shared among members of the group*. Such a sense of commonness of purpose, interests and character increases the *propensity of organization members to defend each other against outside pressures*. This, in turn, solidifies the tendency toward rigid behavior.

The rigidity of behavior has three major consequences. First, it substantially satisfies the original demands for reliability. Thus, it meets an important maintenance need of the system. Further needs of this sort are met by strengthening in-group identification, as previously mentioned. Second, it increases the *defensibility of individual action*. Simple categories rigorously applied to individual cases without regard for personal features can only be challenged at a higher level of the hierarchy. Third, the rigidity of behavior increases the *amount of difficulty with clients* of the organization and complicates the achievement of client satisfaction – a near-universal organizational goal. Difficulty with clients is further

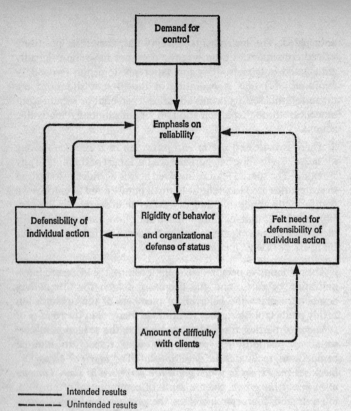

Intended results
------ Unintended results

Figure 2 The simplified Merton model

increased by an increase in the *extent of use of trappings of authority* by subordinates in the organization, a procedure that is encouraged by the in-group's defensiveness.

The maintenance of part of the system by the techniques previously outlined produces a continuing pressure to maintain these techniques, as would be anticipated. It is somewhat more difficult to explain why the organization would continue to apply the same techniques in the face of client dissatisfaction. Why do organizational members fail to behave in each case in a manner appropriate to the situation? For the answer one must extend Merton's explicit statements by providing at least one, and perhaps two, additional feedback loops in the system. (It is not enough to say that such behavior becomes a part of the 'personality'. One must offer some explanation of why this apparently maladaptive learning takes place.)

The second major consequence of rigidity in behavior mentioned above (increased defensibility of individual action) is a deterrent to discrimination that reinforces the emphasis on reliability of behavior. In addition, client dissatisfaction may in itself reinforce rigidity. On the one hand, client pressure at lower levels in the hierarchy tends to increase the *felt need for the defensibility of individual action*. On the other hand, remedial action demanded by clients from higher officials in the hierarchy may be misdirected. To the extent to which clients perceive themselves as being victims of discrimination (a perception that is facilitated in American culture by the importance attached to 'equal treatment'), the proposals of clients or of the officials to whom they complain will probably strengthen the emphasis on reliability of behavior. This conflict between 'service' and 'impartiality' as goals for public organizations seems to lie behind a good deal of the literature on public bureaucracies.

We see that Merton's model is a rather complex set of relations among a relatively large number of variables. A simplified version of the model, designed to illustrate its major features, is provided in Figure 2.

The Selznick model

Where Merton emphasizes rules as a response to the demand for control, Selznick (1949) emphasizes the delegation of authority. Like Merton, however, Selznick wishes to show how the use of a control technique (i.e., delegation) brings about a series of unanticipated consequences. Also, like Merton, Selznick shows how these consequences stem from the problems of maintaining highly interrelated systems of interpersonal relations.

Selznick's model starts with the demand for control made by the top hierarchy. As a result of this demand, an increased *delegation of authority* is instituted.

Delegation, however, has several immediate consequences. As intended, it increases the *amount of training in specialized competences*. Restriction of attention to a relatively small number of problems increases experience within these limited areas and improves the employee's ability to deal with these problems. Operating through this mechanism, delegation tends to decrease the *difference between organizational goals and achievement*, and thus to stimulate more delegation. At the same time, however, delegation results in departmentalization and an increase in the *bifurcation of interests* among the subunits in the organization. The maintenance needs of the subunits dictate a commitment to the subunit goals over and above their contribution to the total organizational program. Many individual needs depend on the continued success and even expansion of the subunit. As in the previous example, the activities originally evaluated in terms of the organization goals are seen to have additional important ramifications for the subunits.

Bifurcation of interests is also stimulated by the specialized training that delegation (intendedly) produces. Training results in increased competence and, therefore, in increased *costs of changing personnel* and this results, in turn, in further differentiation of subunit goals.

The bifurcation within the organization leads to increased *conflict among organizational subunits*. As a consequence, the *content of decisions* made within the organization depends increasingly upon considerations of internal strategy, particularly if there is little *internalization of organizational goals by participants*. As a result there is an increase in the difference between organizational goals and achievement and this results in an increase in delegation. (The general subject of intraorganizational conflict is discussed in Chapter 5.)

This effect on daily decisions is accentuated by two other mechanisms in Selznick's system. The struggle for internal control not only affects directly the content of decisions, but also causes greater *elaboration of subunit ideologies*. Each subunit seeks success by fitting its policy into the official doctrine of the large organization to legitimize its demands. Such a tactic increases the *internalization of subgoals by participants* within subunits.

At the same time, the internalization of subgoals is reinforced by a feedback from the daily decisions it influences. The necessity for making daily decisions creates a system of precedents. Decisions depend primarily on the operational criteria provided by the organization, and, among these criteria, subunit goals are of considerable importance. Precedents tend to become habitual responses to the situations for which they are defined as relevant and thus to reinforce the internalization of subunit goals. Obviously, internalization of subgoals is partially dependent on the *operationality of organizational goals*. By operationality of goals, we mean the extent to which it is possible to observe and test how well goals are being achieved. Variations in the operationality of organizational goals affect the content of daily decisions and thus the extent of subunit goal internalization.

From this it is clear that delegation has both functional and dysfunctional consequences for the achievement of organizational goals. It contributes both to their realization and to their deflection. Surprisingly, the theory postulates that both increases and decreases in goal achievement cause an increase in delegation. Why does not normal learning occur here? The answer seems to be that when goals are not achieved, delegation is – within the framework of the 'machine' model – the correct response, and the model does not consider alternatives to simple delegation. On the other hand, the model offers explicitly at least two 'dampers' that limit the operation of the dysfunctional mechanisms. As is indicated in Figure 3, where the skeleton of the Selznick model is outlined, there are two (not entirely independent) variables treated as independent but potentially amenable to organizational control, each of which restrains the runaway features of daily decision-making. By suitable changes in the extent to which organizational goals are operational or in the internalization of organizational goals by participants, some of the dysfunctional effects of delegation can be reduced. (To be sure, this ignores the possible effect of such procedures on the maintenance problems of the subunits and the consequent results for the larger organizations, but these are problems we are not prepared to attack at the moment.)

The Gouldner model

In terms of number of variables and relations, Gouldner's model (1954) is the simplest of the three presented here; but it exhibits the major features of the two previous systems. Like Merton, Gouldner is concerned with the consequences of bureaucratic rules for the maintenance of organization structure. Like both Merton and

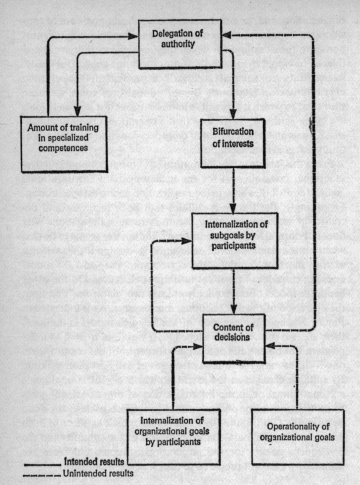

Figure 3 The simplified Selznick model

Selznick, he attempts to show how a control technique designed to maintain the equilibrium of a subsystem disturbs the equilibrium of a larger system, with a subsequent feedback on the subsystem.

In Gouldner's system, the *use of general and impersonal rules* regulating work procedures is part of the response to the demand for control from the top hierarchy. One consequence of such rules is to decrease the *visibility of power relations* within the group. The visibility of authority differences within the work group interacts with the *extent to which equality norms are held* to affect the *legitimacy of the supervisory role*. This, in turn, affects the *level of interpersonal tension* in the work group. In the American culture of egalitarian norms, decreases in power visibility increase the legitimacy of the supervisory position and therefore decrease tension within the group.

Gouldner argues that these anticipated consequences of rule-making do occur, that the survival of the work group as an operating unit is substantially furthered by the creation of general rules, and that consequently the use of such rules is reinforced.

At the same time, however, work rules provide cues for organizational members beyond those intended by the authority figures in the organization. Specifically, by defining unacceptable behavior, they increase *knowledge about minimum acceptable behavior*. In conjunction with a low level of internalization of organizational goals, specifying a minimum level of permissible behavior increases the disparity between organization goals and achievement by depressing behavior to the minimum level.

Performance at the minimum level is perceived by hierarchical superiors as a failure. In short, the internal stabilizing effects of the rules are matched by the unbalance they produce in the larger organization. The response to the unbalance is an increase in the *closeness of supervision* over the work group. This response is based on the 'machine' model of human behavior: low performance indicates a need for more detailed inspection and control over the operation of the 'machine'.

In turn, however, close supervision increases the visibility of power relations within the organization, raises the tension level in the work group, and thereby upsets the equilibrium originally based on the institution of rules. The broad outline of the model is shown in Figure 4.

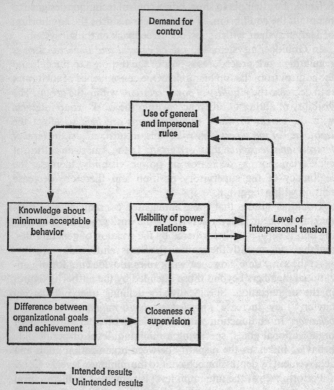

```
                    ┌──────────┐
                    │ Demand for│
                    │  control  │
                    └──────────┘
                          │
                          ▼
                  ┌──────────────┐
          ┌───────│ Use of general│◄──────────┐
          ╎       │and impersonal │◄────┐      │
          ╎       │    rules      │     ╎      │
          ╎       └──────────────┘      ╎      │
          ╎              │              ╎      │
          ▼              ▼              ╎      │
┌──────────────┐  ┌──────────────┐  ┌──────────────┐
│Knowledge about│  │Visibility of  │─►│Level of      │
│minimum        │  │power          │╌►│interpersonal  │
│acceptable     │  │relations      │  │tension        │
│behavior       │  └──────────────┘  └──────────────┘
└──────────────┘          ▲
       ╎                   ╎
       ▼                   ╎
┌──────────────┐  ┌──────────────┐
│Difference     │╌►│Closeness of  │
│between        │  │supervision   │
│organizational │  │              │
│goals and      │  │              │
│achievement    │  │              │
└──────────────┘  └──────────────┘
```

———————— Intended results
‑ ‑ ‑ ‑ ‑ ‑ ‑ ‑ Unintended results

Figure 4 The simplified Gouldner model

Gouldner's model leaves some puzzles unexplained. In particular, why is increased supervision the supervisory response to low performance? It seems reasonable that the tendency to make such a response is affected both by role perceptions and by a third equilibrating process in the system – the individual needs of the supervisors. Thus, the intensity of supervision is a function of the *authoritarianism* of supervisors and a function of the *punitivity of supervisory role perception*.

As in the Selznick model, the existence of 'dampers' on the system poses the question of their treatment as external variables.

Appropriate manipulation of equality norms, perceived commonality of interest, and the needs of supervisors will restrict the operation of the dysfunctional features of the system. The failure of top management to use such techniques of control suggests that the system may be incompletely defined. [. . .]

Implications of the bureaucracy models

Other quite comparable models could be added to those examined here. Bendix (1947) has discussed limits on technical rationality within an organization and pointed out the intriguing complications involved in the use of spy systems as systems of control. Dubin (1949) has presented a model quite similar to that of Merton. Blau (1955) has examined the changes in operating procedures that occur at a relatively low level in the hierarchy under the pressure of work group needs.

In the sample of three cases from the 'bureaucracy' literature we have presented (as well as in the others mentioned), complications arise in each of the three ways predicted from the influence model outlined previously. The elaboration of evoking connections, the presence of unintended cues, and organizationally dysfunctional learning appear to account for most of the unanticipated consequences with which these theories deal.

Many of the central problems for the analysis of human behavior in large-scale organizations stem from the operation of subsystems within the total organizational structure. The sociological studies of the work group analyzed here have focussed on the ways in which the needs of individuals, the primary work group, and the large organization interact to affect each other. [In] the study of morale and productivity, we also find that the study of the psychology of work has focussed on the same interactions, with perhaps a greater emphasis on the relations between the needs of individual personalities and the needs of the organization.

References

BENDIX, R. (1947), 'Bureaucracy: the problem and its setting', *American Sociological Review*, no. 12, pp. 493–507.

BLAU, P. M. (1955), *The Dynamics of Bureaucracy*, Chicago University Press.

DUBIN, R. (1949), 'Decision-making by management in industrial relations', *American Journal of Sociology*, no. 54, pp. 292–7.

GOULDNER, A. W. (1954), *Patterns of Industrial Bureaucracy*, Free Press.

GOULDNER, A. W. (1957), 'Theoretical requirements of the applied social sciences', *American Sociological Review*, no. 22, pp. 91–102.

MERTON, R. K. (1936), 'The unanticipated consequences of purposive social action', *American Sociological Review*, no. 1, pp. 894–904.

MERTON, R. K. (1940), 'Bureaucratic structure and personality', *Social Forces*, no. 18, pp. 560–68.

SELZNICK, P. (1949), *TVA and the Grass Roots*, Berkeley.

WEBER, M. (1946), *From Max Weber: Essays in Sociology*, translated by H. H. Gerth, and C. W. Mills, Oxford University Press.

WEBER, M. (1947), *The Theory of Social and Economic Organisation*, translated and edited by A. M. Henderson and T. Parsons, Oxford University Press.

3 T. Burns

Mechanistic and Organismic Structures

T. Burns, 'Industry in a new age', *New Society*, 31 January 1963, pp. 17–20.

Industry has a long past. We are now near the end of the second century of industrialism in its recognizably modern form. To be conscious of the history of an institution like the industrial concern is to become alive to two essential considerations. First, that like any other institution – government, the church, the family, military forces, for example – industry has undergone substantial changes in its organizational form as well as in the activity or task or objectives it performs. Secondly, and in consequence, unless we realize that industrial organization is still in the process of development, we are liable to be trapped into trying to use out-of-date organizational systems for coping with entirely new situations.

A sense of the past – and the very recent past – is essential to anyone who is trying to perceive the here-and-now of industrial organization. What is happening now is part of a continuing development. A study of this process will at least help firms avoid the traps they often fall into when they try to confront a situation of the newest kind with an organizational system appropriate to an earlier phase of industrial development. Adaptation to new challenge is not an automatic process: there are many factors against it.

What we recognize as industrialism is the product of two technologies, material and social. It has developed in spasmodic fashion from the rudimentary forms of the eighteenth century by alternate advances in first one technology and then the other.

The elementary form of industrialism is Adam Smith's conjunction of the division of labour traditional in advanced society with the extension of its advantages by 'those machines by which labour is so much facilitated and enlarged'.

The modern industrial system was founded at a time when the perception by early mechanical scientists that natural events 'obeyed' certain laws became widely diffused – in the eighteenth century. Samuel Smiles' legend that Arkwright was first struck by the feasibility of mechanical spinning 'by accidentally observing a hot piece of iron become elongated by passing between iron rollers' may be fiction, but it reflects truly the commonplace terms in which the new habits of scientific thought could be used by craftsmen-inventors, who saw not just an interesting analogy but one process obeying a law which might also apply to a different and entirely new process.

At the same time that Adam Smith was observing the archetypal form of the two technologies, a third step was being taken: the creation of the first successful factory by Strutt and Arkwright. By 1835 Ure could already discount the basic principles of division of labour as outdated and misleading. The industrial system was simply the factory system as developed by Arkwright: the term, factory, meaning 'the combined operation of many work people. adult and young, in tending with assiduous skill a system of productive machines continuously impelled by a central power. It is the constant aim and tendency of every improvement in machinery to supersede human labour altogether.'

Factory organization stayed for three generations at the point at which Arkwright had left it. Marx's account contains the same essentials: a collection of machines in a building all driven by one prime mover, and, preferably, of the same type and engaged on the same process. Attending the machines were men and women who themselves were attended by 'feeders', most of them children, who fetched and carried away materials. There was also a 'superior, but numerically unimportant' class of maintenance and repair workers. All of these worked under a master, with perhaps a chief workman or foreman. The primitive social technology of the factory system still confined it, even by the 1850s, largely to the mass production of textiles.

Technical developments in transport and communications, the impact of the international exhibitions in London and Paris, free trade, the armaments revolutions supported by the development of machine tools and of steel, and chemical technology (in Germany first) all combined during the 1850s and 1860s to form the springboard, in material technology, of the next advance in the social techniques of industrial organization.

As yet, there is no account of how that advance took place. All that can be said is that with the extension of the factory system into engineering and chemicals, iron and steel processing, food manufacture and clothing, an organizational development took place which provided for the conduct and control of many complex series of production processes within the same plant. One overt sign of this development is the increase in the number of salaried officials employed in industry. The proportion of 'administrative employees' to 'production employees' in British manufacturing industry had risen to 8·6 per cent by 1907 and to 20 per cent by 1948. Similar increases took place in western Europe and the United States.

The growth in the numbers of industrial administrative officials, or managers, reflects the growth of organizational structures. Production department managers, sales managers, accountants, cashiers, inspectors, training officers, publicity managers, and the rest emerged as specialized parts of the general management function as industrial concerns increased in size. Their jobs were created, in fact, out of the eighteenth-century master's, either directly or at one or two removes. This gives them and the whole social structure which contains their newly created roles its hierarchical character. It is indeed a patrimonial structure. All rights and powers at every level derive from the boss; fealty, or 'responsibility', is owed to him; all benefits are 'as if' dispensed by him. The bond is more easily and more often broken than in pre-feudal polities, but loyalty to the concern, to employers, is still regarded not only as proper, but as essential to the preservation of the system.

Chester Barnard makes this point with unusual emphasis: 'The most important single contribution required of the executive, certainly the most universal qualification. is loyalty, domination by the organization personality.' More recently, A. W. Gouldner has pointed out 'much of W. H. Whyte's recent study of Organization Man is a discussion of the efforts by industry to attach managerial loyalty to the corporation.'

The development of the bureaucratic system made possible the increase in scale of undertakings characteristic of the first part of this century. It had other aspects. The divorce of ownership and management, although by no means absolute, went far enough to render survival of the enterprise (and the survival of the existing management) at least as important a consideration as making the best profit. Profit itself wears a different aspect in the large-scale corporation.

More important, the growth of bureaucracy – the social technology which made possible the second stage of industrialism – was only feasible because the development of material technology was held relatively steady. An industry based on major technological advances shows a high death-rate among enterprises in its early years; growth occurs when the rate of technical advance slows down. What happens is that consumer demand tends to be standardized through publicity and price reductions, and technical progress is consequently restrained. This enables companies to maintain relatively stable conditions, in which large scale production is built up by converting manufacturing processes into routine cycles of activity for machines or semi-skilled assembly hands.

Under such conditions, not only could a given industrial company grow in size, not only could the actual manufacturing processes be routinized, mechanized and quickened, but the various management functions also could be broken down into specialisms and routines. Thus developed specialized management tasks: those of ensuring employee cooperation, of coordinating different departments, of planning and monitoring.

It is this second phase of industrialism which now dominates the institutional life of western societies. But while the greater part of the industrial system is in this second, bureaucratic phase of the historical development (and some older and smaller establishments remain in the first), it is now becoming clear that we have entered a third phase during the past two or three decades. J. K. Galbraith, in his *Affluent Society*, has described the new, more insecure relationship with the consumer which appears as production catches up and overtakes spontaneous domestic demand. The 'propensity to consume' has had to be stimulated by advertising, by styling, and by marketing promotions guided by research into the habits, motives, and potential 'needs' of consumers. At the same time, partly in an effort to maintain expansion, partly because of the stimulus of government spending on new military equipment, industry has admitted a sizeable influx of new technical developments.

There are signs that industry organized according to principles of bureaucracy – by now traditional – is no longer able to accommodate the new elements of industrial life in the affluent second half of the twentieth century. These new demands are made by large-scale research and development and by industry's new relationship with its markets. Both demand a much greater flexibility in internal organization, much higher levels of commitment to the commercial aims of the company from all its members, and an even higher proportion of administrators, controllers and monitors to operatives.

Recently, with G. M. Stalker, I made an attempt to elucidate the situation of concerns in the electronics industry which were confronted with rapidly changing commercial circumstances and a much faster rate of technical progress. I found it necessary to posit two 'ideal types' of working organization, the one mechanistic, adapted to relatively stable conditions, the other, 'organismic', adapted to conditions of change.

In mechanistic systems the problems and tasks which face the concern as a whole are, typically, broken down into specialisms. Each individual carries out his assigned task as something apart from the overall purpose of the company as a whole. 'Somebody at the top' is responsible for seeing that his work is relevant to that of others. The technical methods, duties, and powers attached to each post are precisely defined, and a high value is placed on precision and demarcation. Interaction within the working organization follows vertical lines – i.e., between superiors and subordinates. How a man operates and what he does is prescribed by his functional role and governed by instructions and decisions issued by superiors. This hierarchy of command is maintained by the assumption that the only man who knows – or should know – all about the company is the man at the top. He is the only one, therefore, who knows exactly how the human resources should be properly disposed. The management system, usually visualized as the complex hierarchy familiar in organization charts, operates as a simple control system, with information flowing upwards through a succession of filters, and decisions and instructions flowing downwards through a succession of amplifiers.

Mechanistic systems are, in fact, the 'rational bureaucracy' of an earlier generation of students of organization. For the individual, it provides an ordered world of work. His own decisions and actions occur within a stable constellation of jobs, skills, specialized knowledge, and sectional responsibilities. In a textile mill, or any factory which sees itself turning out any standardized product for a familiar and steady market, one finds decision-making at all levels prescribed by the familiar.

As one descends through the levels of management, one finds more limited information and less understanding of the human capacities of other members of the firm. One also finds each person's task more and more clearly defined by his superior. Beyond a certain limit he has insufficient authority, insufficient information, and usually insufficient technical ability to be able to make decisions. He is informed quite clearly when this limit occurs; beyond it, he has one course open – to report to his superior.

Organismic systems are adapted to unstable conditions, when new and unfamiliar problems and requirements continually arise which cannot be broken down and distributed among specialist roles within a hierarchy. Jobs lose much of their formal definition. The definitive and enduring demarcation of functions becomes impossible. Responsibilities and functions, and even methods and powers, have to be constantly redefined through interaction with others participating in common tasks or in the solution of common problems. Each individual has to do his job with knowledge of overall purpose and situation of the company as a whole. Interaction runs laterally as much as vertically, and communication between people of different rank tends to resemble 'lateral' consultation rather than 'vertical' command. Omniscience can no longer be imputed to the boss at the top.

The head of one successful electronics concern, at the very beginning of the first interview of the whole study, attacked the idea of the organization chart as inapplicable in his concern and as a dangerous method of thinking. The first requirement of a management, according to him, was that it should make the fullest use of the capacities of its members; any individual's job should be as little defined as possible, so that it would 'shape itself' to his special abilities and initiative.

In this company, insistence on the least possible specification for managerial positions was much more in evidence than any devices for ensuring adequate interaction within the system. This did occur, but it was often due to physical conditions rather than to order by top management. A single-storeyed building housed the entire company, two thousand strong, from laboratories to canteen. Access to anyone was, therefore, physically simple and direct; it was easier to walk across to the laboratory door, the office door, or the factory door and look about for the person one wanted, than even to telephone. Written communication inside the factory was actively discouraged. More important than the physical set up however was the need of each individual manager for interaction with others, in order to get his own functions defined, since these were not specified from above.

For the individual, the important part of the difference between the mechanistic and the organismic is in the degree of his commitment to the working organization. Mechanistic systems tell him what he has to attend to, and how, and also tell him what he does *not* have to bother with, what is *not* his affair, what is *not* expected of him – what he can post elsewhere as the responsibility of others. In organismic systems, such boundaries disappear. The individual is expected to regard himself as fully implicated in the discharge of any task appearing over his horizon. He has not merely to exercise a special competence, but to commit himself to the success of the concern's undertakings as a whole.

Mechanistic and organismic systems of management[1]

A mechanistic management system is appropriate to stable conditions. It is characterized by:

1. The *specialized differentiation* of functional tasks into which the problems and tasks facing the concern as a whole are broken down.

2. The *abstract nature* of each individual task, which is pursued with techniques and purposes more or less distinct from those of the concern as a whole.

3. The reconciliation, for each level in the hierarchy, of these distinct performances by the *immediate superiors*.

4. The *precise definition* of rights and obligations and technical methods attached to each functional role.

1. Source: Burns and Stalker (1966).

5. The *translation of rights* and obligations and methods into the responsibilities of a functional position.

6. *Hierarchic structure* of control, authority and communication.

7. A reinforcement of the hierarchic structure by the location of *knowledge* of actualities exclusively *at the top* of the hierarchy.

8. A tendency for *vertical interaction* between members of the concern to be i.e., between superior and subordinate.

9. A tendency for operations and working behaviour to be *governed by superiors*.

10. *Insistence on loyalty* to the concern and obedience to superiors as a condition of membership.

11. A greater importance and prestige attaching to *internal* (local) than to general (cosmopolitan) knowledge, experience and skill.

The organismic form is appropriate to changing conditions, which give rise constantly to fresh problems and unforeseen requirements for action which cannot be broken down or distributed automatically arising from the functional roles defined within a hierarchic structure. It is characterized by:

1. The *contributive nature* of special knowledge and experience to the common task of the concern.

2. The *realistic* nature of the individual task, which is seen as set by the total situation of the concern.

3. The adjustment and *continual redefinition* of individual tasks through interaction with others.

4. The *shedding of responsibility* as a limited field of rights, obligations and methods. (Problems may not be posted upwards, downwards or sideways).

5. The *spread of commitment* to the concern beyond any technical definition.

6. A *network structure* of control, authority, and communication.

7. Omniscience no longer imputed to the head of the concern; *knowledge* may be located anywhere in the network; this location becoming the centre of authority.

8. A *lateral* rather than a vertical direction of communication through the organization.

9. A content of communication which consists of *information and advice* rather than instructions and decisions.

10. *Commitment* to the concern's tasks and to the 'technological ethos' of material progress and expansion is more highly valued than loyalty.

11. Importance and prestige attach to *affiliations and expertise* valid in the industrial and technical and commercial milieux external to the firm.

In studying the electronics industry in Britain, we were occupied for the most part with companies which had been started a generation or more ago, well within the time period of the second phase of industrialization. They were equipped at the outset with working organizations designed by mechanistic principles. The ideology of formal bureaucracy seemed so deeply ingrained in industrial management that the common reaction to unfamiliar and novel conditions was to redefine, in more precise and rigorous terms, the roles and working relationships obtaining within management, along orthodox lines of organization charts and organization manuals. The formal structure was reinforced, not adapted. In these concerns the effort to make the orthodox bureaucratic system work produced what can best be described as pathological forms of the mechanistic system.

Three of these pathological systems are described below. All three were responses to the need for finding answers to new and unfamiliar problems and for making decisions in new circumstances of uncertainty.

First, there is the *ambiguous figure* system. In a mechanistic organization, the normal procedure for dealing with any matter lying outside the boundaries of one individual's functional responsibility is to refer it to the point in the system where such responsibility is known to reside, or, failing that, to lay it before one's superior. If conditions are changing rapidly such episodes occur frequently; in many instances, the immediate superior has to put such matters higher up still. A sizeable volume of matters for solution and decision can thus find their way to the head of the concern. There can, and frequently does, develop a system by which a large number of executives find – or claim – that they can only get matters settled by going to the top man.

So, in some places we studied, an ambiguous system developed of an official hierarchy, and a clandestine or open system of pair relationships between the head of the concern and some dozens of persons at different positions below him in the management. The head of the concern was overloaded with work, and senior managers whose standing depended on the mechanistic formal system felt aggrieved at being bypassed. The managing director told himself – or brought in consultants to tell him – to delegate responsibility and decision making. The organization chart would be redrawn. But inevitably, this strategy promoted its own counter measures from the beneficiaries of the old, latent system as the stream of novel and unfamiliar problems built up anew.

The conflict between managers who saw their standing and prospects depending on the ascendancy of the old system or the new deflected attention and effort into internal politics. All of this bore heavily on the time and effective effort the head of the company was free to apply to his proper function, the more so because political moves focussed on controlling access to him.

Secondly, the *mechanistic jungle*. Some companies simply grew more branches of the bureaucratic hierarchy. Most of the problems which appeared in all these firms with pathological mechanisms manifested themselves as difficulties in communications. These were met, typically, by creating special intermediaries and interpreters: methods engineers, standardization groups, contract managers, post design engineers. Underlying this familiar strategy were two equally familiar clichés of managerial thinking. The first is to look for the solution of a problem, especially a problem of communication in 'bringing somebody in' to deal with it. A new job, or possibly a whole new department, may then be created, which depends for its survival on the perpetuation of the difficulty. The second attitude probably comes from the traditions of productive management: a development engineer is not doing the job he is paid for unless he is at his drawing board, drawing, and so on. Higher management has the same instinctive reaction when it finds people moving about the works, when individuals it wants are not 'in their place'. There managers cannot trust subordinates when they are not demonstrably and physically 'on the job'. Their response, therefore, when there was an admitted need for 'better communication' was to tether functionaries to their posts and to appoint persons who would specialize in 'liaison'.

The third kind of pathological response is the *super-personal* or committee system. It was encountered only rarely in the electronics firms we studied; it appeared sporadically in many of them, but it was feared as the characteristic disease of government administration. The committee is a traditional device whereby *temporary* commitments over and above those encapsulated in a single functional role may be contained within the system and discharged without enlarging the demands on individual functionaries, or upsetting the balance of power.

Committees are often set up where new kinds of work and/or unfamiliar problems seem to involve decisions, responsibilities and powers beyond the capabilities or deserts of any one man or department. Bureaucratic hierarchies are most prone to this defect. Here most considerations, most of the time, are subordinated to the career structure afforded by the concern (a situation by no means confined to the civil service or even to universities). The difficulty of filling a job calling for unfamiliar responsibility is overcome by creating a super-person – a committee.

Why do companies not adapt to new situations by changing their working organization from mechanistic to organismic? The answer seems to lie in the fact that the individual member of the concern is not only committed to the working organization as a whole. In addition, he is a member of a group or a department with sectional interests in conflict with those of other groups, and all of these individuals are deeply concerned with the position they occupy, relative to others, and their future security or betterment are matters of deep concern.

In regard to sectional commitments, he may be, and usually is, concerned to extend the control he has over his own situation, to increase the value of his personal contribution, and to have his resources possibly more thoroughly exploited and certainly more highly rewarded. He often tries to increase his personal power by attaching himself to parties of people who represent the same kind of ability and wish to enhance its exchange value, or to cabals who seek to control or influence the exercise of patronage in the firm. The interest groups so formed are quite often identical with a department, or the dominant groups in it, and their political leaders are heads of departments, or accepted activist leaders, or elected representatives (e.g. shop stewards). They become involved in issues of internal politics arising from the conflicting demands such as those on allocation of capital, on direction of others, and on patronage.

Apart from this sectional loyalty, an individual usually considers his own career at least as important as the well being of the firm, and while there may be little incompatibility in his serving the ends of both, occasions do arise when personal interests outweigh the firm's interests, or even a clear conflict arises.

If we accept the notion that a large number, if not all, of the members of a firm have commitments of this kind to themselves, then it is apparent that the resulting relationships and conduct are adjusted to other self-motivated relationships and conduct throughout the concern. We can therefore speak of the new career structure of the concern, as well as of its working organization and political system. Any concern will contain these three systems. All three will interact: particularly, the political system and career structure will influence the constitution and operation of the working organization.

(There are two qualifications to be made here. The tripartite system of commitments is not exhaustive, and is not necessarily self balancing. Besides commitments to the concern, to 'political' groups, and to his own career prospects, each member of a concern is involved in a multiplicity of relationships. Some arise out of social origin and culture. Others are generated by the encounters which are governed, or seem to be governed, by a desire for the comfort of friendship, or the satisfactions which come from popularity and personal esteem, or those other rewards of inspiring respect, apprehension or alarm. All relationships of this sociable kind, since they represent social values, involve the parties in commitments.)

Neither political nor career preoccupations operate overtly, or even, in some cases, consciously. They give rise to intricate manoeuvres and counter moves, all of them expressed through decisions, or in discussions about decisions, concerning the organization and the policies of the firm. Since sectional interests and preoccupations with advancement only display themselves in terms of the working organization, that organization becomes more or less adjusted to serving the ends of the political and career system rather than those of the concern. Interlocking systems of commitments – to sectional interests and to individual status – generate strong forces. These divert organizations from purposive adaptation. Out of date mechanistic organizations are perpetuated and pathological systems develop, usually because of one or the other of two things: internal politics and the career structure.

Reference

BURNS, T., and STALKER, G. M. (1966), *The Management of Innovation,* Tavistock.

4 J. Woodward

Management and Technology

Excerpt from J. Woodward, *Management and Technology*, H M S O, 1958, p. 4–21.

Introduction

The research described in this booklet was the first attempt in Britain to discover whether the principles of organization laid down by an expanding body of management theory correlate with business success when put into practice.

It was carried out between 1953 and 1957 by the Human Relations Research Unit of the South-East Essex Technical College. The original intention of the research workers was to look at the division of responsibilities between line supervision and the technical specialists who apply technology to the production process, and at the factors which determine the relationships between them. They soon found, however, that this line-staff relationship could not be studied in isolation, so they widened their investigations to include the whole structure of management and supervision. Their basic survey in 91 per cent of the manufacturing firms in south Essex with over 100 employees revealed considerable variations in the pattern of organization which could not be related to size of firm, type of industry or business success.

When, however, the firms were grouped according to similarity of objectives and techniques of production, and classified in order of the technical complexity of their production systems, each production system was found to be associated with a characteristic pattern of organization. It appeared that technical methods were the most important factor in determining organizational structure and in setting the tone of human relationships inside the firms. The widely accepted assumption that there are principles of management valid for all types of production systems seemed very doubtful – a conclusion with wide implications for the teaching of this subject.

After completing the survey the team studied more fully twenty firms selected along a scale of technical complexity, and made detailed case studies of three firms in which production systems were mixed or changing.

This summary covers all three stages of the research. It describes the background survey, giving enough of the information collected to show some of the main differences between the organizational patterns associated with each of the different systems of production. The more descriptive information obtained in the second stage of the research is used to provide explanations of these differences. Finally, the detailed case studies are briefly referred to and an attempt is made to show how the analysis of changes in technical demands due to innovation can help to solve in advance the problems of management organization likely to arise.

The survey
The area

The map shows the area covered by the survey [not included]. Industrial development came comparatively late to south Essex and newer industries such as oil refining, wireless, photography, pharmaceuticals, paperboard and vehicles predominate. Factory buildings are on the whole modern. So is management organization. Most factories here were built when the functions of ownership and management had already been separated and there are few long-established family businesses. A number of family firms did move here, but their history suggests that the move gave most of them an occasion for radical changes in management structure.

The firms

The investigation was confined to manufacturing firms in the area. Those concerned with mining and quarrying, building contracting and laundering were excluded, as were transport undertakings, public utilities and local authorities.

A long search produced a list of 203 manufacturing firms which was as comprehensive as humanly possible; it is unlikely that any firm employing 100 people or more was omitted.

The number employed ranged from a dozen to approximately 35,000 (see Table 1).

There are more large firms in south Essex than in the country generally, 9 per cent employing more than 1000 people as against 1·7 per cent overall. The 203 firms cover a wide range of industries. In most of them the number employed in the area represents between 1 and 2 per cent of the national total. In textiles and leather the percentage is particularly low, but in vehicles and chemicals it is as high as 7 per cent.

Table 1 Size Distribution of Manufacturing Firms in South Essex

Firms employing	Percentage of 203 firms	Percentage of labour force (119,400)
100 or less	46	3
101–250	24	7
251–500	12	8
501–1000	9	11
1001–2000	4	10
2001–4000	3	14
4001–8000	1	9
8000 and over	1	38
Totals	100	100

A 25 per cent sample survey of the ninety-five firms employing less than 100 people showed no clear-cut level of management between board and operators in most of them. The main survey was therefore confined to the 110 firms employing 100 people or more, of which 100, or 91 per cent, were willing and able to take part.

Of these 100 firms, sixty-eight had both their main establishment and their commercial headquarters inside the area; the rest had only branch factories.

Information obtained

A research worker visited each of the firms and obtained information under the following headings:

1. History, background and objectives.
2. Description of the manufacturing processes and methods.

3. Forms and procedures through which the firm was organized and operated.

(a) An organization chart.

(b) A simple analysis of costs into three main divisions: wages, materials and overheads.

(c) An analysis of the labour structure, including the size of the span of control at various levels and the following ratios:

 (i) Direct production workers to total personnel.

(ii) Maintenance workers to direct production workers.

iii) Clerical and administrative to hourly paid personnel.

iv) Managers and supervisory staff to total personnel.

[d) The organization and operation of sales activities, research and development, personnel management, inspection, maintenance and purchasing.

(e) The procedures used in production control and planning.

(f) The procedures used in cost or budgetary control.

(g) The qualifications and training of managers and supervisory staff; management recruitment and training policy.

4. Information helpful in making an assessment of the firm's efficiency.

The assessment of efficiency

It is not easy to assess either the success of a firm or the effectiveness of a particular administrative expedient. The circular argument that an arrangement works because it exists is difficult to avoid. But an assessment was attempted. The firms were classified into three broad categories of success: average, below average and above average. The more obvious factors considered were profitability, market standing, rate of development and future plans. Questions were asked about the unit of measure commonly applied to the product, the volume of the industry's output, the proportion of that volume produced by the firm concerned and the nature of the market. More subjective factors considered included the reputation of the firm, both inside its industry and among local firms, the quality and attitudes of its management and supervisory staff, the rate of this staff's turnover and the opportunity provided for a complete and satisfying career in management.

Results
Organizational differences between firms

The 100 firms in the survey were organized and run in widely different ways. In only about half did the principles and concepts of management theory appear to have had much influence on organizational development.

In thirty-five firms there was an essentially 'line' or 'military' type of organization; two firms were organized functionally, almost exactly as recommended by Taylor fifty years ago (Taylor, 1910). The rest followed in varying degrees a line-staff pattern of organization; that is, they employed a number of functional specialists as 'staff' to advise those in the direct line of authority.

The number of distinct levels of management between board and operators varied from two to twelve; while the span of control of the chief executive[1] ranged from two to nineteen, and that of the first line supervisor[2] from seven to ninety. (An individual's span of control is the number of people directly responsible to him.)

Wages and salaries accounted for anything between 3 per cent and 50 per cent of total costs. Labour forces differed in character from firm to firm too; for example, the ratio of clerical and administrative staff to hourly paid workers ranged between 3:1 and 1:14; and that of direct to indirect labour between 1:3 and 15:1. Exactly half of the firms employed graduates or other professionally qualified staff. Thirty firms promoted their managers entirely from within, five from outside only and the remainder used both sources according to circumstances.

There was no obvious explanation of these differences in organizational structure; they did not appear to be related either to size or type of industry. Also, conformity with the 'rules' of management did not necessarily result in success or non-conformity in commercial failure. Of the twenty firms assessed as 'above average' in success only nine had a clearly defined organizational pattern of the orthodox kind.

1. The chief executive was in some cases the Chairman, in others the Managing Director and in others the General or Works Manager. In every case he presented the highest level of authority operating full-time on the spot.

2. i.e. the first level of authority that spent more than 50 per cent of the time on supervisory duties.

New ideas about management

Did any common thread underlie these differences? One possible explanation was that they reflected the different personalities of the senior managers, another that they arose from the historical background of the firms. While such factors undoubtedly influenced the situation, they did not adequately explain it; they were not always associated with differences in organizational patterns or in the quality of human relations.

A new approach lay in recognizing that firms differed not only in size, kind of industry and organizational structure, but also in objectives. While the firms were all manufacturing goods for sale their detailed objectives depended on the nature of the product and the type of customer. Thus some firms were in more competitive industries than others, some were making perishable goods that could not be stored, some produced for stock and others to orders; in fact, marketing conditions were different in every firm. The underlying purpose varied too. For example, one firm had originally undertaken manufacture to demonstrate that the products of its mines could be effective substitutes for other more commonly used materials.

These differences in objectives controlled and limited the techniques of production that could be employed. A firm whose objective was to build prototypes of electronic equipment, for example, could not employ the technical methods of mass-production engineering. The criterion of the appropriateness of an organizational structure must be the extent to which it furthers the objectives of the firm, not, as management teaching sometimes suggests, the degree to which it conforms to a prescribed pattern. There can be no one best way of organizing a business.

This is perhaps not sufficiently recognized; management theorists have tried to develop a 'science' of administration relevant to all types of production. One result is that new techniques such as operational research and the various tools of automation have been regarded as aids to management and to industrial efficiency rather than as developments which may change the very nature of management.

Evidence is accumulating, particularly in the United States, that automation and other technological changes are often associated with considerable disturbance in the management systems of the firms concerned. New tools begin to change the task and the new task begins to change the organization and the qualities required to carry it out successfully. For example, work done in the United States has shown that the qualities required of the foreman on a motor-car assembly line appear to be very different from those required on transfer-line production (Walker and Guest, 1952). Expressions like 'leadership' or 'the art of foremanship', used so often in management literature, are losing much of their meaning. It is possible, for example, that leadership must be directive, participant, or *laissez-faire* according to circumstances. A good leader in one situation is not necessarily a good leader in another.

Two interesting questions have so far emerged. Are the management organization and supervisory qualities required in a firm in the process of radical technical change different from those required in a stable firm? Does the kind of organization required vary with the technical complexity of the manufacturing methods?

Differences in technical methods

The firms were grouped according to their technical methods. Ten different categories emerged (see Figure 1).

Firms in the same industry did not necessarily fall into the same group. For example, two tailoring firms of approximately equal size had very different production systems; one made bespoke suits, the other mass-produced men's clothing.

Measurement of technical complexity

The ten production groups listed in Figure 1 form a scale of technical complexity. (This term is used here to mean the extent to which the production process is controllable and its results predictable.) For example, targets can be set more easily in a chemical plant than in even the most up-to-date mass-production engineering shops, and the factors limiting production are known more definitely so that continual productivity drives are not needed.

Some of the firms studied used techniques of operational research to increase control over production limitations – but these could be effective only within limits set by technical methods, which were always the major factor determining the extent of control over production.

I Production of simple units to customers' orders
(5 firms)

II Production of technically complex units
(10 firms)

III Fabrication of large equipment in stages
(2 firms)

IV Production of small batches
(7 firms)

V Production of components in large batches
subsequently assembled diversely
(3 firms)

group I
small batch and
unit production

VI Production of large batches, assembly line type
(25 firms)

VII Mass production
(6 firms)

group II
large batch and
mass production

VIII Process production combined with the preparation
of a product for sale by large-batch or
mass-production methods
(9 firms)

IX Process production of chemicals in batches
(13 firms)

X Continuous flow production of liquids gases and solid
shapes
(12 firms)

group III
process production

Figure 1   (8 firms unclassified because too mixed or changing)

Grading firms according to their technical complexity implies no judgement of their progressiveness or backwardness, nor is it any indication of the attitude of their management towards technical innovation. Each production system has its particular applications and limitations. While there remains a demand for the gold-plated limousine or the bespoke suit, while large items of equipment have to be built, or while progress in industries like electronics proceeds too rapidly to permit standardization, there will be a place for unit production even though it is less advanced technically than other systems. Moreover, although continuous-flow production is applicable to the manufacture of single components, it is difficult as yet to foresee its use where many different component parts are assembled.

However, technical developments may from time to time enable a firm to achieve its objectives more effectively through a change in its production system, and a large proportion of manufacturing firms in the future are likely to be process firms. Indeed, although large-batch and mass production is regarded as the typical manufacturing system, less than one third of the firms in south Essex are even now in this production group.

Automatic and other advanced techniques, although more appropriate to some systems than others, are not restricted to any one system. Automatic control can be applied most readily to mass production and continuous-flow process production, but even in unit and small-batch production devices for the control of individual machines can be used.

Sixteen of the firms included in the research had introduced some form of automation. In some of them, for example in those canning food and making mill-board, the production system had changed in consequence; in others it had not. Thus automation can be introduced without a change in the production system, and a change in the production system can be introduced without automation.

Organization and technology

The analysis of the research described in the previous chapter revealed that firms using similar technical methods had similar organizational structures. It appeared that different technologies imposed different kinds of demands on individuals and organizations, and that these demands had to be met through an appropriate form of organization. There were still a number of differences between firms – related to such factors as history, background and personalities – but these were not as significant as the differences between one production group and another and their influence seemed to be limited by technical considerations. For example, there were differences between managers in their readiness to delegate authority; but in general they delegated more in process than in mass-production firms.

Organization and technical complexity

Organization also appeared to change as technology advanced. Some figures showed a direct and progressive relationship with advancing technology (used in this report to mean 'system of techniques'). Others reached their peak in mass production and then decreased, so that in these respects unit and process production resembled each other more than the intermediate stage. Figures 2 and 3 show these two trends. (Details are given for the three main groups of production systems. See Figure 1.)

The number of levels of authority in the management hierarchy increased with technical complexity (see Figure 2).

The span of control of the first-line supervisor on the other hand reached its peak in mass production and then decreased (see Figure 3).

The ratio of managers and supervisory staff to total personnel in the different production systems is shown in some detail in Figure 4 as an indication of likely changes in the demand for managers as process production becomes more widespread. There were over three times as many managers for the same number of personnel in process firms as in unit-production firms. Mass-production firms lay between the two groups, with half as many managers as in process production for the same number of personnel.

The following characteristics followed the pattern shown in Figure 2 – a direct and progressive relationship with technical complexity.

1. *Labour costs* decreased as technology advanced. Wages accounted

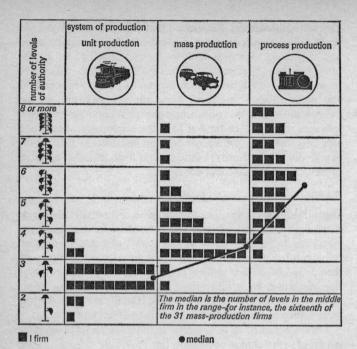

Figure 2

number of levels of authority	system of production unit production	mass production	process production
8 or more		■	■■ ■■ ■■■
7		■ ■■	■■ ■■■
6		■ ■■	■■■ ■■■ ■■
5		■■ ■■■■	■■■ ■■
4	■ ■■	■■■■■■■■■ ■■■■■■■■ ■	
3	■■■■■■■■■ ■■■■■■■■	■	
2	■■ ■	*The median is the number of levels in the middle firm in the range—for instance, the sixteenth of the 31 mass-production firms*	

■ 1 firm   ● median

for an average of 36 per cent of total costs in unit production, 34 per cent in mass production and 14 per cent in process production.

2. *The ratios of indirect labour* and of administrative and clerical staff to hourly paid workers increased with technical advance.

3. *The proportion of graduates* among the supervisory staff engaged on production increased too. Unit-production firms employed more professionally qualified staff altogether than other firms, but mainly on research or development activities. In unit-production and mass-production firms it was the complexity of the product that determined the proportion of professionally qualified staff, while in process industry it was the complexity of the process.

4. *The span of control of the chief executive* widened considerably with technical advance.

66 The Structure of Organizations

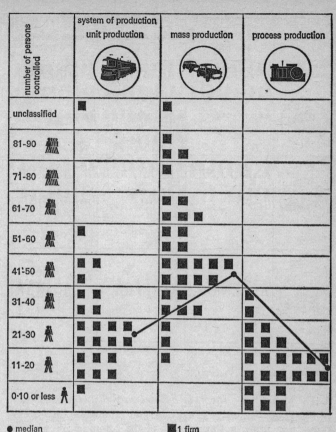

Figure 3

The following organizational characteristics formed the pattern shown in Figure 3. The production groups at the extremes of the technical scale resembled each other, but both differed considerably from the groups in the middle.

1. *Organization was more flexible* at both ends of the scale, duties and responsibilities being less clearly defined.

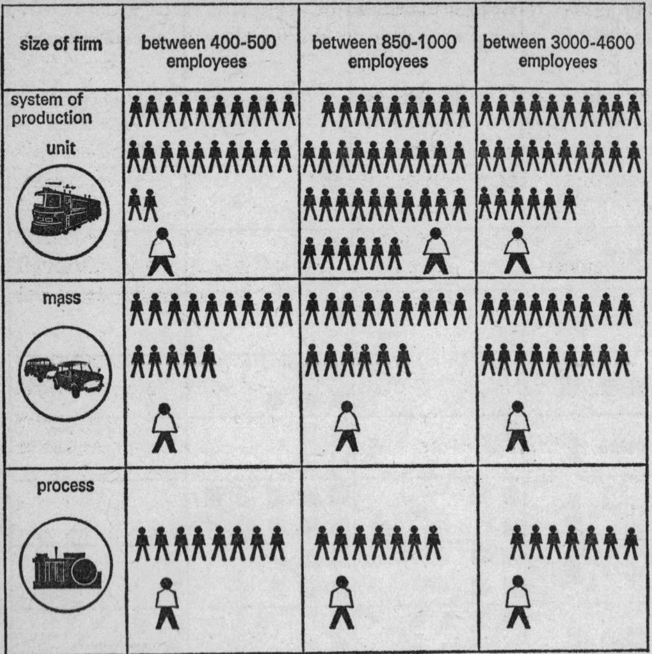

size of firm	between 400-500 employees	between 850-1000 employees	between 3000-4600 employees
system of production
unit			
mass			
process			

supervisory staff shown in white jackets— other personnel shaded

Figure 4

2. The amount of *written, as opposed to verbal, communication* increased up to the stage of assembly-line production. In process-production firms, however, most of the communications were again verbal.

3. *Specialization between the functions of management* was found more frequently in large-batch and mass production than in unit or process production. In most unit-production firms there were few specialists; managers responsible for production were expected to have technical skills, although these were more often based on length of experience and on 'know-how' than on scientific knowledge. When unit production was based on mass-produced components more specialists were employed, however. Large-

batch and mass-production firms generally conformed to the traditional line-and-staff pattern, the managerial and supervisory group breaking down into two sub-groups with separate, and sometimes conflicting, ideas and objectives. In process-production firms the line-and-staff pattern broke down in practice, though it sometimes existed on paper. Firms tended either to move towards functional organization of the kind advocated by Taylor (1910), or to do without specialists and incorporate scientific and technical knowledge in the direct executive hierarchy. As a result, technical competence in line supervision was again important, although now the demand was for scientific knowledge rather than technical 'know-how'.

4. Although production control became increasingly important as technology advanced, *the administration of production* – what Taylor called 'the brainwork of production' – was most widely separated from the actual supervision of production operations in large-batch and mass-production firms, where the newer techniques of production planning and control, methods engineering and work study were most developed. The two functions became increasingly reintegrated beyond this point.

The effect of technology upon human relations

The attitudes and behaviour of management and supervisory staff and the tone of industrial relations in the firms also seemed to be closely related to their technology. In firms at the extremes of the scale, relationships were on the whole better than in the middle ranges. Pressure on people at all levels of the industrial hierarchy seemed to build up as technology advanced, became heaviest in assembly-line production and then relaxed, so reducing personal conflicts. Some factors – the relaxation of pressure, the smaller working groups, the increasing ratio of supervisors to operators, and the reduced need for labour economy – were conducive to industrial peace in process production. Thus, although some management handled their labour problems more skilfully than others, these problems were much more difficult for firms in the middle ranges than for those in unit or process production. The production system seemed more important in determining the quality of human relations than did the numbers employed.

Size and technology

No significant relationship was revealed between the size of the firm and the system of production. There were small, medium and large firms in each of the main production groups.

Table 2 Production Systems Analysed by Number Employed

Production system	Number employed 101–250	251–1000	Over 1000	Total number of firms
Unit	7	13	4	24
Mass	14	12	5	31
Process	12	9	4	25
Totals	33	34	13	80

There were firms which employed relatively few people and yet had all the other characteristics of a large company, including a well-defined and developed management structure, considerable financial resources and a highly paid staff with considerable status in the local industrial community. This was particularly true of the smaller process-production firms. Some of these employed less than 500 people but had more of the characteristics of large-scale industry than unit- or mass-production firms with two or three times as many employees. As indicated already (p. 65) the ratio of management staff to the total number employed was found to increase as technology advanced. It appeared also that the size of the management group was a more reliable measure of the 'bigness' of a firm than its total personnel.

Moreover, although no relationship was found between organization and size in the general classification of firms, some evidence of such a relationship emerged when each of the production groups was considered separately. For example, in the large-batch and mass-production group the number of levels of authority and the span of control of both the chief executive and the first line supervisor both tended to increase with size.

Structure and success

Again, no relationship between conformity with the 'rules' of management and business success appeared in the preliminary analysis of the research data. The twenty firms graded as outstandingly successful seemed to have little in common.

When, however, firms were grouped on a basis of their production systems, the outstandingly successful ones had at least one feature in common. Many of their organizational characteristics approximated to the median of their production group. For example, in successful unit-production firms the span of control of the first line supervisor ranged from twenty-two to twenty-eight, the median for the group as a whole being twenty-three; in successful mass-production firms it ranged from forty-five to fifty, the median for the group being forty-nine; and in successful process-production firms it ranged from eleven to fifteen, the median for the group being thirteen (see Figure 3). Conversely the firms graded as below average in most cases diverged widely from the median.

The research workers also found that when the thirty-one large-batch and mass-production firms were examined separately there was a relationship between conformity with the 'rules' of management and business success. The medians approximated to the pattern of organization advocated by writers on management subjects. Within this limited range of production systems, therefore, observance of these 'rules' does appear to increase administrative efficiency. This is quite understandable because management theory is mainly based on the experience of practitioners in the field, much of which has been in large-batch and mass-production firms. Outside these systems, however, it appears that new 'rules' are needed and it should be recognized that an alternative kind of organizational structure might be more appropriate.

5 H. J. Leavitt

Some Effects of Certain Communication Patterns on Group Performance

H. J. Leavitt, 'Some effects of certain communication patterns on group performance',[1] *Journal of Abnormal and Social Psychology*, no. 46, January 1951, pp. 38–50.

Introduction

Cooperative action by a group of individuals having a common objective requires, as a necessary condition, a certain minimum of communication. This does not mean that all the individuals must be able to communicate with one another. It is enough, in some cases, if they are each touched by some part of a network of communication which also touches each of the others at some point. The ways in which the members of a group may be linked together by such a network of communication are numerous; very possibly only a few of the many ways have any usefulness in terms of effective performance. Which of all feasible patterns are 'good' patterns from this point of view? Will different patterns give different results in the performance of group tasks?

In a free group, the kind of network that evolves may be determined by a multitude of variables. The job to be done by the group may be a determinant, or the particular abilities or social ranks of the group members, or other cultural factors may be involved.

Even in a group in which some parent organization defines the network of communication, as in most military or industrial situations, the networks themselves may differ along a variety of dimensions. There may be differences in number of connections, in the symmetry of the pattern of connections, in 'channel capacity' (how much and what kind of information), and in many other ways.

1. The experiments reported here were conducted at the Massachusetts Institute of Technology. The stimulus for this research derives from the work and the thinking of Professor Alex Bavelas. A great deal of help was also contributed by members of Professor Bavelas' seminar in Advanced Experimental Psychology.

It was the purpose of this investigation to explore experimentally the relationship between the behavior of small groups and the patterns of communication in which the groups operate. It was our further purpose to consider the psychological conditions that are imposed on group members by various communication patterns, and the effects of these conditions on the organization and the behavior of its members. We tried to do this for small groups of a constant size, using two-way written communication and a task that required the simple collection of information.

Some characteristics of communication structures

The stimulus for this research lies primarily in the work of Bavelas (1948), who considered the problem of defining some of the dimensions of group structures. In his study, the structures analysed consist of cells connected to one another. If we make persons analogous to 'cells' and communication channels analogous to 'connections', we find that some of the dimensions that Bavelas defines are directly applicable to the description of communication patterns. Thus, one way in which communication patterns vary can be described by the sum of the neighbors that each individual member has, neighbors being defined as individuals to whom a member has communicative access. So, too, the concept of *centrality*, as defined by Bavelas, is of value in describing differences within and between structures. The most central position in a pattern is the position closest to all other positions. Distance is measured by number of communicative links which must be utilized to get, by the shortest route, from one position to another.

Bavelas also introduced a *sum of neighbors* measure – sum of neighbors being a summation, for the entire pattern, of the number of positions one link away from each position. Similarly, *sum of distances* is the summation, for all positions, of the shortest distances (in links) from every position to every other one.

Unfortunately, these dimensions we have mentioned do not in themselves uniquely define a pattern of communication. What defines a pattern is the *way* the cells are connected, regardless of how they are represented on paper. In essence, our criterion is this: if two patterns cannot be 'bent' into the same shape without breaking a link, they are different patterns. A more precise definition of unique patterns would require the use of complex topological concepts.

Some operational characteristics of communication patterns

Consider the pattern depicted as A in Figure 1. If at each dot or cell (lettered a, b, etc.) we place a person; if each link (line between dots) represents a two-way channel for written communications; and if we assign to the five participants a task requiring that *every* member get an answer to a problem which can be solved only by pooling segments of information originally held separately by each member, then it is possible *a priori* to consider the ways in which the problem can be solved.

Pattern flexibility. First we note that the subjects (Ss) need not always use all the channels potentially available to them in order to reach an adequate solution of the problem. Although pattern A (Figure 1) contains potentially seven links or channels of communication, it can be solved as follows with three of the seven channels ignored.

Step 1: a and e each send their separate items of information to b and d respectively.

Step 2: b and d each send their separate items of information, along with those from a and b respectively, to c.

Step 3: c organizes all the items of information, arrives at a answer, and sends the answer to b and then to d.

Step 4: b and d then send the answer to a and e respectively.

The use of these particular four channels yielsd pattern C (Figure 1). The original seven-link pattern (A) can be used as a four-link pattern in various ways. For instance, each of the four Ss diagrammatically labelled c, b, a and e might send his item of information to d who would organize the items, arrive at the answer, and send it back to each respectively. Use of these particular four channels would yield the pattern B in Figure 1. The problem could also be solved by the Ss using five, six or all of the seven potential channels.

Operational flexibility. Secondly, with the specification that a given number of links be used, any pattern can be operated in a variety of ways. Thus the pattern D (Figure 1), which has no pattern flexibility, can be used as shown in D-1, with information

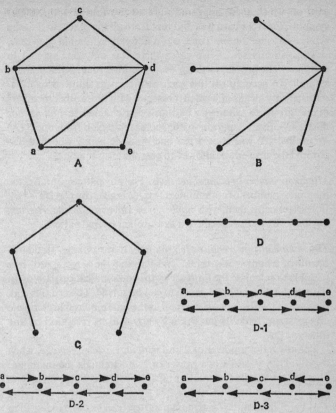

Figure 1 Communication patterns (see text)

funnelled in to C and the answer sent out from C. It is also possible to use it, as in D-2, with E as the key position; or as in D-3. These are operational differences that can be characterized in terms of the roles taken by the various positions. Thus in D-1, C is the decision-making position. In D-2, it is E or A. Some patterns can be operated with two or three decision-makers.

The definition of maximum theoretical efficiency

Before going further it may be helpful to state the task used in this research. To each *S*, labelled by color (see Figure 2), was given a card on which there appeared a set of five (out of six possible) symbols. Each S's card was different from all the others in that the symbol lacking, the sixth one, was a different symbol in each case.

Thus, in any set of five cards there was only one symbol in common. The problem was for every member to find the common symbol. To accomplish this each member was allowed to communicate, by means of written messages, with those other members of the group to whom he had an open channel (a link in our diagrams). Every separate written communication from one S (A) to another (B) was considered one message. An S who had discovered the answer was allowed to pass the answer along.

Minimum number of communications. For any pattern of n Ss, the minimum number of communications, C, is given by $C = 2(n-1)$.

Theoretically, then, with *number of messages as the sole criterion*, any pattern of n Ss is as efficient as any other n-sized pattern.

The minimum time required for solution. If we assume 'standard' Ss, all of whom work, think, and write at the same speed, it is possible to calculate the limit set by the communication pattern on the speed with which the problem can be solved. Toward this end, we can arbitrarily define a *time unit* as the time required to complete any message, from its inception by any S to its reception by any other.

For any n not a power of 2 and *with unrestricted linkage*, when $2^x < n < 2^{x+1}$ and x is a power of 2, $x+1$ equals the minimum possible time units for solution of the problem. Thus, for a five-man group we have $2^x < 5 < 2^{x+1}$ becoming $2^2 < 5 < 2^3$, and $x + 1 = 3$ time units. *No* five-man pattern can be done in less than three time units, although several require more than three time units. When n is an even power of 2, the formula $2^x = n$ holds, and $x = $ minimum time.[2]

2. This is an empirical generalization derived chiefly from an analysis of a four-man square pattern. In such a pattern, A and B, and C and D may swap information in one time unit. Then A and C, and B and D may swap in two time units to yield a complete solution. For an eight-man ladder pattern the same simultaneous swapping process yields a minimum time. For the intervening ns, at least 'part' of a time unit is required, in addition to the minimum time for the four-man pattern. A detailed account of this analysis may be found in a paper, as yet unpublished, by J. P. Macy, Jr.

Figure 2 Symbol distribution by trial

Six symbols used: ● ▲ ◆ ■ ✚ ★

Trial No.	Symbol missing from: White	Red	Brown	Yellow	Blue	Common symbol
1	▲	◆	★	●	■	✚
2	◆	●	■	▲	✚	★
3	✚	★	■	▲	◆	●
4	■	◆	▲	★	✚	●
5	●	★	✚	▲	■	◆
6	▲	●		★	◆	✚
7	■	✚	●	◆	▲	★
8	◆	★	■	✚	●	▲
9	★	◆	■	▲	●	✚
10	✚	●	■	★	◆	▲
11	●	✚	▲	◆	★	■
12	★	●	■	▲	✚	◆
13	▲	●	◆	■	✚	★
14	■	◆	✚	★	▲	●
15	✚	●	■	◆	★	▲

It will be noted that, although some patterns require fewer time units than others, they may also require more message (*m*) units. This phenomenon, effectively the generalization that it requires increased messages to save time units, holds for all the patterns we have examined. It is, however, true that certain patterns requiring different times can be solved in the same number of message units.

Some possible effects of various patterns on the performance of individuals

There are two general kinds of reasons which dictate against our theoretically perfect performance from real people. The first of these is the obvious one that people are not standardized. There are also the forces set up by the patterns themselves to be considered. The problem becomes one of analysing the forces operating on an individual in any particular position in a communication pattern and then predicting how the effects of these forces will be translated into behavior.

It is our belief that the primary source of differential forces will be *centrality*. Centrality will be the chief (though perhaps not the sole) determinant of behavioral differences because centrality reflects the extent to which one position is strategically located relative to other positions in the pattern.

Our selection of centrality derives from the belief that availability of information necessary for the solution of the problem will be of prime importance in affecting one's behavior. Centrality is a measure of one's closeness to all other group members and, hence, is a measure of the availability of the information necessary for solving the problem.

Availability of information should affect behavior, in turn, by determining one's role in the group. An individual who can rapidly collect information should see himself and be seen by others in a different way from an individual to whom vital information is not accessible. Such roles should be different in the extent to which they permit independence of action, in the responsibility they entail, and in the monotony they impose. Finally, differences in independence, in responsibility, and in monotony should affect the speed, the accuracy, the aggressiveness, and the flexibility of behavior.

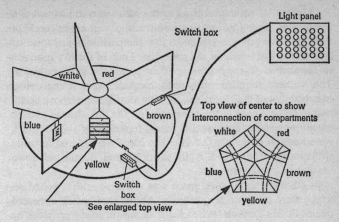

Figure 3 Apparatus

Method
The problem to be solved

We have already described the task to be given our *S*s – a task of discovering the single common symbol from among several symbols. When *all five* men indicated that they knew the common symbol, a trial was ended. Another set of cards, with another common symbol, was then given to the *S*s, and another trial was begun.

Each group of *S*s was given fifteen consecutive trials. The composition of the standard sets of cards, used for all groups, is indicated in Figure 2, which indicates the symbol *not* on each person's card for each trial. By referring this missing symbol to the set of six symbols at the top, the reader may reconstruct the symbols actually on each man's card. The common symbol (the right answer) is also shown in Figure 2.

The apparatus

The *S*s were seated around a circular table (Figure 3) so that each was separated from the next by a vertical partition from the center to six inches beyond the table's edge. The partitions had slots permitting subjects to push written message cards to the men on either side of them.

To allow for communication to the other men in the group, a five-layered pentagonal box was built and placed at the center of the table. The box was placed so that the partitions just touched each of the five points of the pentagon. Each of the five resulting wedge-shaped work-spaces was then painted a different color. The Ss were supplied with blank message cards whose colors matched that of their work spaces. Any message sent from a booth had to be on a card of the booth's color. On the left wall of each partition, sixteen large symbol cards, representing sixteen trials, were hung in loose-leaf fashion. The cards were placed in order with numbered backs to S. At the starting signal, S could pull down the first card and go to work.

In addition, each work space was provided with a board on which were mounted six switches. Above each switch appeared one of the six symbols. When S got an answer to the problem, he was to throw the proper switch, which would turn on an appropriate light on a master board of thirty lights in the observer's room. When five lights (whether or not they were under the correct symbol), representing five different Ss, were lit, the observer called a halt to the trial. The observer could tell by a glance at the light panel whether (a) five different Ss had thrown their switches, (b) whether all five had decided on the same answer, and (c) whether the answer decided on was right or wrong. The same detailed instructions were given to all Ss.

A preliminary series of four problems, in which each S was given all the information required for solution, was used. This was done to note the extent of differences among Ss in the time required to solve such problems.

The procedure

One hundred male undergraduates of MIT,[3] drawn from various classes at the Institute, served as Ss for these experiments. These hundred were split up into twenty groups of five men each. These twenty groups were then further subdivided so that five groups could be tested on each of four experimental patterns.

Each group was given fifteen consecutive trials on *one* pattern, a

3. Data on female graduate students are being gathered at MIT by Smith and Bavelas, and the indications are that their behavior differs in some ways from the behavior of our male Ss.

process which required one session of about fifty minutes. These *S*s were *not used again*. The order in which we used our patterns was also randomized. Just in case the color or geographical position of one's work-space might affect one's behavior, we shifted positions for each new group. After a group had completed its fifteen trials, and before members were permitted to talk with one another, each member was asked to fill out a questionnaire.

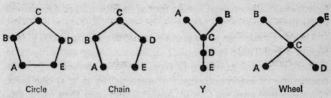

    Circle   Chain   Y   Wheel

Figure 4 The experimental patterns

The patterns selected

The four five-man patterns selected for this research are shown in Figure 4.

These four patterns represented extremes in centrality (as in the circle *v.* the wheel), as well as considerable differences in other characteristics (Table 1).

Table 1 Characteristics of the Experimental Patterns

Pattern	No. of links	Most central position	Sum of neighbors	Sum of distances	Min. time units	Min. messages
Chain	4	C(6·7)	8	40	5(8m)	8(5t)
Y	4	C(7·2)	8	36	4(8m)	8(4t)
Wheel	4	C(8·0)	8	32	5(8m)	8(5t)
Circle	5	All(5·0)	10	30	3(14m)	8(5t)

Results

The data which have been accumulated are broken down in the pages that follow into (a) a comparison of total patterns and (b) a comparison of positions within patterns.

H. J. Leavitt 81

A. Differences among patterns

It was possible to reconstruct a picture of the operational methods actually used by means of: (a) direct observations, (b) post-experimental analysis of messages, and (c) post-experimental talks with Ss.

The *wheel* operated in the same way in all five cases. The peripheral men funnelled information to the center where an answer decision was made and the answer sent out. This organization had usually evolved by the fourth or fifth trial and remained in use throughout.

The Y operated so as to give the most central position, C (see Figure 4 and Table 1), complete decision-making authority. The next-most-central position, D (see Figure 4), served only as a transmitter of information and of answers. In at least one case, C transmitted answers first to A and B and only then to D. Organization for the Y evolved a little more slowly than for the wheel, but, once achieved, it was just as stable.

In the *chain* information was usually funnelled in from both ends to C, whence the answer was sent out in both directions. There were several cases, however, in which B or D reached an answer decision and passed it to C. The organization was slower in emerging than the Y's or the wheel's, but consistent once reached.

The *circle* showed no consistent operational organization. Most commonly messages were just sent in both directions until any S received an answer or worked one out. In every case, all available links were used at some time during the course of each trial.

Direct measures of differences among patterns

Time. The curves in Figure 5 are for *correct* trials only, that is, for trials in which all five switches represented the correct common symbols. In most cases, the medians shown are for distributions of five groups, but in no case do they represent less than three groups.

The variability of the distributions represented by these medians is considerable. In the fifteenth trial, the distribution for the circle has a range of 50–96 seconds; for the chain, 28–220 seconds; for the Y, 24–52 seconds; and for the wheel, 21–46 seconds. More-

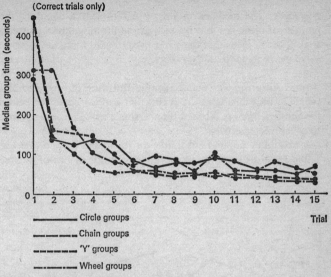

(Correct trials only)

Median group time (seconds)

Trial

— — — Circle groups

— — — Chain groups

— — — 'Y' groups

— — — Wheel groups

Figure 5 Median group-times per trial

over, much of the time that went to make up each trial was a constant consisting of writing and passing time. Any differences attributable to pattern would be a small fraction of this large constant and would be easily obscured by accidents of misplacing or dropping of messages.

Despite all these factors, one measure of speed did give statistically significant differences. A measure of the *fastest single trial* of each group indicates that the wheel was considerably faster (at its fastest) than the circle (Table 2).

Table 2 Fastest Single Correct Trial

	Circle	Chain	Y	Wheel	Diff.	p^*
Mean	50·4	53·2	35·4	32·0	Ci–W	< ·01
Median	55·0	57·0	32·0	36·0	Ch–W	< ·10
Range	44–59	19–87	22–53	20–41	Ci–Y	< ·05
					Ch–Y	< ·20

* Significance of differences between means were measured throughout

Messages. The medians in Figure 6 represent a count of the number of messages sent by each group during a given (correct) trial. It seems clear that the circle pattern used more messages to solve the problem than the others.

Errors. An error was defined as the throwing of any incorrect switch by an S during a trial. Errors that were *not* corrected before the end of a trial are labelled 'final errors'; the others are referred to as 'corrected errors'.

It should be pointed out that the error figures for the wheel in Table 3 are distorted by the peculiar behavior of one of the five

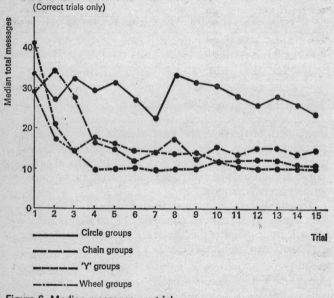

Figure 6 Median messages per trial

___

by t-tests. The p-values are based on distributions of t which include both tails of the distribution (see Freeman, 1942). Where differences are between proportions, p is derived from the usual measure of significance of differences between proportions. Ci–W means the circle-wheel difference, and so on.

wheel groups. The center man in this group took the messages which he received to be *answers* rather than simple information, and, in addition to throwing his own switch, passed the information on *as an answer*. This difficulty was cleared up after a few trials, and the figures for the last eight trials are probably more representative than the figures for the full fifteen trials.

In addition to the differences in errors, there are differences in the proportion of total errors that were corrected. Although

Table 3 Errors

Pattern	Total errors (15 trials)		Total errors (last 8 trials)		Final errors		Mean no. of trials with at least one final error
	mean	range	mean	range	mean	range	
Circle	16·6	9–33	7·6	1–18	6·4	2–14	3·4
Chain	9·8	3–19	2·8	0–11	6·2	1–19	1·8
Y	2·6	1–8	0	0	1·6	0–5	0·8
Wheel	9·8	0–34	0·6	0–2	2·2	0–7	1·2

p–Values Ci–Y < ·02

more errors were made in the circle pattern than any other, a greater proportion of them (61 per cent) were corrected than in any other pattern. Too, the frequency of unanimous five-man final errors is lower, both absolutely and percentage-wise, for the circle than for the chain.

Questionnaire results

1. '*Did your group have a leader? If so, who?*' Only thirteen of twenty-five people who worked in the circle named a leader, and those named were scattered among all the positions in the circle. For all patterns, the total frequency of people named increased in the order *circle, chain, Y, wheel*. Similarly, the unanimity of opinion increased in the same order so that, for the wheel pattern, all twenty-three members who recognized any leader agreed that position C was that leader.

2. '*Describe briefly the organization of your group.*' The word 'organization' in this question was ambiguous. Some of the *S*s understood the word to mean pattern of communication, while

others equated it with their own duties or with status difference.

These differences in interpretation were not random, however. Sixteen people in the wheel groups fully reproduced the wheel structure in answer to this question, while only one circle member reproduced the circle pattern.

3. '*How did you like your job in the group?*' In this question Ss were asked to place a check on a rating scale marked 'disliked it' at one end and 'liked it' at the other. For purposes of analysis, the scale was translated into numerical scores from 0 at the dislike end to 100. Each rating was estimated only to the closest decile.

Again, we find the order *circle, chain, Y, wheel,* with circle members enjoying their jobs significantly more than the wheel members.

4. '*See if you can recall how you felt about the job as you went along. Draw the curve below.*' The Ss were asked to sketch a curve into a space provided for it. We measured the height of these curves on a six-point scale at trials 1, 5, 10, and 15. These heights were averaged for each group, and the averages of the group averages were plotted.

Although the differences between groups are not statistically significant, trends of increasing satisfaction in the circle and decreasing satisfaction in the wheel seem to corroborate the findings in the question on satisfaction with one's job. Except for a modest Y-chain reversal, the order is, as usual, from circle to wheel.

5. '*Was there anything, at any time, that kept your group from performing at its best? If so, what?*' The answers to this question were categorized as far as possible into several classes.

None of the circle members feels that 'nothing' was wrong with his group; a fact that is suggestive of an attitute different from that held by members of the other patterns. So, too, is the finding that insufficient knowledge of the pattern does not appear as an obstacle to the circle member but is mentioned at least five times in each of the other patterns.

6. '*Do you think your group could improve its efficiency? If so, how?*' Circle members place great emphasis on *organizing* their groups, on working out a 'system' (mentioned seventeen times). Members

of the other patterns, if they felt that any improvement at all was possible, emphasized a great variety of possibilities.

7. '*Rate your group on the scale below.*' For purposes of analysis, these ratings (along a straight line) were transposed into numbers from 0, for 'poor', to 100.

The same progression of differences that we have already encountered, the progression *circle, chain, Y, wheel*, holds for this question. Once again the circle group thinks less well of itself (Mean $= 56$) than do the other patterns ($M_{ch} = 60$; $M_Y = 70$; $M_w = 71$).

Message analysis

The messages sent by all Ss were collected at the end of each experimental run and their contents coded and categorized. Some of these categories overlapped with others, and hence some messages were counted in more than one category.

The now familiar progression, *circle, chain, Y, wheel*, continues into this area. Circle members send many more informational messages than members of the other patterns ($M_{ci} = 283$; $M_w = 101$). Circle members also send more answers ($M_{ci} = 91$; $M_w = 65$).

The same tendency remains in proportion to total errors as well as absolutely. The circle has a mean of 4·8 recognition-of-error messages for a mean of 16·6 errors; the chain has a mean of 1 recognition-of-error messages for a mean of 9·8 errors.

We were concerned, before beginning these experiments, lest Ss find short cuts for solving the problem, thus making certain comparisons among patterns difficult. One such short cut we have called 'elimination'. Instead of taking time to write their five symbols, many Ss, after discovering that only six symbols existed in all, wrote just the missing symbol, thus saving considerable time. This method was used by at least one member in two of the circle groups, in all the chain groups, in three of the Y groups, and in four of the wheel groups. In *both* the circle cases, the method was used by *all five members* during final trials. In the chain, though present in every group, elimination was used only once by all five members, twice by three members, and twice by just one member. In the Y, the method was adopted once by four members (the fifth man was *not* the center) and twice by two members. There was at

Table 4 Number of Messages Sent by Each Position

		A	B	C	D	E	Diff.	p
Circle	Mean	78·4	90·0	83·6	86·2	81·0	A–B	< ·30
	Range	64–101	63–102	60–98	60–122	72–90		
Chain	Mean	24·8	70·8	82·4	71·8	27·6	C–E	< ·01
	Range	20–34	43–112	45–113	42–101	22–43		
Y	Mean	28·0	23·8	79·8	63·8	25·6	A–C	< ·01
							D–C	< ·20
	Range	20–44	21–28	65–104	43–78	21–37	D–E	< ·01
Wheel	Mean	29·4	26·2	102·8	26·6	30·2	C–E	< ·01
	Range	19–48	17–40	78–138	17–39	22–43		

least one case (in the wheel) in which a member who suggested the use of elimination was ordered by another member not to use it.

The questions here are two. Is the idea of elimination more likely to occur in some patterns than in others? Is an innovation like elimination likely to be more readily accepted in some patterns than in others? To neither of these questions do we have an adequate answer.

B. A positional analysis of the data

Observation of the experimental patterns indicates that every position in the circle is indistinguishable from every other one. No one has more neighbors, is more central, or is closer to anyone than anyone else. In the wheel, the four peripheral positions are alike, and so on. Despite our inability to differentiate these positions from one another, we have set up the data in the following sections as if all positions in each pattern were actually different from one another.

Direct observations

Messages. The most central positions, it will be seen from Table 4, send the greatest number of messages; the least central ones send the fewest.

Errors. The analysis of total errors made in each position showed nothing of significance.

Questionnaire results by position

1. '*How much did you enjoy your job?*' The most central positions in other patterns enjoy their jobs more than any circle position. Peripheral positions, on the other hand, enjoy the job less than any circle position (Table 5).

2. '*See if you can recall how you felt about the job as you went along. Draw the curve below.*' The data for this question are gathered after all most-peripheral and all most-central positions are combined.

Finally, it should be pointed out that differences in speed between patterns were subject to major fluctuations for reasons of differences in writing speed, dexterity in passing messages, and other extraneous factors.

The relation of the centrality measure to behavior

Our second and more important question is: Are the behavioral differences among patterns and among positions related consistently to the centrality index? An examination of Table 1 indicates that the centrality index shows the same progression, *circle, chain, Y, wheel,* as do most of the behavioral differences. On a positional basis, centrality also differentiates members of a pattern in the same order that their behavior does.

Because such a relationship does exist between behavior and centrality, a more detailed consideration of the centrality concept is in order.

The central region of a structure is defined by Bavelas as 'the class of all cells with the smallest p to be found in the structure'. The quantity, p, in turn, is defined as the largest distance between one cell and any other cell in the structure. Distance is measured in link units. Thus the distance from A to B in the chain is one link; from A to C the distance is two links. The most central position in a pattern is the position that is closest to all other positions. Quantitatively, an index of the centrality of position A in any pattern can be found by (a) summing the shortest distances from *each* position to every other one and (b) dividing this summation by the total of the shortest distances from position A to every other position.

Centrality, then, is a function of the size of a pattern as well as of its structure. Thus, in a five-man circle, the centrality of each man is 5·0. In a six-man circle, the centrality of each man jumps to 6·0.

The two most peripheral men in a five-man chain each have a centrality of 4·0. But in a seven-man chain, the two most peripheral men have centralities of 5·3.

In Figure 7 are given the centralities of each position in each of our four test patterns. The sum of centralities is also given. Both total centrality and distribution of centralities fall in the order *circle, chain, Y, wheel*.

These centrality figures correlate with the behavior we have observed. But it seems unreasonable to assume that the correlation would hold for larger *n*s. Certainly we would not expect *more* message activity or *more* satisfaction from peripheral positions in a chain of a larger *n* than from a five-man chain.

To obviate this difficulty, a measure we have called 'relative peripherality' may be established. The relative peripherality of

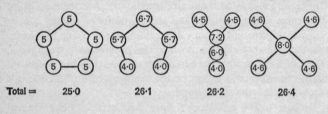

Total =   25·0   26·1   26·2   26·4

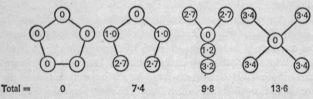

Total =   0   7·4   9·8   13·6

Figure 7 Centrality indices (above) and peripherality indices (below)

any position in a pattern is the difference between the centrality of that position and the centrality of the most central position in that pattern. Thus, for the two end men in a five-man chain, the peripherality index is 2·7 (the difference between their centralities of 4·0 and the centrality of the most central position, 6·7). For a total pattern, the peripherality index may be taken by summating all the peripherality indices in the pattern (Figure 7).

Examination of the data will show that observed differences in behavior correlate positively with these peripherality measures. *By total pattern*, messages, satisfaction and errors (except for the wheel) vary consistently with total peripherality index. Similarly, by position, messages and satisfaction vary with peripherality. Errors, however, show no clear relationship with peripherality of position, a finding which is discussed in detail later in this section.

Recognition of a leader also seems to be a function of peripherality, but in a somewhat different way. A review of our leadership findings will show that leadership becomes more clear-cut as the differences in peripherality *within a pattern become greater*. Recognition of a leader seems to be determined by the extent of the difference in centrality between the most central and next-most-central man.

There arises next the question: What is the mechanism by which the peripherality of a pattern or a position affects the behavior of persons occupying that pattern or position?

A reconstruction of the experimental situation leads us to this analysis of the peripherality-behavior relationship:

First, let us asume standard *S*s, motivated to try to solve our experimental problem as quickly as possible. Let them be 'intelligent' *S*s who do not send the same information more than once to any neighbor. Let them also be *S*s who, given several neighbors, will send, with equal probability, their first message to any one of those neighbors.

Given such standard *S*s, certain specific positions will probably get an answer to the problem before other positions. In the chain, position C will be most likely to get the answer first, but, in the circle, all positions have an equal opportunity.

To illustrate, consider the chain pattern (see Figure 4): During the first time unit, A may send only to B. B may send either to C or to A. C may send either to B or to D. D may send either to C or to E. E may send only to D. No matter where B, C and D send their messages, B and D will have, at the end of one time unit, A's and E's information. During the second time unit, if B and/or D had sent to C the first time, they will now send to A and E. If they sent to A and E the first time, they will send to C, and C will have the answer. Even if B and D do not send to C until the third time unit, C will either get the answer before or simultaneously with B and D.

In *no* case can any other position beat C to the answer. In the wheel, C cannot even be tied in getting an answer. He will *always* get it first.

Our second concern is with Ss' perceptions of these answer-getting potentials. We suggest that these random differences in answer-getting potentials rapidly structure members' perceptions of their own roles in the group. These differences affect one's independence from, or dependence on, the other members of the group. In the wheel, for example, a peripheral S perceives, at first, only that he gets the answer and information from C and can send only to C. C perceives that he gets information from everyone and must send the answer to everyone. The recognition of roles is easy. The peripheral men are dependent on C. C is autonomous and controls the organization.

In the circle, an S's perception must be very different. He gets information from both sides; sometimes he gets the answer, sometimes he sends it. He has two channels of communication. He is exclusively dependent on no one. His role is not clearly different from anyone else's.

Thirdly, having closed the gap between structural pattern and Ss' perceptions of their roles in the group, the problem reduces to one purely psychological. The question becomes: How do differences in one's perception of one's own dependence or independence bring about specific behavior differences of the sort we have observed?

Differences in satisfaction level are relatively easy to relate to independence. In our culture, in which needs for autonomy, recognition, and achievement are strong, it is to be expected that positions which limit independence of action (peripheral positions) would be unsatisfying.

A fairly direct relationship between centrality (and, hence, independence) and the speed with which a group gets organized is also perceptible. In the wheel, unless Ss act 'unintelligently', an organization, with C as center, is forced on the wheel groups by the structural pattern. In the circle, no such differences in role and, hence, in organization are forced on the group.

Message-activity can also be related to centrality by means of the independence-of-action concept. A peripheral person in any pattern can send messages to only one other position. Only one informational message is called for. Extra messages would be repetitions. Central positions, however, are free to send more than one non-repetitious informational message until an organization evolves. Once the most central man perceives that he is most central, he need send *no* informational messages. But so long as the most central man does not perceive his own position, it is intelligent to send informational messages to whomever he feels may require some information. It is in keeping with this analysis that the circle should yield maximum messages and the wheel minimum messages. Peripheral positions were: positions A and E, in the chain; position E in the Y; and positions A, B, D, and E in the wheel. Central positions were all C positions with the exception of C in the circle. The data thus combined highlight the trend toward higher satisfaction with increasing centrality. The central positions progress from a mean of 2·1 at trial 1 to a mean of 3·9 at trial 15. Peripheral positions decline from 3·9 to 2·3.

Message analysis by position

One of the things that immediately stands out from an examination of the messages is an apparent peculiarity in the *informational message* category. Although the most central man in the chain sends more informational messages (fifty-two) than the other positions in that pattern, the same is not true of the most central men in the Y and the wheel. In the Y, it is position D, the next-most-central position, that sends most; while in the wheel all positions are about equal. This peculiarity becomes quite understandable if we take into account (a) the kind of organization used in each pattern and (b) the fact that these figures represent the entire fifteen trials, some of which occurred before the group got itself stably organized. In the wheel, the Y, and the chain, the center man really needed to send *no* informational messages, only answers; but in the *early* trials, before his role was clarified, he apparently sent enough to bring his total up to or higher than the level of the rest.

It can also be noted that the number of *organizational messages* (messages which seek to establish some plan of action for future trials) is negatively correlated with positional centrality. The most peripheral men send the greatest numbers of organizational messages, the most central men least.

Table 5 Enjoyment of the Job

		A	B	C	D	E	Diff.	p
Circle	Mean	58·0	64·0	70·0	65·0	71·0	A–E	< ·70
	Range	0–100	0–100	20–100	40–100	25–100		
Chain	Mean	45·0	82·5	78·0	70·0	24·0	C–E	< ·02
	Range	25–55	50–100	50–100	40–100	0–70	C–AE	< ·01
Y	Mean	46·0	49·0	95·0	71·0	31·0	C–A	< ·02
							C–AB	< ·01
	Range	0–100	25–100	75–100	30–100	0–75	D–E	< ·10
Wheel	Mean	37·5	20·0	97·0	25·0	42·5	B–C	< ·01
							C–E	< ·02
	Range	0–50	0–40	85–100	0–75	0–100	ABED–C	< ·01

Discussion

Patternwise, the picture formed by the results is of differences almost always in the order *circle, chain, Y, wheel*.

We may grossly characterize the kinds of differences that occur in this way: the circle, one extreme, is active, leaderless, unorganized, erratic, and yet is enjoyed by its members. The wheel, at the other extreme, is less active, has a distinct leader, is well and stably organized, is less erratic, and yet is unsatisfying to most of its members.

There are two questions raised by these behavioral differences. First, what was wrong with our *a priori* time-unit analysis? The results measured in clock time do not at all match the time-unit figures. And second, to what extent are behavioral differences matched by centrality differences?

The time unit

It was hypothesized earlier that the time taken to solve a problem should be limited at the lower end by the structure of the pattern of communication. If pattern does set such a limitation on speed, the limitation is not in the direction we would have predicted. Our analysis (Table 1), based on a theoretical time unit, led us falsely to expect greatest speed from the circle pattern.

There are three outstanding reasons for the failure of the time-unit analysis to predict clock time. First, the time unit itself was too gross a measure. We defined the time unit as the time required for the transmission of one message from its inception to its reception. In actuality, different kinds of messages required very different clock times for transmission. *S*s could send two messages simultaneously. They could also lay out and write several messages before sending any.

A second reason for the failure of the time-unit analysis was the assumption that *S*s would gravitate to the theoretically 'best'-operating organization. Only the wheel groups used the theoretically 'best' method (the minimum time method) consistently.

If the behavior of one of the wheel groups can be discounted, then an explanation, in terms of peripherality, is also possible for both differences in tendencies to correct errors and total error differences.

If peripherality determines one's independence of action, it seems very likely that positions most limited in independence should begin to perceive themselves as subordinates whose sole function is to send information and await an answer. That they should then uncritically accept whatever answer they receive is perfectly in keeping with their subordinate, relatively unresponsible positions – hence, very little correction of errors in the patterns in which there are great differences in peripherality.

Total errors, it will be recalled, were correlated with total peripherality indices but showed no clear relationship with the relative peripherality of particular positions. A consideration of our definition of error may shed some light on this apparent anomaly.

The 'errors' that we recorded were signals from the *S* that indicated a wrong answer. But these wrong answers derived from a variety of sources. First, *S*s might wrongly interpret the correct information they received. They might also make errors in throwing switches; and they might also *correctly* interpret *wrong* information. In all three cases, 'errors' were recorded.

We submit that this broad definition of error should yield a total pattern relationship with peripherality, but no positional relationship. Our reasoning can be illustrated by an example. Suppose that the central man in the wheel wrongly interprets information sent to him and, hence, throws an incorrect switch. This is a 'real' error. He then funnels out the wrong answer to the other members. At least three of these intelligently conclude that the answer sent them is correct and also throw the wrong switches. We then have three 'false' errors consequent to our single 'real' one. When several independent answer decisions are made (as in the circle), we should expect several real errors, multiplication of these by a factor of about three and a larger total of errors. This process should lead to a correlation between total pattern behavior and peripherality but not to a correlation between positional behavior and peripherality. The process simply multiplies real errors more or less constantly for a whole pattern but obscures positional differences because the 'real' and the 'false' errors are indistinguishable in our data.

We submit, further, that pattern differences in real errors, if such there be, may be attributable to 'over-information'; too much information to too many members which, under pressure, leads to errors. Central positions or positions which are no less central than others in the pattern should be the ones to yield the greatest number of real errors, while peripheral positions, which require no such rapid collation of information, should be the false error sources. Such an hypothesis would be in keeping with our total pattern findings and might also clarify our positional findings. Only an experiment designed to differentiate real from false errors can answer this question.

It is in keeping with this peripherality-independence analysis, also, that we should find the recognition of a single leader occurring most frequently in the wheel and Y groups. It is also to be expected that we should find circle members emphasizing need for organization and planning and seldom giving a complete picture of their pattern. Perhaps, too, it is reasonable to expect that the whole group should be considered good in the highly organized wheel (and not so good in the unorganized circle) even though one's own job is considered poor.

In summary, then, it is our feeling that centrality determines behavior by limiting independence of action, thus producing differences in activity, accuracy, satisfaction, leadership, recognition of pattern, and other behavioral characteristics.

Summary and conclusions

Within the limits set by the experimental conditions – group size, type of problem, source of Ss – these conclusions seem warranted:

1. The communication patterns within which our groups worked

affected their behavior. The major behavioral differences attributable to communication patterns were differences in accuracy, total activity, satisfaction of group members, emergence of a leader and organization of the group. There may also be differences among patterns in speed of problem solving, self-correcting tendencies and durability of the group as a group.

2. The positions which individuals occupied in a communication pattern affected their behavior while occupying those positions. One's position in the group affected the chances of becoming a leader of the group, one's satisfaction with one's job and with the group, the quantity of one's activity, and the extent to which one contributed to the group's functional organization.

3. The characteristic of communication patterns that was most clearly correlated with behavioral differences was *centrality*. Total pattern differences in behavior seemed to be correlated with a measure of centrality we have labelled the *peripherality index*. Positional differences in behavior seemed to be correlated with the positional peripherality indices of the various positions within patterns.

4. It is tentatively suggested that centrality affects behavior via the limits that centrality imposes upon independent action. Independence of action, relative to other members of the group is, in turn, held to be the primary determinant of the definition of who shall take the leadership role, total activity, satisfaction with one's lot, and other specific behaviors.

More precisely, it is felt that where centrality and, hence, independence are evenly distributed, there will be no leader, many errors, high activity, slow organization, and high satisfaction. Whatever frustration occurs will occur as a result of the inadequacy of the group, not the inadequacy of the environment.

Where one position is low in centrality relative to other members of the group, that position will be a follower position, dependent on the leader, accepting his dictates, falling into a role that allows little opportunity for prestige, activity, or self-expression.

References

BAVELAS, A. (1948), 'A mathematical model for group structures', *Applied Anthropology*, vol. 7, pp. 16–30.

FREEMAN, H. (1942), *Industrial Statistics*, Wiley.

Part Two The Management of Organizations

All organizations have to be managed, and the tasks and the processes which this involves have been the subject of much thought. In particular, attempts have been made to generalize the analyses so that they may be of use to managers in a large variety of organizations in their attempts to manage better. The contributors to this section have tried to present overall principles distilled from their experience, all of which have attracted much support and much criticism.

Fayol (Reading 6) was the first of the modern management writers to propound a theoretical analysis of what managers have to do and by what principles they have to do it; an analysis which has withstood half a century of critical discussion. His principles of authority and responsibility, unity of command, good order, *esprit de corps*, etc. are the common currency of management parlance. Taylor (Reading 7) set out to challenge management with his approach of 'scientific management', which promised increased efficiency through extreme specialization and tight control of tasks (including managers' as well as workers' tasks). His ideas made him a controversial figure in his own day, and he has remained so since, but from him has flowed the approach to management through time study, work study, industrial engineering, which are important parts of the control procedures of many organizations.

Mary Parker Follett's analysis (Reading 8) opened the way for the consideration of management as a continuous process rather than a series of discrete events. She saw the working out of this process as leading beyond the interplay of personalities to a rational appreciation by all of what is required by the situation, thus depersonalizing and making more acceptable the giving of orders – the example which the present reading discusses. Barnard (Reading 9) is also concerned with the processes which are necessary for an organization to function well, and particularly with the tasks which devolve on the executive. His practical managerial wisdom combined with his deep and insightful knowledge of the social sciences have made him a most influential analyst. Sloan (Reading 10) from his years of experience as head of the largest industrial corporation in the world – General Motors of America – advocates a basic managerial process of 'coordinated decentralization' which is practised in his organization and has had considerable influence on many others. Simon (Reading 11) is a leading representative of the Carnegie approach to management, which focuses on the processes and procedures of decision making. Through their mathematical decision-making approach, the group has had a considerable influence in linking operational research, the economic theory of the firm, and organization theory firmly to modern computer-based methods of analysis.

6 H. Fayol

General Principles of Management

H. Fayol, *General Industrial Management*, Pitman, 1949,
chapter 4, pp. 19–42.

The managerial function finds its only outlet through the members
of the organization (body corporate). Whilst the other functions
bring into play material and machines the managerial function
operates only on the personnel. The soundness and good working
order of the body corporate depend on a certain number of conditions termed indiscriminately principles; laws, rules. For preference I shall adopt the term principles whilst dissociating it from
any suggestion of rigidity, for there is nothing rigid or absolute in
management affairs, it is all a question of proportion. Seldom do
we have to apply the same principle twice in identical conditions;
allowance must be made for different changing circumstances, for
men just as different and changing and for many other variable
elements.

Therefore principles are flexible and capable of adaptation to
every need; it is a matter of knowing how to make use of them,
which is a difficult art requiring intelligence, experience, decision
and proportion. Compounded of tact and experience, proportion
is one of the foremost attributes of the manager. There is no limit
to the number of principles of management, every rule or managerial procedure which strengthens the body corporate or facilitates its functioning has a place among the principles so long, at
least, as experience confirms its worthiness. A change in the state
of affairs can be responsible for change of rules which had been
engendered by that state.

I am going to review some of the principles of management
which I have most frequently had to apply; viz.

1. Division of work.
2. Authority.

3. Discipline.
4. Unity of command.
5. Unity of direction.
6. Subordination of individual interests to the general interest.
7. Remuneration.
8. Centralization.
9. Scalar chain (line of authority).
10. Order.
11. Equity.
12. Stability of tenure of personnel.
13. Initiative.
14. *Esprit de corps*.

Division of work

Specialization belongs to the natural order; it is observable in the animal world, where the more highly developed the creature the more highly differentiated its organs; it is observable in human societies where the more important the body corporate[1] the closer is the relationship between structure and function. As society grows, so new organs develop destined to replace the single one performing all functions in the primitive state.

The object of division of work is to produce more and better work with the same effort. The worker always on the same part, the manager concerned always with the same matters, acquire an ability, sureness and accuracy which increase their output. Each change of work brings in its train an adaptation which reduces output. Division of work permits of reduction in the number of objects to which attention and effort must be directed and has been recognized as the best means of making use of individuals and of groups of people. It is not merely applicable to technical work, but without exception to all work involving a more or less considerable number of people and demanding abilities of various types, and it

1. '*Body corporate*.' Fayol's term 'corps social', meaning all those engaged in a given corporate activity in any sphere, is best rendered by this somewhat unusual term because [a] it retains his implied biological metaphor; [b] it represents the structure as distinct from the process of organization.

The term will be retained in all contexts where these two requirements have to be met. (*Translator's note*.)

results in specialization of functions and separation of powers. Although its advantages are universally recognized and although possibility of progress is inconceivable without the specialized work of learned men and artists, yet division of work has its limits which experience and a sense of proportion teach us may not be exceeded.

Authority and responsibility

Authority is the right to give orders and the power to exact obedience. Distinction must be made between a manager's official authority deriving from office and personal authority, compounded of intelligence, experience, moral worth, ability to lead, past services, etc. In the make up of a good head personal authority is the indispensable complement of official authority. Authority is not to be conceived of apart from responsibility, that is apart from sanction – reward or penalty – which goes with the exercise of power. Responsibility is a corollary of authority, it is its natural consequence and essential counterpart, and wheresoever authority is exercised responsibility arises.

The need for sanction, which has its origin in a sense of justice, is strengthened and increased by this consideration, that in the general interest useful actions have to be encouraged and their opposite discouraged. Application of sanction to acts of authority forms part of the conditions essential for good management, but it is generally difficult to effect, especially in large concerns. First, the degree of responsibility must be established and then the weight of the sanction. Now, it is relatively easy to establish a workman's responsibility for his acts and a scale of corresponding sanctions; in the case of a foreman it is somewhat difficult, and proportionately as one goes up the scalar chain of businesses, as work grows more complex, as the number of workers involved increases, as the final result is more remote, it is increasingly difficult to isolate the share of the initial act of authority in the ultimate result and to establish the degree of responsibility of the manager. The measurement of this responsibility and its equivalent in material terms elude all calculation.

Sanction, then, is a question of kind, custom, convention, and judging it one must take into account the action itself, the attendant circumstances and potential repercussions. Judgment demands high moral character, impartiality and firmness. If these all conditions are not fulfilled there is a danger that the sense of responsibility may disappear from the concern.

Responsibility valiantly undertaken and borne merits some consideration; it is a kind of courage everywhere much appreciated. Tangible proof of this exists in the salary level of some industrial leaders, which is much higher than that of civil servants of comparable rank but carrying no responsibility. Nevertheless, generally speaking, responsibility is feared as much as authority is sought after, and fear of responsibility paralyses much initiative and destroys many good qualities. A good leader should possess and infuse into these around him courage to accept responsibility.

The best safeguard against abuse of authority and against weakness on the part of a higher manager is personal integrity and particularly high moral character of such a manager, and this integrity, it is well known, is conferred neither by election nor ownership.

Discipline

Discipline is in essence obedience, application, energy, behaviour and outward marks of respect observed in accordance with the standing agreements between the firm and its employees, whether these agreements have been freely debated or accepted without prior discussion, whether they be written or implicit, whether they derive from the wish of the parties to them or from rules and customs, it is these agreements which determine the formalities of discipline.

Discipline, being the outcome of different varying agreements, naturally appears under the most diverse forms; obligations of obedience, application, energy, behaviour, vary, in effect, from one firm to another, from one group of employees to another, from one time to another. Nevertheless, general opinion is deeply convinced that discipline is absolutely essential for the smooth running of business and that without discipline no enterprise could prosper.

This sentiment is very forcibly expressed in military handbooks, where it runs that 'Discipline constitutes the chief strength of armies.' I would approve unreservedly of this aphorism were it followed by this other, 'Discipline is what leaders make it.' The first one inspires respect for discipline, which is a good thing, but it tends to eclipse from view the responsibility of leaders, which is undesirable, for the state of discipline of any group of people depends essentially on the worthiness of its leaders.

When a defect in discipline is apparent or when relations between superiors and subordinates leave much to be desired, responsibility for this must not be cast heedlessly, and without going further afield, on the poor state of the team, because the ill mostly results from the ineptitude of the leaders. That, at all events, is what I have noted in various parts of France, for I have always found French workmen obedient and loyal provided thay are ably led.

In the matter of influence upon discipline, agreements must be set side by side with command. It is important that they be clear and, as far as is possible, afford satisfaction to both sides. This is not easy. Proof of that exists in the great strikes of miners, railwaymen and civil servants which, in these latter years, have jeopardized national life at home and elsewhere and which arose out of agreements in dispute or inadequate legislation.

For half a century a considerable change has been effected in the mode of agreements between a concern and its employees. The agreements of former days fixed by the employer alone are being replaced, in ever increasing measure, by understandings arrived at by discussion between an owner or group of owners and workers' associations. Thus each individual owner's responsibility has been reduced and is further diminished by increasingly frequent State intervention in labour problems. Nevertheless, the setting up of agreements binding a firm and its employees from which disciplinary formalities emanate, should remain one of the chief preoccupations of industrial heads.

The well-being of the concern does not permit, in cases of offence against discipline, of the neglect of certain sanctions capable of preventing or minimizing their recurrence. Experience and tact on the part of a manager are put to the proof in the choice and degree of sanctions to be used, such as remonstrances, warnings, fines, suspensions, demotion, dismissal. Individual people and attendant circumstances must be taken into account. In fine, discipline is respect for agreements which are directed at achieving obedience, application, energy, and the outward marks of respect.

It is incumbent upon managers at high levels as much as upon humble employees, and the best means of establishing and maintaining it are:

1. Good superiors at all levels.
2. Agreements as clear and fair as possible.
3. Sanctions (penalties) judiciously applied.

Unity of command

For any action whatsoever, an employee should receive orders from one superior only. Such is the rule of unity of command, arising from general and ever-present necessity and wielding an influence on the conduct of affairs, which to my way of thinking, is at least equal to any other principle whatsoever. Should it be violated, authority is undermined, discipline is in jeopardy, order disturbed and stability threatened. This rule seems fundamental to me and so I have given it the rank of principle. As soon as two superiors wield their authority over the same person or department, uneasiness makes itself felt and should the cause persist, the disorder increases, the malady takes on the appearance of an animal organism troubled by a foreign body, and the following consequences are to be observed: either the dual command ends in disappearance or elimination of one of the superiors and organic well-being is restored, or else the organism continues to wither away. In no case is there adaptation of the social organism to dual command.

Now dual command is extremely common and wreaks havoc in all concerns, large or small, in home and in State. The evil is all the more to be feared in that it worms its way into the social organism on the most plausible pretexts. For instance

1. In the hope of being better understood or gaining time or to put a stop forthwith to an undesirable practice, a superior S^2 may give orders directly to an employee E without going via the superior S^1. If this mistake is repeated there is dual command with its consequences, viz., hesitation on the part of the subordinate, irritation and dissatisfaction on the part of the superior set aside, and disorder in the work. It will be seen later, that it is possible to by-pass the scalar chain when necessary, whilst avoiding the drawbacks of dual command.

2. The desire to get away from the immediate necessity of dividing up authority as between two colleagues, two friends, two members of one family, results at times in dual command reigning at the top of a concern right from the outset. Exercising the same powers and having the same authority over the same men, the two colleagues end up inevitably with dual command and its consequences. Despite harsh lessons, instances of this sort are still numerous. New colleagues count on their mutual regard, common interest and good sense to save them from every conflict, every serious disagreement and, save for rare exceptions, the illusion is short-lived. First an awkwardness makes itself felt, then a certain irritation and, in time, if dual command exists, even hatred. Men cannot bear dual command. A judicious assignment of duties would have reduced the danger without entirely banishing it, for between two superiors on the same footing there must always be some question ill-defined. But it is riding for a fall to set up a business organization with two superiors on equal footing without assigning duties and demarcating authority.

3. Imperfect demarcation of departments also leads to dual command: two superiors issuing orders in a sphere which each thinks his own, constitutes dual command.

4. Constant linking up as between different departments, natural intermeshing of functions, duties often badly defined, create an ever-present danger of dual command. If a knowledgeable superior does not put it in order, footholds are established which later upset and compromise the conduct of affairs.

In all human associations, in industry, commerce, army, home, State, dual command is a perpetual source of conflicts, very grave sometimes, which have special claim on the attention of superiors of all ranks.

Unity of direction

This principle is expressed as: one head and one plan for a group of activities having the same objective. It is the condition essential to unity of action, coordination of strength and focusing of effort. A body with two heads is in the social as in the animal sphere a monster, and has difficulty in surviving. Unity of direction (one head one plan) must not be confused with unity of command (one employee to have orders from one superior only). Unity of direction is provided for by sound organization of the body corporate, unity of command turns on the functioning of the personnel. Unity of command cannot exist without unity of direction, but does not flow from it.

Subordination of individual interest to general interest

This principle calls to mind the fact that in a business the interest of one employee or group of employees should not prevail over that of the concern, that the interest of the home should come before that of its members and that the interest of the State should have pride of place over that of one citizen or group of citizens.

It seems that such an admonition should not need calling to mind. But ignorance, ambition, selfishness, laziness, weakness, and all human passions tend to cause the general interest to be lost sight of in favour of individual interest and a perpetual struggle has to be waged against them. Two interests of a different order, but claiming equal respect, confront each other and means must be found to reconcile them. That represents one of the great difficulties of management. Means of effecting it are

1. Firmness and good example on the part of superiors.
2. Agreements as fair as is possible.
3. Constant supervision.

Remuneration of personnel

Remuneration of personnel is the price of services rendered. It should be fair and, as far as is possible, afford satisfaction both to personnel and firm (employee and employer). The rate of remuneration depends, firstly, on circumstances independent of the employer's will and employee's worth, viz. cost of living, abundance or shortage of personnel, general business conditions, the economic position of the business, and after that it depends on the value of the employee and mode of payment adopted. Appreciation of the factors dependent on the employer's will and on the value of employees, demands a fairly good knowledge of business, judgment, and impartiality. Later on in connection with selecting personnel we shall deal with assessing the value of employees; here only the mode of payment is under consideration as a factor operating on remuneration. The method of payment can exercise considerable influence on business progress, so the choice of this method is an important problem. It is also a thorny problem which in practice has been solved in widely different ways, of which so far none has proved satisfactory. What is generally looked for in the method of payment is that

1. It shall assure fair remuneration.
2. It shall encourage keenness by rewarding well-directed effort.
3. It shall not lead to over-payment going beyond reasonable limits.

I am going to examine briefly the modes of payment in use for workers, junior managers, and higher managers.

Workers

The various modes of payment in use for workers are

1. Time rates.
2. Job rates.
3. Piece rates.

These three modes of payment may be combined and give rise to important variations by the introduction of bonuses, profit-sharing schemes, payment in kind, and non-financial incentives.

1. *Time rates.* Under this system the workman sells the employer, in return for a pre-determined sum, a day's work under definite conditions. This system has the disadvantage of conducing to negligence and of demanding constant supervision. It is inevitable where the work done is not susceptible to measurement and in effect it is very common.

2. *Job rates.* Here payment made turns upon the execution of a definite job set in advance and may be independent of the length of the job. When payment is due only on condition that the job be completed during the normal work spell, this method merges into time rate. Payment by daily job does not require as close a supervision as payment by the day, but it has the drawback of levelling the output of good workers down to that of mediocre ones. The good ones are not satisfied, because they feel that they could earn more; the mediocre ones find the task set too heavy.

3. *Piece rates.* Here payment is related to work done and there is no limit. This system is often used in workshops where a large number

of similar articles have to be made, and is found where the product can be measured by weight, length or cubic capacity, and in general is used wherever possible. It is criticized on the grounds of emphasizing quantity at the expense of quality and of provoking disagreements when rates have to be revised in the light of manufacturing improvements. Piece-work becomes contract work when applied to an important unit of work. To reduce the contractor's risk, sometimes there is added to the contract price a payment for each day's work done.

Generally, piece rates give rise to increased earnings which act for some time as a stimulus, then finally a system prevails in which this mode of payment gradually approximates to time rates for a pre-arranged sum.

The above three modes of payment are found in all large concerns; sometimes time rates prevail, sometimes one of the other two. In a workshop the same workman may be seen working now on piece rates, now on time rates. Each one of these methods has its advantages and drawbacks, and their effectiveness depends on circumstances and the ability of superiors. Neither method nor rate of payment absolves management from competence and tact, and keenness of workers and peaceful atmosphere of the workshop depend largely upon it.

Bonuses

To arouse the worker's interest in the smooth running of the business, sometimes an increment in the nature of a bonus is added to the time, job or piece rate: for good time keeping, hard work, freedom from machine breakdown, output, cleanliness, etc. The relative importance, nature and qualifying conditions of these bonuses are very varied. There are to be found the small daily supplement, the monthly sum, the annual award, shares or portions of shares distributed to the most meritorious, and also even profit-sharing schemes such as, for example, certain monetary allocations distributed annually among workers in some large firms. Several French collieries started some years back the granting of a bonus proportional to profits distributed or to extra profits. No contract is required from the workers save that the earning of the bonus is subject to certain conditions, for instance, that there shall have been no strike during the year, or that absenteeism shall not have exceeded a given number of days. This type of bonus introduced an element of profit-sharing into miners' wages without any prior discussion as between workers and employer. The workman did not refuse a gift, largely gratuitous, on the part of the employer, that is, the contract was a unilateral one. Thanks to a successful trading period the yearly wages have been appreciably increased by the operation of the bonus. But what is to happen in lean times? This interesting procedure is as yet too new to be judged, but obviously it is no general solution of the problem.

In the mining industry there is another type of bonus, dependent upon the selling price of coal. The sliding scale of wages depending on a basic rate plus a bonus proportionate to the local selling price, which had long flourished in Wales, but was discontinued when minimum wages legislation came into force, is today the principle regulating the payment of miners in the Nord and Pas de Calais *départements*, and has also been adopted in the Loire region. This system established a certain fixed relationship between the prosperity of the colliery and the miner's wage. It is criticized on the grounds that it conduces to limitation of production in order to raise selling price. So we see that it is necessary to have recourse to a variety of methods in order to settle wages questions. The problem is far from being settled to everyone's satisfaction and all solutions are hazardous.

Profit-sharing

Workers. The idea of making workers share in profits is a very attractive one and it would seem that it is from there that harmony as between Capital and Labour should come. But the practical formula for such sharing has not yet been found. Workers' profit-sharing has hitherto come up against insurmountable difficulties of application in the case of large concerns. Firstly, let us note that it cannot exist in enterprises having no monetary objective (State services, religions, philanthropic, scientific societies) and also that it is not possible in the case of businesses running at a loss. Thus profit-sharing is excluded from a great number of concerns. There remain the prosperous business concerns and of these latter the desire to reconcile and harmonize workers' and employers' interests is nowhere so great as in French mining and metallurgical industries. Now, in these industries I know of no clear application of workers' profit-sharing, whence it may be concluded forthwith that the matter is difficult, if not impossible. It is very difficult indeed. Whether a business is making a profit or not the worker must have an immediate wage assured him, and a system which would make workers' payment depend entirely on eventual future profit is unworkable. But perhaps a part of wages might come from business profits. Let us see. Viewing all contingent factors, the worker's greater or lesser share of activity or ability in the final outcome of a large concern is impossible to assess and is, moreover, quite insignificant. The portion accruing to him of distributed dividend would at the most be a few centimes on a wage of five francs for instance, that is to say the smallest extra effort, the stroke of a pick or of a file operating directly on his wage, would prove of greater advantage to him. Hence the worker has no interest in being rewarded by a share in profits proportionate to the effect he has upon profits. It is worthy of note that, in most large concerns, wage increases, operative now for some twenty years, represent a total sum greater than the amount of capital shared out. In effect, unmodified real profit-sharing by workers of large concerns has not yet entered the sphere of practical business politics.

Junior Managers. Profit-sharing for foremen, superintendents, engineers, is scarcely more advanced than for workers. Nevertheless, the influence of these employees on the results of a business is quite considerable, and if they are not consistently interested in profits the only reason is that the basis for participation is difficult to establish. Doubtless managers have no need of monetary incentive to carry out their duties, but they are not indifferent to material satisfactions and it must be acknowledged that the hope of extra profit is capable of arousing their enthusiasm. So employees at middle levels should, where possible, be induced to have an interest in profits. It is relatively easy in businesses which are starting out or on trial, where exceptional effort can yield outstanding results. Sharing may then be applied to overall business profits or merely to the running of the particular department of the employee in question. When the business is of long standing and well run the zeal of a junior manager is scarcely apparent in the general outcome, and it is very hard to establish a useful basis on which he may participate. In fact, profit-sharing among junior managers in

France is very rare in large concerns. Production or workshop output bonuses – not to be confused with profit-sharing – are much more common.

Higher Managers. It is necessary to go right up to top management to find a class of employee with frequent interest in the profits of large-scale French concerns. The head of the business, in view of his knowledge, ideas and actions, exerts considerable influence on general results, so it is quite natural to try and provide him with an interest in them. Sometimes it is possible to establish a close connection between his personal activity and its effects. Nevertheless, generally speaking, there exist other influences quite independent of the personal capability of the manager which can influence results to a greater extent than can his personal activity. If the manager's salary were exclusively dependent upon profits, it might at times be reduced to nothing. There are besides, businesses being built up, wound up or merely passing through temporary crisis, wherein management depends no less on talent than in the case of prosperous ones, and wherein profit-sharing cannot be a basis for remuneration for the manager. In fine, senior civil servants cannot be paid on a profit-sharing basis. Profit-sharing, then, for either higher managers or workers, is not a general rule of remuneration. To sum up, then: profit-sharing is a mode of payment capable of giving excellent results in certain cases, but is not a general rule. It does not seem to me possible, at least for the present, to count on this mode of payment for appeasing conflict between Capital and Labour. Fortunately, there are other means which hitherto have been sufficient to maintain relative social quiet. Such methods have not lost their power and it is up to managers to study them, apply them, and make them work well.

Payment in kind, welfare work, non-financial incentives

Whether wages are made up of money only or whether they include various additions such as heating, light, housing, food, is of little consequence provided that the employee be satisfied.

From another point of view, there is no doubt that a business will be better served in proportion as its employees are more energetic, better educated, more conscientious and more permanent. The employer should have regard, if merely in the interests of the business, for the health, strength, education, morale, and stability of his personnel. These elements of smooth running are not acquired in the workshop alone, they are formed and developed as well, and particularly, outside it, in the home and school, in civil and religious life. Therefore, the employer comes to be concerned with his employees outside the works and here the question of proportion comes up again. Opinion is greatly divided on this point. Certain unfortunate experiments have resulted in some employers stopping short their interest at the works gate and at the regulation of wages. The majority consider that the employer's activity may be used to good purpose outside the factory confines provided that there be discretion and prudence, that it be sought after rather than imposed, be in keeping with the general level of education and taste of those concerned and that it have absolute respect for their liberty. It must be benevolent collaboration, not tyrannical stewardship, and therein lies an indispensable condition of success.

The employer's welfare activities may be of various kinds. In the works they bear on matters of hygiene and comfort: ventilation, lighting, cleanliness, canteen facilities. Outside the works they bear on housing accommodation, feeding, education, and training. Provident schemes come under this head.

Non-financial incentives only come in in the case of large scale concerns and may be said to be almost exclusively in the realm of government work. Every mode of payment likely to make the personnel more valuable and improve its lot in life, and also to inspire keenness on the part of employees at all levels, should be a matter for managers' constant attention.

Centralization

Like division of work, centralization belongs to the natural order; this turns on the fact that in every organism, animal or social, sensations converge towards the brain or directive part, and from the brain or directive part orders are sent out which set all parts of the organism in movement. Centralization is not a system of management good or bad of itself, capable of being adopted or discarded at the whim of managers or of circumstances; it is always present to a greater or less extent. The question of centralization or decentralization, is a simple question of proportion, it is a matter of finding the optimum degree for the particular concern.

In small firms, where the manager's orders go directly to subordinates, there is absolute centralization; in large concerns, where a long scalar chain is interposed between manager and lower grades, orders and counter-information, too, have to go through a series of intermediaries. Each employee, intentionally or unintentionally, puts something of himself into the transmission and execution of orders and of information received too. He does not operate merely as a cog in a machine. What appropriate share of initiative may be left to intermediaries depends on the personal character of the manager, on his moral worth, on the reliability of his subordinates, and also on the condition of the business. The degree of centralization must vary according to different cases. The objective to pursue is the optimum utilization of all faculties of the personnel.

If the moral worth of the manager, his strength, intelligence, experience and swiftness of thought allow him to have a wide span of activities he will be able to carry centralization quite far and reduce his seconds in command to mere executive agents. If, conversely, he prefers to have greater recourse to the experience, opinions, and counsel of his colleagues whilst reserving to himself the privilege of giving general directives, he can effect considerable decentralization.

Seeing that both absolute and relative value of manager and employees are constantly changing, it is understandable that the degree of centralization or decentralization may itself vary constantly. It is a problem to be solved according to circumstances, to the best satisfaction of the interests involved. It arises, not only in the case of higher authority, but for superiors at all levels and not one but can extend or confine, to some extent, his subordinates' initiative.

The finding of the measure which shall give the best overall yield: that is the problem of centralization or decentralization. Everything which goes to increase the importance of the subordinate's role is decentralization, everything which goes to reduce it is centralization.

Scalar chain

The scalar chain is the chain of superiors ranging from the ultimate authority to the lowest ranks. The line of authority is the route followed – via every link in the chain – by all communications which start from or go to the ultimate authority. This path is dictated both by the need for some transmission and by the principle of unity of command, but it is not always the swiftest. It is even at times disastrously lengthy in large concerns, notably in governmental ones. Now, there are many activities whose success turns on speedy execution, hence respect for the line of authority must be reconciled with the need for swift action.

Let us imagine that section F has to be put into contact with section P in a business whose scalar chain is represented by the double ladder G–A–Q thus

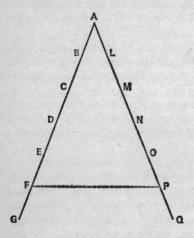

By following the line of authority the ladder must be climbed from F to A and then descended from A to P, stopping at each rung, then ascended again from P to A, and descended once more from A to F, in order to get back to the starting point. Evidently it is much simpler and quicker to go directly from F to P by making use of FP as a 'gang plank' and that is what is most often done. The scalar principle will be safeguarded if managers E and O have authorized their respective subordinates F and P to treat directly, and the position will be fully regularized if F and P inform their respective superiors forthwith of what they have agreed upon. So long as F and P remain in agreement, and so long as their actions are approved by their immediate superiors, direct contact may be maintained, but from the instant that agreement ceases or there is no approval from the superiors direct contact comes to an end, and the scalar chain is straightway resumed. Such is the actual procedure to be observed in the great majority of businesses. It provides for the usual exercise of some measure of initiative at all levels of authority. In the small concern, the general interest, viz. that of the concern proper, is easy to grasp, and the employer is present to recall this interest to those tempted to lose sight of it. In government enterprise the general interest is such a complex, vast, remote thing, that it is not easy to get a clear idea of it, and for the majority of civil servants the employer is somewhat mythical and unless the sentiment of general interest be constantly revived by higher authority, it becomes blurred and weakened and each section tends to regard itself as its own aim and end and forgets that it is only a cog in a big machine, all of whose parts must work in concert. It becomes isolated, cloistered, aware only of the line of authority.

The use of the 'gang plank' is simple, swift, sure. It allows the two employees F and P to deal at one sitting, and in a few hours, with some question or other which via the scalar chain would pass through twenty transmissions, inconvenience many people, involve masses of paper, lose weeks or months to get to a conclusion less satisfactory generally than the one which could have been obtained via direct contact as between F and P.

Is it possible that such practices, as ridiculous as they are devastating, could be in current use? Unfortunately there can be little doubt of it in government department affairs. It is usually acknowledged that the chief cause is fear of responsibility. I am rather of the opinion that it is insufficient executive capacity on the part of those in charge. If supreme authority A insisted that his assistants B and L made use of the 'gang plank' themselves and made its use incumbent upon their subordinates C and M, the habit and courage of taking responsibility would be established and at the same time the custom of using the shortest path.

It is an error to depart needlessly from the line of authority, but it is an even greater one to keep to it when detriment to the business ensues. The latter may attain extreme gravity in certain conditions. When an employee is obliged to choose between the two practices, and it is impossible for him to take advice from his superior, he should be courageous enough and feel free enough to adopt the line dictated by the general interest. But for him to be in this frame of mind there must have been previous precedent, and his superiors must have set him the example – for example must always come from above.

Order

The formula is known in the case of material things 'A place for everything and everything in its place'. The formula is the same for human order 'A place for everyone and everyone in his place'.

Material order

In accordance with the preceding definition, so that material order shall prevail, there must be a place appointed for each thing and each thing must be in its appointed place. Is that enough? Is it not also necessary that the place shall have been well chosen? The object of order must be avoidance of loss of material, and for this object to be completely realized not only must things be in their place suitably arranged but also the place must have been chosen so as to facilitate all activities as much as possible. If this last condition be unfulfilled, there is merely the appearance of order. Appearance of order may cover over real disorder. I have seen a works yard used as a store for steel ingots in which the material was well stacked, evenly arranged and clean and which gave a pleasing impression of orderliness. On close inspection it could be noted that the same heap included five or six types of steel intended for different manufacture all mixed up together. Whence useless handling, lost time, risk of mistakes because each thing was not in its place. It happens, on the other hand, that the appearance of disorder may actually be true order. Such is the case with papers scattered about at a master's whim which a well-meaning but incompetent servant rearranges and stacks in neat piles. The master can no longer find his way about them. Perfect order presupposes a judiciously chosen place and the appearance of order is merely a false or imperfect image of real order. Cleanliness is a corollary of orderliness, there is no appointed place for dirt. A diagram representing the entire premises divided up into as many sections as there are employees responsible facilitates considerably the establishing and control of order.

Social order

For social order to prevail in a concern there must, in accordance with the definition, be an appointed place for every employee and every employee be in his appointed place. Perfect order requires, further, that the place be suitable for the employee and the employee for the place – in English idom, 'The right man in the right place.'

Thus understood, social order presupposes the successful execution of the two most difficult managerial activities: good organization and good selection. Once the posts essential to the smooth running of the business have been decided upon and those to fill such posts have been selected, each employee occupies that post wherein he can render most service. Such is perfect social order 'A place for each one and each one in his place.' That appears simple, and naturally we are so anxious for it to be so that when we hear for the twentieth time a government departmental head assert this principle, we conjure up straightway a concept of perfect administration. This is a mirage.

Social order demands precise knowledge of the human requirements and resources of the concern and a constant balance between these requirements and resources. Now this balance is most difficult to establish and maintain and all the more difficult the bigger the business, and when it has been upset and individual interests resulted in neglect or sacrifice of the general interest, when ambition, nepotism, favouritism or merely ignorance, has multiplied positions without good reason or filled them with incompetent employees, much talent and strength of will and more persistence than current instability of ministerial appointments presupposes, are required in order to sweep away abuses and restore order.

As applied to government enterprise the principle of order 'a place for each one and each one in his place', takes on an astounding breadth. It means national responsibility towards each and all, everyone's destiny mapped out, national solidarity, the whole problem of society. I will stay no longer over this disturbing extension of the principle of order. In private businesses and especially in those of restricted scope it is easier to maintain proportion as between selection and requirements. As in the case of orderly material arrangement, a chart or plan makes the establishment and control of human arrangement much more easy. This represents the personnel in entirety, and all sections of the concern together with the people occupying them. This chart will come up again in the chapter on Organization [not included].

Equity

Why equity and not justice? Justice is putting into execution established conventions, but conventions cannot foresee everything, they need to be interpreted or their inadequacy supplemented. For the personnel to be encouraged to carry out its duties with all the devotion and loyalty of which it is capable it must be treated with kindliness, and equity results from the combination of kindliness and justice. Equity excludes neither forcefulness nor sternness and the application of it requires much good sense, experience and good nature.

Desire for equity and equality of treatment are aspirations to be taken into account in dealing with employees. In order to satisfy these requirements as much as possible without neglecting any principle or losing sight of the general interest, the head of the business must frequently summon up his highest faculties. He should strive to instil sense of equity throughout all levels of the scalar chain.

Stability of tenure of personnel

Time is required for an employee to get used to new work and succeed in doing it well, always assuming that he possesses the requisite abilities. If when he has got used to it, or before then, he is removed, he will not have had time to render worthwhile service. If this be repeated indefinitely the work will never be properly done. The undesirable consequences of such insecurity of tenure are especially to be feared in large concerns, where the settling in of managers is generally a lengthy matter. Much time is needed indeed to get to know men and things in a large concern in order to be in a position to decide on a plan of action, to gain confidence in oneself and inspire it in others. Hence it has often been recorded that a mediocre manager who stays is infinitely preferable to outstanding managers who merely come and go.

Generally the managerial personnel of prosperous concerns is stable, that of unsuccessful ones is unstable. Instability of tenure is at one and the same time cause and effect of bad running. The apprenticeship of a higher manager is generally a costly matter.

Nevertheless, changes of personnel are inevitable; age, illness, retirement, death, disturb the human make-up of the firm; certain employees are no longer capable of carrying out their duties, whilst others become fit to assume greater responsibilities. In common with all the other principles, therefore, stability of tenure of personnel is also a question of proportion.

Initiative

Thinking out a plan and ensuring its success is one of the keenest satisfactions for an intelligent man to experience. It is also one of the most powerful stimulants of human endeavour. This power of thinking out and executing is what is called initiative, and freedom to propose and to execute belongs, too, each in its way, to initiative. At all levels of the organizational ladder zeal and energy on the part of employees are augmented by initiative. The initiative of all, added to that of the manager, and supplementing it if need be, represents a great source of strength for business. This is particularly apparent at difficult times; hence it is essential to encourage and develop this capacity to the full.

Much tact and some integrity are required to inspire and maintain everyone's initiative, within the limits imposed, by respect for authority and for discipline. The manager must be able to sacrifice some personal vanity in order to grant this sort of satisfaction to subordinates. Other things being equal, moreover, a manager able to permit the exercise of initiative on the part of subordinates is infinitely superior to one who cannot do so.

Esprit de corps

'Union is strength.' Business heads would do well to ponder on this proverb. Harmony, union among the personnel of a concern, is great strength in that concern. Effort, then, should be made to establish it. Among the countless methods in use I will single out specially one principle to be observed and two pitfalls to be avoided. The principle to be observed is unity of command; the dangers to be avoided are (1) a misguided interpretation of the motto 'divide and rule', (2) the abuse of written communications.

1 Personnel must not be split up

Dividing enemy forces to weaken them is clever, but dividing one's own team is a grave sin against the business. Whether this error results from inadequate managerial capacity or imperfect grasp of things, or from egoism which sacrifices general interest to personal interest, it is always reprehensible because harmful to the business. There is no merit in sowing dissension among subordinates; any beginner can do it. On the contrary, real talent is needed to co-ordinate effort, encourage keenness, use each man's abilities, and reward each one's merit without arousing possible jealousies and disturbing harmonious relations.

2 Abuse of written communications

In dealing with a business matter or giving an order which requires explanation to complete it, usually it is simpler and quicker to do so verbally than in writing. Besides, it is well known that differences and misunderstandings which a conversation could clear up, grow more bitter in writing. Thence it follows that, wherever possible, contacts should be verbal; there is a gain in speed, clarity and harmony. Nevertheless, it happens in some firms that employees of neighbouring departments with numerous points of contact, or even employees within a department, who could quite easily meet, only communicate with each other in writing. Hence arise increased work and complications and delays harmful to the business. At the same time, there is to be observed a certain animosity prevailing between different departments or different employees within a department. The system of written communications usually brings this result. There is a way of putting an end to this deplorable system and that is to forbid all communications in writing which could easily and advantageously be replaced by verbal ones. There again, we come up against a question of proportion.

It is not merely by the satisfactory results of harmony obtaining as between employees of the same department that the power of unity is shown: commercial agreements, unions, associations of every kind, play an important part in business management.

The part played by association has increased remarkably in half a century. I remember, in 1860, workers of primary industries without cohesion, without common bond, a veritable cloud of individual dust particles; and out of that the union has produced collective associations, meeting employers on equal terms. At that same time, bitter rivalry prevailed between large firms, closely similar, which has given place gradually to friendly relations, permitting of the settlement of most common interests by joint agreement. It is the beginning of a new era which already has profoundly modified both habits and ideas, and industrial heads should take this development into account.

There I bring to an end this review of principles, not because the list is exhausted – this list has no precise limits – but because to me it seems at the moment especially useful to endow management theory with a dozen or so well-established principles, on which it is appropriate to concentrate general discussion. The foregoing principles are those to which I have most often had recourse. I have simply expressed my personal opinion in connection with them. Are they to have a place in the management code which is to be built up? General discussion will show.

This code is indispensable. Be it a case of commerce, industry, politics, religion, war or philanthropy, in every concern there is a management function to be performed, and for its performance there must be principles, that is to say acknowledged truths regarded as proven on which to rely. And it is the code which represents the sum total of these truths at any given moment.

Surprise might be expressed at the outset that the eternal moral principles, the laws of the Decalogue and Commandments of the Church are not sufficient guide for the manager, and that a special code is needed. The explanation is this: the higher laws of religious or moral order envisage the individual only, or else interests which are not of this world, whereas management principles aim at the success of associations of individuals and at the satisfying of economic interests. Given that the aim is different, it is not surprising that the means are not the same. There is no identity, so there is no contradiction. Without principles one is in darkness and chaos; interest, experience and proportion are still very handicapped, even with the best principles. The principle is the lighthouse fixing the bearings but it can only serve those who already know the way into port.

7 F. Taylor

Scientific Management[1]

F. Taylor, *Scientific Management*, Harper & Row, 1947, pp. 39–73.

What I want to try to prove to you and make clear to you is that the principles of scientific management when properly applied, and when a sufficient amount of time has been given to make them really effective, must in all cases produce far larger and better results, both for the employer and the employees, than can possibly be obtained under even this very rare type of management which I have been outlining, namely, the management of 'initiative and incentive', in which those on the management's side deliberately give a very large incentive to their workmen, and in return the workmen respond by working to the very best of their ability at all times in the interest of their employers.

I want to show you that scientific management is even far better than this rare type of management.

The first great advantage which scientific management has over the management of initiative and incentive is that under scientific management the initiative of the workmen – that is, their hard work, their good will, their ingenuity – is obtained practically with absolute regularity, while under even the best of the older type of management this initiative is only obtained spasmodically and somewhat irregularly. This obtaining, however, of the initiative of the workmen is the lesser of the two great causes which make scientific management better for both sides than the older type of management. By far the greater gain under scientific management comes from the new, the very great and the extraordinary burdens and duties which are voluntarily assumed by those on the management's side.

These new burdens and new duties are so unusual and so great

1. Testimony to the House of Representatives Committee, 1912.

that they are to the men used to managing under the old school almost inconceivable. These duties and burdens voluntarily assumed under scientific management, by those on the management's side, have been divided and classified into four different groups and these four types of new duties assumed by the management have (rightly or wrongly) been called the 'principles of scientific management'.

The first of these four groups of duties taken over by the management is the deliberate gathering in on the part of those on the management's side of all of the great mass of traditional knowledge, which in the past has been in the heads of the workmen, and in the physical skill and knack of the workmen, which he has acquired through years of experience. The duty of gathering in of all this great mass of traditional knowledge and then recording it, tabulating it and, in many cases, finally reducing it to laws, rules and even to mathematical formulae, is voluntarily assumed by the scientific managers. And later, when these laws, rules and formulae are applied to the everyday work of all the workmen of the establishment, through the intimate and hearty cooperation of those on the management's side, they invariably result, first, in producing a very much larger output per man, as well as an output of a better and higher quality; and, second, in enabling the company to pay much higher wages to their workmen; and, third, in giving to the company a larger profit. The first of these principles, then, may be called the development of a science to replace the old rule-of-thumb knowledge of the workmen; that is, the knowledge which the workmen had, and which was, in many cases, quite as exact as that which is finally obtained by the management, but which the workmen nevertheless in nine hundred and ninety-nine cases out of a thousand kept in their heads, and of which there was no permanent or complete record.

A very serious objection has been made to the use of the word 'science' in this connection. I am much amused to find that this objection comes chiefly from the professors of this country. They resent the use of the word science for anything quite so trivial as the ordinary, every-day affairs of life. I think the proper answer to this criticism is to quote the definition recently given by a professor who is, perhaps, as generally recognized as a thorough scientist as any man in the country – President McLaurin, of the Institute of

Technology, of Boston. He recently defined the word science as 'classified or organized knowledge of any kind'. And surely the gathering in of knowledge which, as previously stated, has existed, but which was in an unclassified condition in the minds of workmen, and then the reducing of this knowledge to laws and rules and formulae, certainly represents the organization and classification of knowledge, even though it may not meet with the approval of some people to have it called science.

The second group of duties which are voluntarily assumed by those on the management's side, under scientific management, is the scientific selection and then the progressive development of the workmen. It becomes the duty of those on the management's side to deliberately study the character, the nature, and the performance of each workman with a view to finding out his limitations on the one hand, but even more important, his possibilities for development on the other hand; and then, as deliberately and as systematically to train and help and teach this workman, giving him, wherever it is possible, those opportunities for advancement which will finally enable him to do the highest and most interesting and most profitable class of work for which his natural abilities fit him, and which are open to him in the particular company in which he is employed. This scientific selection of the workman and his development is not a single act; it goes on from year to year and is the subject of continual study on the part of the management.

The third of the principles of scientific management is the bringing of the science and the scientifically selected and trained workmen together. I say 'bringing together' advisedly, because you may develop all the science that you please, and you may scientifically select and train workmen just as much as you please, but unless some man or some men bring the science and the workman together all your labor will be lost. We are all of us so constituted that about three-quarters of the time we will work according to whatever method suits us best; that is, we will practice the science or we will not practice it; we will do our work in accordance with the laws of the science or in our own old way, just as we see fit unless some one is there to see that we do it in accordance with the principles of the science. Therefore I use advisedly the words 'bringing the science and the workman together'. It is unfortunate, however, that this word 'bringing' has rather a disagreeable sound, a rather forceful sound; and, in a way, when it is first heard it puts one out of touch with what we have come to look upon as the modern tendency. The time for using the word 'bringing', with a sense of forcing, in relation to most matters, has gone by; but I think that I may soften this word down in its use in this particular case by saying that nine-tenths of the trouble with those of us who have been engaged in helping people to change from the older type of management to the new management – that is, to scientific management – that nine-tenths of our trouble has been to 'bring' those on the management's side to do their fair share of the work and only one-tenth of our trouble has come on the workman's side. Invariably we find very great opposition on the part of those on the management's side to do their new duties and comparatively little opposition on the part of the workmen to cooperate in doing their new duties. So that the word 'bringing' applies much more forcefully to those on the management's side than to those on the workman's side.

The fourth of the principles of scientific management is perhaps the most difficult of all of the four principles of scientific management for the average man to understand. It consists of an almost equal division of the actual work of the establishment between the workmen, on the one hand, and the management, on the other hand. That is, the work which under the old type of management practically all was done by the workman, under the new is divided into two great divisions, and one of these divisions is deliberately handed over to those on the management's side. This new division of work, this new share of the work assumed by those on the management's side, is so great that you will, I think, be able to understand it better in a numerical way when I tell you that in a machine shop, which, for instance, is doing an intricate business – I do not refer to a manufacturing company, but, rather, to an engineering company; that is, a machine shop which builds a variety of machines and is not engaged in manufacturing them, but, rather, in constructing them – will have one man on the management's side to every three workmen; that is, this immense share of the work – one-third – has been deliberately taken out of the workman's hands and handed over to those on the management's side. And it is due to this actual sharing of the work between the two sides more than to any other one element that there has never (until this last summer) been a single strike under scientific management. In a machine shop, again, under this new type of management there is hardly a single act or piece of work done by any workman in the shop which is not preceded and followed by some act on the part of one of the men in management. All day long every workman's acts are dovetailed in between corresponding acts of the management. First, the workman does something, and then a man on the management's side does something; then the man on the management's side does something, and then the workman does something; and under this intimate, close, personal cooperation between the two sides it becomes practically impossible to have a serious quarrel.

Of course I do not wish to be understood that there are never any quarrels under scientific management. There are some, but they are the very great exception, not the rule. And it is perfectly evident that while the workmen are learning to work under this new system, and while the management is learning to work under this new system, while they are both learning, each side to cooperate in this intimate way with the other, there is plenty of chance for disagreement and for quarrels and misunderstandings, but after both sides realize that it is utterly impossible to turn out the work of the establishment at the proper rate of speed and have it correct without this intimate, personal cooperation, when both sides realize that it is utterly impossible for either one to be successful without the intimate, brotherly cooperation of the other, the friction, the disagreements, and quarrels are reduced to a minimum. So I think that scientific management can be justly and truthfully characterized as management in which harmony is the rule rather than discord.

There is one illustration of the application of the principles of scientific management with which all of us are familiar and with which most of us have been familiar since we were small boys, and I think this instance represents one of the best illustrations of the application of the principles of scientific management. I refer to the management of a first-class American baseball team. In such a team you will find almost all of the elements of scientific management.

You will see that the science of doing every little act that is done by every player on the baseball field has been developed. Every single element of the game of baseball has been the subject of the most intimate, the closest study of many men, and finally, the best way of doing each act that takes place on the baseball field has been fairly well agreed upon and established as a standard throughout the country. The players have not only been told the best way of making each important motion or play, but they have been taught, coached and trained to it through months of drilling. And I think that every man who has watched first-class play, or who knows anything of the management of the modern baseball team, realizes fully the utter impossibility of winning with the best team of individual players that was ever gotten together unless every man on the team obeys the signals or orders of the coach and obeys them at once when the coach gives those orders; that is, without the intimate cooperation between all members of the team and the management, which is characteristic of scientific management.

Now, I have so far merely made assertions; I have merely stated facts in a dogmatic way. The most important assertion I have made is that when a company, when the men of a company and the management of a company have undergone the mental revolution that I have referred to earlier in my testimony, and that when the principles of scientific management have been applied in a correct way in any particular occupation or industry that the results must, inevitably, in all cases, be far greater and better than they could possibly be under the best of the older types of management, even under the especially fine management of 'initiative and incentive', which I have tried to outline.

I want to try and prove the above-stated fact to you gentlemen. I want to try now and make good in this assertion. My only hope of doing so lies in showing you that whenever these four principles are correctly applied to work, either large or small, to work which is either of the most elementary or the most intricate character, that inevitably results follow which are not only greater, but enormously greater, than it is possible to accomplish under the old type of management. Now, in order to make this clear I want to show the application of the four principles first to the most elementary, the simplest kind of work that I know of, and then to give a series of further illustrations of one class of work after another, each a little more difficult and a little more intricate than the work which preceded it, until I shall finally come to an illustration of the application of these same principles to about the most intricate type of mechanical work that I know of. And in all of these illustrations I hope that you will look for and see the application of the four principles I have described. Other elements of the stories may interest you, but the thing that I hope you will see and have before you in all cases is the effect of the four following elements in each particular case: First, the development of the science, i.e., the gathering in on the part of those on the management's side of all the knowledge which in the past has been kept in the heads of the workmen; second, the scientific selection and the progressive development of the workmen; third, the bringing of the science and the scientifically selected and trained men together; and, fourth, the constant and intimate cooperation which always occurs between the men on the management's side and the workmen.

I ordinarily begin with a description of the pig-iron handler. For some reason, I don't know exactly why, this illustration has been talked about a great deal, so much, in fact, that some people seem to think that the whole of scientific management consists in handling pig-iron. The only reason that I ever gave this illustration, however, was that pig-iron handling is the simplest kind of human effort; I know of nothing that is quite so simple as handling pig-iron. A man simply stoops down and with his hands picks up a piece of iron, and then walks a short distance and drops it on the ground. Now, it doesn't look as if there was very much room for the development of a science; it doesn't seem as if there was much room here for the scientific selection of the man nor for his progressive training, nor for cooperation between the two sides; but, I can say, without the slightest hesitation, that the science of handling pig-iron is so great that the man who is fit to handle pig-iron as his daily work cannot possibly understand that science; the man who is physically able to handle pig-iron and is sufficiently phlegmatic and stupid to choose this for his occupation is rarely able to comprehend the science of handling pig-iron; and this inability of the man who is fit to do the work to understand the science of doing his work becomes more and more evident as the work becomes more complicated, all the way up the scale. I assert, without the slightest hesitation, that the high-class mechanic has a far smaller chance of ever thoroughly understanding the science of his work than the pig-iron handler has of understanding the science of his work, and I am going to try and prove to your satisfaction, gentlemen, that the law is almost universal – not entirely so, but nearly so – that the man who is fit to work at any particular trade is unable to understand the science of that trade without the kindly help and cooperation of men of a totally different type of education, men whose education is not necessarily higher but a different type from his own.

I dare say most of you gentlemen are familiar with pig-iron handling and with the illustration I have used in connection with it, so I won't take up any of your time with that. But I want to show you how these principles may be applied to some one of the lower classes of work. You may think I am a little highfalutin when I speak about what may be called the atmosphere of scientific management, the relations that ought to exist between both sides, the intimate and friendly relations that should exist between employee and employer. I want, however, to emphasize this as one of the most important features of scientific management, and I can hardly do so without going into detail, without explaining minutely the duties of both sides, and for this reason I want to take some of your time in explaining the application of these four principles of scientific management to one of the cheaper kinds of work, for instance, to shoveling. This is one of the simplest kinds of work, and I want to give you an illustration of the application of these principles to it.

Now, gentlemen, shoveling is a great science compared with pig-iron handling. I dare say that most of you gentlemen know that a good many pig-iron handlers can never learn to shovel right; the ordinary pig-iron handler is not the type of man well suited to shoveling. He is too stupid; there is too much mental strain, too much knack required of a shoveler for the pig-iron handler to take kindly to shoveling.

You gentlemen may laugh, but that is true, all right; it sounds ridiculous, I know, but it is a fact. Now, if the problem were put up to any of you men to develop the science of shoveling as it was put up to us, that is, to a group of men who had deliberately set out to develop the science of doing all kinds of laboring work, where do you think you would begin? When you started to study the science of shoveling I make the assertion that you would be within two days – just as we were within two days – well on the way toward development of the science of shoveling. At least you would have outlined in your minds those elements which required careful, scientific study in order to understand the science of shoveling. I do not want to go into all of the details of shoveling, but I will give you some of the elements, one or two of the most important elements of the science of shoveling; that is, the elements that reach further and have more serious consequences than any other. Probably the most important element in the science of shoveling is this: There must be some shovel load at which a first-class shoveler will do his biggest day's work. What is that load? To illustrate: When we went to the Bethlehem Steel Works and observed the shovelers in the yard of that company, we found that each of the good shovelers in that yard owned his own shovel; they preferred to buy their own shovels rather than to have the company furnish them. There was a larger tonnage of ore shoveled in that works than of any other material and rice coal came next in tonnage. We would see a first-class shoveler go from shoveling rice coal with a load of $3\frac{1}{2}$ pounds to the shovel to handling ore from the Massaba Range, with 38 pounds to the shovel. Now, is $3\frac{1}{2}$ pounds the proper shovel load or is 38 pounds the proper shovel load? They cannot both be right. Under scientific management the answer to this question is not a matter of anyone's opinion; it is a question for accurate, careful, scientific investigation.

Under the old system you would call in a first-rate shoveler and say, 'See here, Pat, how much ought you to take on at one shovel load?' And if a couple of fellows agreed, you would say that's about the right load and let it go at that. But under scientific management absolutely every element in the work of every man in your establishment, sooner or later, becomes the subject of exact, precise, scientific investigation and knowledge to replace the old, 'I believe so', and 'I guess so'. Every motion, every small fact becomes the subject of careful, scientific investigation.

What we did was to call in a number of men to pick from, and from these we selected two first-class shovelers. Gentlemen, the words I used were 'first-class shovelers'. I want to emphasize that. Not poor shovelers. Not men unsuited to their work, but first-class shovelers. These men were then talked to in about this way, 'See here, Pat and Mike, you fellows understand your job all right; both of you fellows are first-class men; you know what we think of you; you are all right now; but we want to pay you fellows double wages. We are going to ask you to do a lot of damn fool things, and when you are doing them there is going to be someone out alongside of you all the time, a young chap with a piece of paper and a stop watch and pencil, and all day long he will tell you to do these fool things, and he will be writing down what you are doing and snapping the watch on you and all that sort of business. Now, we just want to know whether you fellows want to go into that bargain or not? If you want double wages while that is going on all right, we will pay you double; if you don't, all right, you needn't take the job unless you want to; we just called you in to see whether you want to work this way or not.

'Let me tell you fellows just one thing: If you go into this bargain, if you go at it, just remember that on your side we want no monkey business of any kind; you fellows will have to play square; you fellows will have to do just what you are supposed to be doing; not a damn bit of soldiering on your part; you must do a fair day's work; we don't want any rushing, only a fair day's work and you know what that is as well as we do. Now, don't take this job unless you agree to these conditions, because if you start to try to fool this same young chap with the pencil and paper he will be onto you in fifteen minutes from the time you try to fool him, and just as surely as he reports you fellows as soldiering you will go out of this works and you will never get in again. Now, don't take this job unless you want to accept these conditions; you need not do it unless you want to; but if you do, play fair.'

Well, these fellows agreed to it, and, as I have found almost universally to be the case, they kept their word absolutely and faithfully. My experience with workmen has been that their word is just as good as the word of any other set of men that I know of, and all you have to do is to have a clear, straight, square understanding with them and you will get just as straight and fair a deal from them as from any other set of men. In this way the shoveling experiment was started. My remembrance is that we first started them on work that was very heavy, work requiring a very heavy shovel load. What we did was to give them a certain kind of heavy material ore, I think, to handle with a certain size of shovel. We sent these two men into different parts of the yard, with two different men to time and study them, both sets of men being engaged on the same class of work. We made all the conditions the same for both pairs of men, so as to be sure that there was no error in judgement on the part of either of the observers and that they were normal, first-class men.

The number of shovel loads which each man handled in the course of the day was counted and written down. At the end of the day the total tonnage of the material handled by each man was weighed and this weight was divided by the number of shovel loads handled, and in that way, my remembrance is, our first experiment showed that the average shovel load handled was 38 pounds, and that with this load on the shovel the man handled, say, about 25 tons per day. We then cut the shovel off, making it somewhat shorter, so that instead of shoveling a load of 38 pounds it held a load of approximately 34 pounds. The average, then, with the 34 pound load, of each man went up, and instead of handling 25 he had handled thirty tons per day. These figures are merely relative, used to illustrate the general principles, and I do not mean that they were the exact figures. The shovel was again cut off, and the load made approximately 30 pounds, and again the tonnage ran up, and again the shovel load was reduced, and the tonnage handled per day increased, until at about 21 or 22 pounds per shovel we found that these men were doing their largest day's work. If you cut the shovel load off still more, say until it averages 18 pounds instead of $21\frac{1}{2}$, the tonnage handled per day will begin to fall off, and at 16 pounds it will be still lower, and so on right down. Very well; we now have developed the scientific fact that a workman well suited to his job, what we call a first-class shoveler, will do his largest day's work when he has a shovel load of $21\frac{1}{2}$ pounds.

Now, what does that fact amount to? At first it may not look to be a fact of much importance, but let us see what it amounted to right there in the yard of the Bethlehem Steel Co. Under the old system, as I said before, the workmen owned their shovels, and the shovel was the same size whatever the kind of work. Now, as a matter of common sense, we saw at once that it was necessary to furnish each workman each day with a shovel which would hold just $21\frac{1}{2}$ pounds of the particular material which he was called upon to shovel. A small shovel for the heavy material, such as ore, and a large scoop for light material, such as ashes. That meant, also, the building of a large shovel room, where all kinds of laborers' implements were stored. It meant having an ample supply of each type of shovel, so that all the men who might be called upon to use a certain type in any one day could be supplied with a shovel of the size desired that would hold just $21\frac{1}{2}$ pounds. It meant, further, that each day each laborer should be given a particular kind of work to which he was suited, and that he must be provided with a particular shovel suited to that kind of work, whereas in the past all the laborers in the yard of the Bethlehem Steel Co. had been handled in masses, or in great groups of men, by the old-fashioned foreman, who had from twenty-five to one hundred men under him and walked them from one part of the yard to another. You must realize that the yard of the Bethlehem Steel Co. at that time was a very large yard. I should say that it was at least $1\frac{1}{2}$ or 2 miles long and, we will say, a quarter to a half mile wide, so it was a good large yard; and in that yard at all times an immense variety of shoveling was going on.

There was comparatively little standard shoveling which went on uniformly from day to day. Each man was likely to be moved from place to place about the yard several times in the course of the day. All of this involved keeping in the shovel room ten or fifteen kinds of shovels, ranging from a very small flat shovel for handling ore up to immense scoops for handling rice coal, and forks with which to handle the coke, which, as you know, is very light. It meant the study and development of the implement best suited to each type of material to be shoveled, and assigning, with the minimum of trouble, the proper shovel to each one of the four to six hundred laborers at work in that yard. Now, that meant mechanism, human mechanism. It meant organizing and planning work at least a day in advance. And, gentlemen, here is an important fact, that the greatest difficulty which we met with in this planning did not come from the workmen. It came from the management's side. Our greatest difficulty was to get the heads of the various departments each day to inform the men in the labor office what kind of work and how much of it was to be done on the following day.

This planning the work one day ahead involved the building of a labor office where before there was no such thing. It also involved the equipping of that office with large maps showing the layout of the yards so that the movements of the men from one part of the yard to another could be laid out in advance, so that we could assign to this little spot in the yard a certain number of men and to another part of the yard another set of men, each group to do a certain kind of work. It was practically like playing a game of chess in which four to six hundred men were moved about so as to be in the right place at the right time. And all this, gentlemen, follows from the one idea of developing the science of shoveling; the idea that you must give each workman each day a job to which he is well suited and provide him with just that implement which will enable him to do his biggest day's work. All this, as I have tried to make clear to you, is the result that followed from the one act of developing the science of shoveling.

In order that our workmen should get their share of the good that came from the development of the science of shoveling and that we should do what we set out to do with our laborers – namely, pay them 60 per cent higher wages than were paid to any similar workmen around that whole district. Before we could pay them these extra high wages it was necessary for us to be sure that we had first-class men and that each laborer was well suited to his job, because the only way in which you can pay wages 60 per cent higher than other people pay and not overwork your men is by having each man properly suited and well trained to his job. Therefore, it became necessary to carefully select these yard laborers; and in order that the men should join with us heartily and help us in their selection it became necessary for us to make it possible for each man to know each morning as he came in to work that on the previous day he had earned his 60 per cent premium, or that he had failed to do so. So here again comes in a lot of work to be done by the management that had not been done before. The first thing each workman did when he came into the yard in the morning – and I may say that a good many of them could not read and write – was to take two pieces of paper out of his pigeonhole; if they were both white slips of paper, the workman knew he was all right. One of those slips of paper informed the man in charge of the tool room what implement the workman was to use on his first job and also in what part of the yard he was to work. It was in this way that each one of the 600 men in that yard received his orders for the kind of work he was to do and the implement with which he was to do it, and he was also sent right to the part of the yard where he was to work, without any delay whatever. The old-fashioned way was for the workmen to wait until the foreman got good and ready and had found out by asking some of the heads of departments what work he was to do, and then he would lead the gang off to some part of the yard and go to work. Under the new method each man gets his orders almost automatically; he goes right to the tool room, gets the proper implement for the work he is to do, and goes right to the spot where he is to work without any delay.

The second piece of paper, if it was a white piece of paper, showed this man that he had earned his 60 per cent higher wages; if it was a yellow piece of paper the workman knew that he had not earned enough to be a first-class man, and that within two or three days something would happen, and he was absolutely certain what this something would be. Every one of them knew that after he had received three or four yellow slips a teacher would be sent down to him from the labor office. Now, gentlemen, this teacher was no college professor. He was a teacher of shoveling; he understood the science of shoveling; he was a good shoveler himself, and he knew how to teach other men to be good shovelers. This is the sort of man who was sent out of the labor office. I want to emphasize the following point, gentlemen: The workman, instead of hating the teacher who came to him – instead of looking askance at him and saying to himself, 'Here comes one of those damn nigger drivers to drive me to work' – looked upon him as one of the best friends he had around there. He knew that he came out there to help him, not to nigger drive him. Now, let me show you what happens. The teacher comes, in every case, not to bulldoze the man, not to drive him to harder work than he can do, but to try in a friendly, brotherly way to help him, so he says, 'Now, Pat, something has gone wrong with you. You know no workman who is not a high-priced workman can stay on this gang, and you will have to get off of it if we can't find out what is the matter with you. I believe you have forgotten how to shovel right. I think that's all there is the matter with you. Go ahead and let me watch you awhile. I want to see if you know how to do the damn thing, anyway.'

Now, gentlemen, I know you will laugh when I talk again about the science of shoveling. I dare say some of you have done some shoveling. Whether you have or not, I am going to try to show you something about the science of shoveling, and if any of you have done much shoveling, you will understand that there is a good deal of science about it.

There is a good deal of refractory stuff to shovel around a steel works; take ore, or ordinary bituminous coal, for instance. It takes a good deal of effort to force the shovel down into either of these materials from the top of the pile, as you have to when you are unloading a car. There is one right way of forcing the shovel into materials of this sort, and many wrong ways. Now, the way to shovel refractory stuff is to press the forearm hard against the upper part of the right leg just below the thigh, like this (indicating), take the end of the shovel in your right hand and when you push the shovel into the pile, instead of using the muscular effort of your arms, which is tiresome, throw the weight of your body on the shovel like this (indicating); that pushes your shovel in the pile with hardly any exertion and without tiring the arms in the least. Nine out of ten workmen who try to push a shovel in a pile of that sort will use the strength of their arms, which involves more than twice the necessary exertion. Any of you men who don't know this fact just try it. This is one illustration of what I mean when I speak of the science of shoveling, and there are many similar elements of this science. Now, this teacher would find, time and time again, that the shoveler had simply forgotten how to shovel; that he had drifted back to his old wrong and inefficient way of shoveling, which prevented him from earning his 60 per cent higher wages. So he would say to him, 'I see all that is the matter with you is that you have forgotten how to shovel; you have forgotten what I showed you about shoveling some time ago. Now, watch me,' he says, 'this is the way to do the thing.' And the teacher would stay by him two, three, four or five days, if necessary, until he got the man back again into the habit of shoveling right.

Now, gentlemen, I want you to see clearly that, because that is one of the characteristic features of scientific management; this is not nigger driving; this is kindness; this is teaching; this is doing what I would like mighty well to have done to me if I were a boy trying to learn how to do something. This is not a case of cracking a whip over a man and saying, 'Damn you, get there'. The old way of treating with workmen, on the other hand, even with a good foreman, would have been something like this: 'See here, Pat, I have sent for you to come up here to the office to see me; four or five times now you have not earned your 60 per cent increase in wages; you know that every workman in this place has got to earn 60 per cent more wages than they pay in any other place around here, but you're no good and that's all there is to it; now, get out of this.' That's the old way. 'You are no good; we have given you a fair chance; get out of this', and the workman is pretty lucky if it isn't 'get to hell out of this', instead of 'get out of this'.

The new way is to teach and help your men as you would a brother; to try to teach him the best way and show him the easiest way to do his work. This is the new mental attitude of the management toward the men, and that is the reason I have taken so much of your time in describing this cheap work of shoveling. It may seem to you a matter of very little consequence, but I want you to see, if I can, that this new mental attitude is the very essence of scientific management; that the mechanism is nothing if you have not got the right sentiment, the right attitude in the minds of the men, both on the management's side and on the workman's side. Because this helps to explain the fact that until this summer there has never been a strike under scientific management.

The men who developed the science of shoveling spent, I should say, four or five months studying the subject and during that time they investigated not only the best and most efficient movements that the men should make when they are shoveling right, but they also studied the proper time for doing each of the elements of the science of shoveling. There are many other elements which go to make up this science, but I will not take up your time describing them.

Now, all of this costs money. To pay the salaries of men who are studying the science of shoveling is an expensive thing. As I remember it there were two college men who studied this science of shoveling and also the science of doing many other kinds of laboring work during a period of about three years; then there were a lot of men in the labor office whose wages had to be paid, men who were planning the work which each laborer was to do at least a day in advance; clerks who worked all night so that each workman might know the next morning when he went to work just what he had accomplished and what he had earned the day before; men who wrote out the proper instructions for the day's work for each workman. All of this costs money; it costs money to measure or weigh up the materials handled by each man each day. Under the old method the work of fifty or sixty men was weighed up together; the work done by a whole gang was measured together. But under scientific management we are dealing with individual men and not with gangs of men. And in order to study and develop each man you must measure accurately each man's work. At first we were told that this would be impossible. The former managers of this work told me 'You cannot possibly measure up the work of each individual laborer in this yard; you might be able to do it in a small yard, but our work is of such an intricate nature that it is impossible to do it here.'

I want to say that we had almost no trouble in finding some cheap way of measuring up each man's work, not only in that yard but throughout the entire plant.

But all of that costs money, and it is a very proper question to ask whether it pays or whether it doesn't pay, because, let me tell you, gentlemen, at once, and I want to be emphatic about it, scientific management has nothing in it that is philanthropic; I am not objecting to philanthropy, but any scheme of management which has philanthropy as one of its elements ought to fail; philanthropy has no part in any scheme of management. No self-respecting workman wants to be given things, every man wants to earn things, and scientific management is no scheme for giving people something they do not earn. So, if the principles of scientific management do not pay, then this is a miserable system. The final test of any system is, does it pay?

At the end of some three and a half years we had the opportunity of proving whether or not scientific management did pay in its application to yard labor. When we went to the Bethlehem Steel Co. we found from 400 to 600 men at work in that yard, and when we got through 140 men were doing the work of the 400 to 600, and these men handled several million tons of material a year.

We were very fortunate to be able to get accurate statistics as to the cost of handling a ton of materials in that yard under the old system and under the new. Under the old system the cost of handling a ton of materials had been running between seven and eight cents, and all you gentlemen familiar with railroad work know that this is a low figure for handling materials. Now, after paying for all the clerical work which was necessary under the new system for the time study and the teachers, for building and running the labor office and the implement room, for constructing a telephone system for moving men about the yard, for a great variety of duties not performed under the old system, after paying for all these things incident to the development of the science of shoveling and managing the men the new way, and including the wages of the workmen, the cost of handling a ton of material was brought down from between seven and eight cents to between three and four cents, and the actual saving, during the last six months of the three and one-half years I was there, was at the rate of $78,000 a year. That is what the company got out of it; while the men who were on the labor gang received an average of sixty per cent more wages than their brothers got or could get anywhere around that part of the country. And none of them were overworked, for it is no part of scientific management ever to overwork any man; certainly overworking these men could not have been done with the knowledge of anyone connected with scientific management, because one of the first requirements of scientific management is that no man shall ever be given a job which he cannot do and thrive under through a long term of years. It is no part of scientific management to drive anyone. At the end of three years we had men talk to and investigate all of these yard laborers and we found that they were almost universally satisfied with their jobs.

Of course certain men are permanent grouches and when we run across that kind we all know what to expect. But, in the main, they were the most satisfied and contented set of laborers I have ever seen anywhere; they lived better than they did before, and most of them were saving a little money; their families lived better, and as to having any grouch against their employers, those fellows, every one, looked upon them as the best friends they ever had, because they taught them how to earn 60 per cent more wages than they had ever earned before. This is the round-up of both sides of this question. If the use of the system does not make both sides happier, then it is no good.

To give you one illustration of the application of scientific management to a rather high class of work, gentlemen, bricklaying, so far as I know, is one of the oldest of the trades, and it is a truly extraordinary fact that bricks are now laid just about as they were two thousand years before Christ. In England they are laid almost exactly as they were then; in England the scaffold is still built with timbers lashed together – in many cases with the bark still on it – just as we see that the scaffolds were made in old stone-cut pictures of bricklaying before the Christian era. In this country we have gone beyond the lashed scaffold, and yet in most respects it is almost literally true that bricks are still laid as they were four thousand years ago. Virtually the same trowel, virtually the same brick, virtually the same mortar, and, from the way in which they were laid, according to one of my friends, who is a brick work contractor and a student of the subject, who took the trouble to take down some bricks laid four thousand years ago to study the way in which the mortar was spread, etc., it appears that they even spread the mortar in the same way then as we do now. If, then, there is any trade in which one would say that the principles of scientific management would produce but small results, that the development of the science would do little good, it would be in a trade which thousands and thousands of men through successive generations had worked and had apparently reached, as far as methods and principles were concerned, the highest limit of efficiency four thousand years ago. In bricklaying this would seem to be true since practically no progress has been made in this art since that time. Therefore, viewed broadly, one would say that there was a smaller probability that the principles of scientific management could accomplish notable results in this trade than in almost any other.

Mr Frank Gilbreth is a man who in his youth worked as a brick-layer; he was an educated man and is now a very successful contractor. He said to me, some years ago, 'Now, Taylor, I am a contractor, putting up all sorts of buildings, and if there is one thing I know it is bricklaying; I can go out right now, and I am not afraid to back myself, to beat any man I know of laying bricks for ten minutes, both as to speed and accuracy; you may think I am blowing, but that is one way I got up in the world. I cannot stand it now for more than ten minutes; I'm soft; my hands are tender, I haven't been handling bricks for years, but for ten minutes I will back myself against anyone. I want to ask you about this scientific management; do you think it can be applied to bricklaying? Do you believe that these things you have been shouting about (at that time it was called the 'task system'), do you believe these principles can be applied to bricklaying?' 'Certainly,' I said, 'some day some fellow will make the same kind of study about bricklaying that we have made of other things, and he will get the same results.' 'Well,' he said, 'if you really think so, I will just tell you who is going to do it, his name is Frank Gilbreth.'

I think it was about three years later that he came to me and said: 'Now, I'm going to show you something about bricklaying. I have spent three years making a motion and time study of bricklaying, and not I alone did it; my wife has also spent almost the same amount of her time studying the problems of bricklaying, and I think she has made her full share of the progress which has been made in the science of bricklaying.' Then he said, 'I will show you just how we went to work at it. Let us assume that I am now standing on the scaffold in the position that the bricklayer occupies when he is ready to begin work. The wall is here on my left, the bricks are there in a pile on the scaffold to my right, and the mortar is here on the mortar-board alongside of the bricks. Now, I take my stand as a bricklayer and am ready to start to lay bricks, and I said to myself, "What is the first movement that I make when I start to lay bricks?" I take a step to the right with the right foot. Well, is that movement necessary? It took me a year and a half to cut out that motion – that step to the right – and I will tell you later how I cut it out. Now, what motion do I make next? I stoop down to the floor to the pile of bricks and disentangle a brick from the pile and pick it up off the pile. "My God," I said, "that is nothing short of barbarous." Think of it! Here I am a man weighing over 250 pounds, and every time I stoop down to pick up a brick I lower 250 pounds of weight down two feet so as to pick up a brick weighing 4 pounds, and then raise my 250 pounds of weight up again, and all of this to lift up a brick weighing 4 pounds. Think of this waste of effort. It is monstrous. It took me – it may seem to you a pretty long while – but it took a year and a half of thought and work to cut out that motion; when I finally cut it out, however, it was done in such a simple way that anyone in looking at the method which I adopted would say, "There is no invention in that, any fool could do that; why did you take a year and a half to do a little thing like that?" Well, all I did was to put a table on the scaffold right alongside of me here on my right side and put the bricks and mortar on it, so as to keep them at all times at the right height, thus making it unnecessary to stoop down in picking them up. This table was placed in the middle of the scaffold with the bricklayer on one side of it, and with a walkway on the other side along which the bricks were brought by wheelbarrow or by hod to be placed on the table without interfering with the bricklayer or even getting in his way.' Then Mr Gilbreth made his whole scaffold adjustable, and a laborer was detailed to keep all of the scaffolds at all times at such a height that as the wall goes up the bricks, the mortar, and the men will occupy that position in which the work can be done with the least effort.

Mr Gilbreth has studied out the best position for each of the bricklayer's feet and for every type of bricklaying the exact position for the feet is fixed so that the man can do his work without unnecessary movements. As a result of further study both on the part of Mr and Mrs Gilbreth, after the bricks are unloaded from the cars and before bringing them to the bricklayer they are carefully sorted by a laborer and placed with their best edges up on a simple wooden frame, constructed so as to enable him to take hold of each brick in the quickest time and in the most advantageous position. In this way the bricklayer avoids either having to turn the brick over or end for end to examine it before laying it, and he saves also the time taken in deciding which is the best edge and end to place on the outside of the wall. In most cases, also, he saves the time taken in disentangling the brick from a disorderly pile on the scaffold. This 'pack of bricks', as Mr Gilbreth calls his loaded wooden frames, is placed by the helper in its proper position on the adjustable scaffold close to the mortar box.

We have all been used to seeing bricklayers tap each brick after it is placed on its bed of mortar several times with the end of the handle of the trowel so as to secure the right thickness for the joint. Mr Gilbreth found that by tempering the mortar just right the bricks could be readily bedded to the proper depth by a downward pressure of the hand which lays them. He insisted that the mortar mixers should give special attention to tempering the mortar and so save the time consumed in tapping the brick.

In addition to this he taught his bricklayers to make simple motions with both hands at the same time, where before they completed a motion with the right hand before they followed it later with one made by the left hand. For example, Mr Gilbreth taught his bricklayers to pick up a brick in the left hand at the same time that he takes a trowel of mortar with the right hand. This work with two hands at the same time is, of course, made possible by substituting a deep mortar box for the old mortar-board, on which the mortar used to spread out so thin that a step or two had to be taken to reach it, and then placing the mortar box and the brick pile close together and at the proper height on his new scaffold.

Now, what was the practical outcome of all this study? To sum it up he finally succeeded in teaching his bricklayers, when working under the new method, to lay bricks with five motions per brick, while with the old method they used eighteen motions per brick. And, in fact, in one exceedingly simple type of bricklaying he reduced the motions of his bricklayers from eighteen to two motions per brick. But in the ordinary bricklaying he reduced the motions from eighteen to five. When he first came to me, after he had made this long and elaborate study of the motions of brick-layers, he had accomplished nothing in a practical way through this study, and he said, 'You know, Fred, I have been showing all my friends these new methods of laying bricks and they say to me, "Well, Frank, this is a beautiful thing to talk about, but what in the devil do you think it amounts to? You know perfectly well the unions have forbidden their members to lay more than so many bricks per day; you know they won't allow this thing to be carried out."' But Gilbreth said, 'Now, my dear boy, that doesn't make an iota of difference to me. I'm just going to see that the bricklayers do the right thing. I belong to the bricklayers' union in Boston, and the next job that I get in Boston this thing goes through. I'm not going to do it in any underhanded way. Everyone knows that I have always paid higher wages than the union scale in Boston. I've got a lot of friends at the head of the unions in Boston, and I'm not afraid of having any trouble.'

He got his job near Boston, and he went to the leaders of the union and told them just what you can tell any set of sensible men. He said to them, 'I want to tell you fellows some things that you ought to know. Most of my contracts around here used to be brick jobs; now, most of my work is in reinforced concrete or some other type of construction, but I am first and last a bricklayer; that is what I am interested in, and if you have any sense you will just keep your hands off and let me show you bricklayers how to compete with the reinforced concrete men. I will handle the bricklayers myself. All I want of you leaders is to keep your hands off and I will show you how bricklayers can compete with reinforced concrete or any other type of construction that comes along.'

Well, the leaders of the union thought that sounded all right, and then he went to the workmen and said to them, 'No fellow can work for me for less than $6.50 a day – the union rate was $5 a day – but every man who gets on this job has got to lay bricks my way; I will put a teacher on the job to show you all my way of laying bricks and I will give every man plenty of time to learn, but after a bricklayer has had a sufficient trial at this thing, if he won't do my way or cannot do my way, he must get off the job.' Any number of bricklayers were found to be only too glad to try the job, and I think he said that before the first story of the building was up he had the whole gang trained to work in the new way, and all getting their $6.50 a day when before they only received $5 per day; I believe those are the correct figures; I am not absolutely sure about that, but at least he paid them a very liberal premium above the average bricklayer's pay.

It is one of the principles of scientific management to ask men to do things in the right way, to learn something new, to change their ways in accordance with the science, and in return to receive an increase of from 30 to 100 per cent in pay, which varies according to the nature of the business in which they are engaged.

8 M. P. Follett

The Giving of Orders[1]

M. P. Follett, 'The giving of orders', in H. C. Metcalf and L. Urwick (eds.), *Dynamic Administration*, Harper, 1941, chapter 2, pp. 50–70. (Footnotes as in the original.)

The chief thing I have to say to you in this paper is that I wish we could all take a responsible attitude toward our experience – a conscious and responsible attitude.[2] Let us take one of the many activities of the business man, and see what it would mean to take a responsible attitude toward our experience in regard to that one thing. I am going to take the question of giving orders: what are the principles underlying the different ways of giving orders, which of these principles have you decided to follow? Most people have not decided, have not even thought out what the different principles are. Yet we all give orders every day. Surely this is a pity. To know what principles may underlie any given activity of ours is to take a conscious attitude toward our experience.

The second step is to take a responsible attitude, by deciding, after we have recognized the different principles, which ones we will follow. In the matter of giving orders, I wish we might all of us decide now, if we have not already done so, on the way we think orders should be given. We shall not arrive at the same conclusions, there may be a good deal of difference of opinion among us. What I urge is not that you adopt my principles, but that you stop to think what principles you are acting on or what principles you intend to act on in this matter, and then try giving orders in accordance with those principles as far as the methods of your firm permit.

And next I urge you to note results; for our first decision should be tentative. We should try experiments and note whether they succeed or fail and, most important of all, why they succeed or fail. This is taking an experimental attitude toward experience.

1. This paper was presented in January 1925.
2. Cf. Follett (1924) p. xi: 'But we wish to do far more than observe our experience, we wish to make it yield up for us its riches.'

We have then three steps: (1) a conscious attitude – realize the principles which it is possible to act on in this matter; (2) a responsible attitude – decide which we will act on; (3) an experimental attitude – try experiments and watch results. We might add a fourth step: pool our results.

In doing all this we should observe carefully what opportunities the methods of our particular firm afford for giving orders in the way we have decided provisionally is best, and come to some conclusion as to how far and in what way those methods would have to be changed if our principles were adopted. This will increase our consciousness in the matter.

Behaviour patterns and obedience to orders

To some men the matter of giving orders seems a very simple affair; they expect to issue their orders and have them obeyed without question. Yet, on the other hand, the shrewd common sense of many a business executive has shown him that the issuing of orders is surrounded by many difficulties; that to demand an unquestioning obedience to orders not approved, not perhaps even understood, is bad business policy. Moreover, psychology, as well as our own observation, shows us not only that you cannot get people to do things most satisfactorily by ordering them or exhorting them; but also that even reasoning with them, even convincing them intellectually, may not be enough. Even the 'consent of the governed' will not do all the work it is supposed to do, an important consideration for those who are advocating employee representation. For all our past life, our early training, our later experience, all our emotions, beliefs, prejudices, every desire that we have, have formed certain habits of mind, what the psychologists call habit-patterns, action-patterns, motor-sets.

Therefore it will do little good merely to get intellectual agreement; unless you change the habit-patterns of people, you have not really changed your people. Business administration, industrial organization, should build up certain habit-patterns, that is, certain mental attitudes. For instance, the farmer has a general disposition to 'go it alone', and this is being changed by the activities of the cooperatives, that is, note, *by the farmer's own activities.* So the workman has often a general disposition of antagonism to his employers which cannot be changed by argument or exhortation, but only through certain activities which will create a different disposition. One of my trade union friends told me that he remembered when he was a quite small boy hearing his father, who worked in a shoe-shop, railing daily against his boss. So he grew up believing that it was inherent in the nature of things that the workman should be against his employer. I know many working men who have a prejudice against getting college men into factories. You could all give me examples of attitudes among your employees which you would like to change. We want, for instance, to create an attitude of respect for expert opinion.

If we analyse this matter a little further we shall see that we have to do three things, I am now going to use psychological language: (1) build up certain attitudes; (2) provide for the release of these attitudes; (3) augment the released response as it is being carried out. What does this mean in the language of business? A psychologist has given us the example of the salesman. The salesman first creates in you the attitude that you want his article; then, at just the 'psychological' moment, he produces his contract blank which you may sign and thus release that attitude; then if, as you are preparing to sign, some one comes in and tells you how pleased he has been with his purchase of this article, that augments the response which is being released.

If we apply this to the subject of orders and obedience, we see that people can obey an order only if previous habit-patterns are appealed to or new ones created. When the employer is considering an order, he should also be thinking of the way to form the habits which will ensure its being carried out. We should first lead the salesmen selling shoes or the bank clerk cashing cheques to see the desirability of a different method. Then the rules of the store or bank should be so changed as to make it possible for salesman or cashier to adopt the new method. In the third place they could be made more ready to follow the new method by convincing in advance some one individual who will set an example to the others. You can usually convince one or two or three ahead of the rank and file. This last step you all know from your experience to be good tactics; it is what the psychologists call intensifying the attitude to be released. But we find that the released attitude is not by one release fixed as a habit; it takes a good many responses to do that.

This is an important consideration for us, for from one point of view business success depends largely on this – namely, whether our business is so organized and administered that it tends to form certain habits, certain mental attitudes. It has been hard for many old-fashioned employers to understand that *orders will not take the place of training*. I want to italicize that. Many a time an employer has been angry because, as he expressed it, a workman 'wouldn't' do so and so, when the truth of the matter was that the workman couldn't, actually couldn't, do as ordered because he could not go contrary to life-long habits. This whole subject might be taken up under the heading of education, for there we could give many instances of the attempt to make arbitrary authority take the place of training. In history, the aftermath of all revolutions shows us the results of the lack of training.

In this matter of prepared-in-advance behaviour patterns – that is, in preparing the way for the reception of orders, psychology makes a contribution when it points out that the same words often rouse in us a quite different response when heard in certain places and on certain occasions. A boy may respond differently to the same suggestion when made by his teacher and when made by his schoolmate. Moreover, he may respond differently to the same suggestion made by the teacher in the schoolroom and made by the teacher when they are taking a walk together. Applying this to the giving of orders, we see that the place in which orders are given, the circumstances under which they are given, may make all the difference in the world as to the response which we get.[3] Hand them down a long way from President or Works Manager and the effect is weakened. One might say that the strength of favourable response to an order is in inverse ratio to the distance the order travels. Production efficiency is always in danger of being affected whenever the long-distance order is substituted for the face-to-face suggestion. There is, however, another reason for that which I shall consider in a moment.

All that we said in the foregoing paper of integration and circular

3. Cf. Follett (1924) p. 65: '. . . we shall have to keep in mind – first, the objective situation as a constituent part of the behaviour process; secondly, that internal conditioning is of equal importance with external conditioning. . . . Often for instance we see the head of an industrial plant trying to solve a situation by studying his men rather than by considering men and situation, and the reciprocal effect of one on the other.'

behaviour applies directly to the anticipation of response in giving orders. We spoke then of what the psychologists call linear and circular behaviour. Linear behaviour would be, to quote from Dr Cabot's review of my book, *Creative Experience*, when an order is accepted as passively as the woodshed accepts the wood. In circular behaviour you get a 'come-back'. But we all know that we get the comeback every day of our life, and we must certainly allow for it, or for what is more elegantly called circular behaviour, in the giving of orders. Following out the thought of the previous paper, I should say that the giving of orders and the receiving of orders ought to be a matter of integration through circular behaviour, and that we should seek methods to bring this about.[4] The rest of this lecture could profitably be spent on this point, with further explanation and with illustration, but I am trying to cover a good deal of ground in these talks by making suggestions for you to expand for yourselves.

Psychology has another important contribution to make on this subject of issuing orders or giving directions: before the integration can be made between order-giver and order-receiver, there is often an integration to be made within one or both of the individuals concerned. There are often two dissociated paths in the individual; if you are clever enough to recognize these, you can sometimes forestall a Freudian conflict, make the integration appear before there is an acute stage.

To explain what I mean, let me run over briefly a social worker's case. The girl's parents had been divorced and the girl placed with a jolly, easy-going, slack and untidy family, consisting of the father and mother and eleven children, sons and daughters. Gracie was very happy here, but when the social worker in charge of the case found that the living conditions involved a good deal of promiscuity, she thought the girl should be placed elsewhere. She therefore took her to call on an aunt who had a home with some

4. Cf. Follett (1924) p. 69: 'We cannot study the "psychology" of the workman, the "psychology" of the employer, and then the "facts" of the situation, as so often seems to be the process of the investigation. We must study the workman and the employer in their relation to the facts – and then the facts themselves become as active as any other part of the "total situation". We can never understand the total situation without taking into account the evolving situation. And when a situation changes we have not a new variation under the old fact, but a new fact.'

refinement of living, where they had 'high tastes', as one of the family said. This aunt wished to have Gracie live with her, and Gracie decided that she would like to do so. The social worker, however, in order to test her, said, 'But I thought you were so happy where you are.' 'Can't I be happy and high, too?' the girl replied. There were two wishes here, you see. The social worker by removing the girl to the aunt may have forestalled a Freudian conflict, the dissociated paths may have been united. I do not know the outcome of this story, but it indicates a method of dealing with our codirectors – make them 'happy and high, too'.

Business administration has often to consider how to deal with the dissociated paths in individuals or groups, but the methods of doing this successfully have been developed much further in some departments than in others. We have as yet hardly recognized this as part of the technique of dealing with employees, yet the clever salesman knows that it is the chief part of his job. The prospective buyer wants the article and does not want it. The able salesman does not suppress the arguments in the mind of the purchaser against buying, for then the purchaser might be sorry afterwards for his purchase, and that would not be good salesmanship. Unless he can unite, integrate, in the purchaser's mind, the reasons for buying and the reasons for not buying, his future sales will be imperilled, he will not be the highest grade salesman.

Please note that this goes beyond what the psychologist whom I quoted at the beginning of this section told us. He said, 'The salesman must create in you the attitude that you want his article.' Yes, but only if he creates this attitude by integration not by suppression.

Apply all this to orders. An order often leaves the individual to whom it is given with two dissociated paths; an order should seek to unite, to integrate, dissociated paths. Court decisions often settle arbitrarily which of two ways is to be followed without showing a possible integration of the two, that is, the individual is often left with an internal conflict on his hands. This is what both courts and business administration should try to prevent, the internal conflicts of individuals or groups.

In discussing the preparation for giving orders, I have not spoken at all of the appeal to certain instincts made so important by many writers. Some writers, for instance, emphasize the instinct of self-assertion; this would be violated by too rigid orders or too clumsily-exercised authority. Other writers, of equal standing, tell us that there is an instinct of submission to authority. I cannot discuss this for we should first have to define instincts, too long an undertaking for us now. Moreover, the exaggerated interest in instincts of recent years, an interest which in many cases has received rather crude expression, is now subsiding. Or, rather, it is being replaced by the more fruitful interest in habits.

There is much more that we could learn from psychology about the forming of habits and the preparation for giving orders than I can even hint at now. But there is one point, already spoken of by implication, that I wish to consider more explicitly – namely, the manner of giving orders. Probably more industrial trouble has been caused by the manner in which orders are given than in any other way. In the *Report on Strikes and Lockouts*,[5] a British Government publication, the cause of a number of strikes is given as 'alleged harassing conduct of the foreman', 'alleged tyrannical conduct of an under-foreman', 'alleged overbearing conduct of officials'. The explicit statement, however, of the tyranny of superior officers as the direct cause of strikes is, I should say, unusual, yet resentment smoulders and breaks out in other issues. And the demand for better treatment is often explicit enough. We find it made by the metal and woodworking trades in an aircraft factory, who declared that any treatment of men without regard to their feelings of self-respect would be answered by a stoppage of works. We find it put in certain agreements with employers that 'the men must be treated with proper respect, and threats and abusive language must not be used'.

What happens to a man, *in* a man, when an order is given in a disagreeable manner by foreman, head of department, his immediate superior in store, bank or factory? The man addressed feels that his self-respect is attacked, that one of his most inner sanctuaries is invaded. He loses his temper or becomes sullen or is on the defensive; he begins thinking of his 'rights' – a fatal attitude for any of us. In the language we have been using, the wrong behaviour pattern is aroused, the wrong motor-set; that is,

5. This is probably a reference to the *Annual Reports and Comparative Statistics of Strikes and Lockouts*, subsequently incorporated in the Annual Reports of the Ministry of Labour.

he is now 'set' to act in a way which is not going to benefit the enterprise in which he is engaged.

There is a more subtle psychological point here, too, the more you are 'bossed' the more your activity of thought will take place within the bossing-pattern, and your part in that pattern seems usually to be opposition to the bossing.

This complaint of the abusive language and the tyrannical treatment of the one just above the worker is an old story to us all, but there is an opposite extreme which is far too little considered. The immediate superior officer is often so close to the worker that he does not exercise the proper duties of his position. Far from taking on himself an aggressive authority, he has often evaded one of the chief problems of his job: how to do what is implied in the fact that he has been put in a position over others. The head of the woman's cloak department in a store will call out, 'Say, Sadie, you're thirty-six aren't you? There's a woman down in the Back Bay kicking about something she says you promised yesterday.' 'Well, I like that,' says Sadie. 'Some of those Back Bay women would kick in Heaven.' And that perhaps is about all that happens. Of course, the Back Bay lady has to be appeased, but there is often no study of what has taken place for the benefit of the store. I do not mean that a lack of connection between such incidents and the improvement of store technique is universal, but it certainly exists far too often and is one of the problems of those officials who are just above the heads of departments. Naturally, a woman does not want to get on bad terms with her fellow employees with whom she talks and works all day long. Consider the chief operator of the telephone exchanges, remembering that the chief operator is a member of the union, and that the manager is not.

Depersonalizing orders – obeying the law of the situation

Now what is our problem here? How can we avoid the two extremes: too great bossism in giving orders, and practically no orders given? I am going to ask how *you* are avoiding these extremes. My solution is to depersonalize the giving of orders, to unite all concerned in a study of the situation, to discover the law of the situation and obey that.[6] Until we do this I do not think we

6. Cf. *Creative Experience*, p. 122: 'We should notice, too, what is some-times forgotten, that in the social situation two processes always go on

shall have the most successful business administration. This is what does take place, what has to take place, when there is a question between two men in positions of equal authority. The head of the sales departments does not give orders to the head of the production department, or vice versa. Each studies the market and the final decision is made as the market demands. This is, ideally, what should take place between foremen and rank and file, between any head and his subordinates. One *person* should not give orders to another *person*, but both should agree to take their orders from the situation. If orders are simply part of the situation, the question of someone giving and someone receiving does not come up. Both accept the orders given by the situation. Employers accept the orders given by the situation; employees accept the orders given by the situation. This gives, does it not, a slightly different aspect to the whole of business administration through the entire plant?

We have here, I think, one of the largest contributions of scientific management: it tends to depersonalize orders. From one point of view, one might call the essence of scientific management the attempt to find the law of the situation. With scientific management the managers are as much under orders as the workers, for both obey the law of the situation. Our job is not how to get people to obey orders, but how to devise methods by which we can best *discover* the order integral to a particular situation. When that is found, the employee can issue it to the employer, as well as employer to employee. This often happens easily and naturally. My cook or my stenographer points out the law of the situation, and I, if I recognize it as such, accept it, even although it may reverse some 'order' I have given.

If those in supervisory positions should depersonalize orders, then there would be no overbearing authority on the one hand, nor on the other that dangerous *laissez-aller* which comes from the fear of exercising authority. Of course we should exercise authority, but always the authority of the situation. I do not say that we have found the way to a frictionless existence, far from it, but we now understand the place which we mean to give to friction. We intend

---

together: the adjustment of man and man, and the adjustment of man and the situation.'

to set it to work for us as the engineer does when he puts the belt over the pulley. There will be just as much, probably more, room for disagreement in the method I am advocating. The situation will often be seen differently, often be interpreted differently. But we shall know what to do with it, we shall have found a method of dealing with it.

I call it depersonalizing because there is not time to go any further into the matter. I think it really is a matter of *repersonalizing*. We, persons, have relations with each other, but we should find them in and through the whole situation. We cannot have any sound relations with each other as long as we take them out of that setting which gives them their meaning and value. This divorcing of persons and the situation does a great deal of harm. I have just said that scientific management depersonalizes; the deeper philosophy of scientific management shows us personal relations within the whole setting of that thing of which they are a part.

There is much psychology, modern psychology particularly, which tends to divorce person and situation. What I am referring to is the present zest for 'personality studies'. When some difficulty arises we often hear the psychologist whose specialty is personality studies say, 'Study the psychology of that man.' And this is very good advice, but only if at the same time we study the entire situation. To leave out the whole situation, however, is so common a blunder in the studies of these psychologists that it constitutes a serious weakness in their work. And as those of you who are personnel directors have more to do, I suppose, with those psychologists who have taken personality for their specialty than with any others, I wish you would watch and see how often you find that this limitation detracts from the value of their conclusions.

I said above that we should substitute for the long-distance order the face-to-face suggestion. I think we can now see a more cogent reason for this than the one then given. It is not the face-to-face suggestion that we want so much as the joint study of the problem, and such joint study can be made best by the employee and his immediate superior or employee and special expert on that question.

I began this talk by emphasizing the advisability of preparing in advance the attitude necessary for the carrying out of orders, as in the previous paper we considered preparing the attitude for integration; but we have now, in our consideration of the joint study of situations, in our emphasis on obeying the law of the situation, perhaps got a little beyond that, or rather we have now to consider in what sense we wish to take the psychologist's doctrine of prepared-in-advance attitudes. By itself this would not take us far, for everyone is studying psychology nowadays, and our employees are going to be just as active in preparing us as we in preparing them! Indeed, a girl working in a factory said to me, 'We had a course in psychology last winter, and I see now that you have to be pretty careful how you put things to the managers if you want them to consider favourably what you're asking for.' If this prepared-in-advance idea were all that the psychologists think it, it would have to be printed privately as secret doctrine. But the truth is that the best preparation for integration in the matter of orders or in anything else, is a joint study of the situation. We should not try to create the attitude *we want*, although that is the usual phrase, but the attitude required for cooperative study and decision. This holds good even for the salesman. We said above that when the salesman is told that he should create in the prospective buyer the attitude that he wants the article, he ought also to be told that he should do this by integration rather than by suppression. We have now a hint of *how* he is to attain this integration.

I have spoken of the importance of changing some of the language of business personnel relations. We considered whether the words 'grievances', 'complaints' or Ford's 'trouble specialists' did not arouse the wrong behaviour-patterns. I think 'order' certainly does. If that word is not to mean any longer external authority, arbitrary authority but the law of the situation, then we need a new word for it. It is often the order that people resent as much as the thing ordered. People do not like to be ordered even to take a holiday. I have often seen instances of this. The wish to govern one's own life is, of course, one of the most fundamental feelings in every human being. To call this 'the instinct of self-assertion', 'the instinct of initiative', does not express it wholly. I think it is told in the life of some famous American that when he was a boy and his mother said, 'Go get a pail of water', he always replied, 'I won't', before taking up the pail and fetching the water. This is significant; he resented the command, the command of a person; but he went and got the water, not, I believe, because he had to, but because he recognized the demand of the situation. *That*, he knew he had to obey; *that*, he was willing to obey. And this kind of obedience is not opposed to the wish to govern one's self, but each is involved in the other; both are part of the same fundamental urge at the root of one's being. We have here something far more profound than 'the egoistic impulse' or 'the instinct of self-assertion'. We have the very essence of the human being.

This subject of orders has led us into the heart of the whole question of authority and consent. When we conceive of authority and consent as parts of an inclusive situation, does that not throw a flood of light on this question? The point of view here presented gets rid of several dilemmas which have seemed to puzzle people in dealing with consent. The feeling of being 'under' someone, of 'subordination', of 'servility', of being 'at the will of another', comes out again and again in the shop stewards movement and in the testimony before the Coal Commission. One man said before the Coal Commission, 'It is all right to work *with* anyone; what is disagreeable is to feel too distinctly that you are working *under* anyone.' *With* is a pretty good preposition, not because it connotes democracy, but because it connotes functional unity,⁷ a much more profound conception than that of democracy as usually held. The study of the situation involves the *with* preposition. Then Sadie is not left alone by the head of the cloak department, nor does she have to obey her. The head of the department says, 'Let's see how such cases had better be handled, then we'll abide by that.' Sadie is not under the head of the department, but both are *under* the situation.

Twice I have had a servant applying for a place ask me if she would be treated as a menial. When the first woman asked me that, I had no idea what she meant, I thought perhaps she did not want to do the roughest work, but later I came to the conclusion that to be treated as a menial meant to be obliged to be under someone, to follow orders without using one's own judgement. If we believe that what heightens self-respect increases efficiency, we shall be on our guard here.

Very closely connected with this is the matter of pride in one's

7. If it is understood as indicating an interweaving, not mere addition (M. P. F.). *Note.* To distinguish between Miss Follett's own notations and the editorial notes, we are initialling the former, as here.

work. If an order goes against what the craftsman or the clerk thinks is the way of doing his work which will bring the best results he is justified in not wishing to obey that order. Could not that difficulty be met by a joint study of the situation? It is said that it is characteristic of the British workman to feel, 'I know my job and won't be told how.' The peculiarities of the British workman might be met by a joint study of the situation, it being understood that he probably has more to contribute to that study than anyone else.

(I should like to say incidentally here, that what I am talking about when I say joint study is entirely different from what is being advocated in England, and tried out in mine and factory, as 'the independent investigation of the worker', 'independent workers' control'. I think they are on quite the wrong track in this matter, and this I shall try to show in a later paper.)

There is another dilemma which has to be met by everyone who is in what is called a position of authority: how can you expect people merely to obey orders and at the same time to take that degree of responsibility which they should take? Indeed, in my experience, the people who enjoy following orders blindly, without any thought on their own part, are those who like thus to get rid of responsibility. But the taking of responsibility, each according to his capacity, each according to his function in the whole (all that we shall take up in the next paper under the title of *Business as an Integrative Unity*), this taking of responsibility is usually the most vital matter in the life of every human being, just as the allotting of responsibility is the most important part of business administration.

A young trade unionist said to me, 'How much dignity can I have as a mere employee?' He can have all the dignity in the world if he is allowed to make his fullest contribution to the plant *and to assume definitely the responsibility therefor*.

I think one of the gravest problems before us is how to make the reconciliation between receiving orders and taking responsibility. And I think the reconciliation can be made through our conception of the law of the situation.

Obedience and liberty

I have spoken of several dilemmas: how to take orders and yet not to be 'under' someone, how to take orders and yet to keep one's pride in one's work, how to take orders and yet to have a share in responsibility. There is still another dilemma troubling many people which our present point of view helps to solve – namely, whether you can have obedience *and* liberty.[8] That group of political scientists and guild socialists who are denying the power of the State, say that we cannot have obedience *and* liberty. I think they are wholly wrong, but I think we should ask ourselves to what we owe obedience. Surely only to a functional unity of which we are a part, to which we are contributing. I agree with the guild socialists that the State is not that now. Those who are concerned with the reorganization of industry should take warning from the failures of the state.

James Myers, author of *Representative Government in Industry*,[9] comes near involving himself in this dilemma of the political scientists when he tells us that men in industry have so long merely obeyed orders that we have there a real social danger. He says, 'We must reawaken the instinct of self-assertion.' While I think Myers recognizes a real problem here, I certainly do not think that the instinct of self-assertion needs to be reawakened in many of us.

We have considered the subject of symbols. It is often very apparent that an order is a symbol. The referee in the game stands watch in hand, and says, 'Go.' It is an order, but order only as a symbol. I may say to an employee, 'Do so and so,' but I should say it only because we have both agreed, openly or tacitly, that that which I am ordering done is the best thing to be done. The order is then a symbol. And if it is a philosophical and psychological truth that we owe obedience only to a functional unity to which we are contributing, we should remember that a more accurate way of stating that would be to say that our obligation is to a unify*ing*, to a process.

This brings us now to one of our most serious problems in this matter of orders. It is important, but we can touch on it only briefly; it is what we spoke of in the foregoing paper as the evolving situation. I am trying to show here that the order must be integral to the situation and must be recognized as such. But we saw that the situation was always developing. If the situation is never stationary, then the order should never be stationary, so to speak; how to

8. Cf. *The New State*, chapters XXVIII–XXXII, on political pluralism.
9. Doubleday-Doran, New York, 1924.

prevent it from being so is our problem. The situation is changing while orders are being carried out, because, by and through orders being carried out. How is the order to keep up with the situation? External orders never can, only those drawn fresh from the situation.

Moreover, if taking a *responsible* attitude toward experience involves recognizing the evolving situation, a *conscious* attitude toward experience means that we note the change which the developing situation makes in ourselves; the situation does not change without changing us.

To summarize, what have we learned from these two papers on the subject of the giving of orders? That, integration being the basic law of life, orders should be the composite conclusion of those who give and those who receive them; more than this, that they should be the integration of the people concerned and the situation; more even than this, that they should be the integrations involved in the evolving situation. If you accept my three fundamental statements on this subject: (1) that the order should be the law of the situation; (2) that the situation is always evolving; (3) that orders should involve circular not linear behaviour – then we see that our old conception of orders has somewhat changed, and that there should therefore follow definite changes in business practice.

There is a problem so closely connected with the giving of orders that I want to put it before you for future discussion. After we have decided on our orders, we have to consider how much and what kind of supervision is necessary or advisable in order that they shall be carried out. We all know that many workers object to being watched. What does that mean, how far is it justifiable? How can the objectionable element be avoided and at the same time necessary supervision given? I do not think that this matter has been studied sufficiently. When I asked a very intelligent girl what she thought would be the result of profit-sharing and employee representation in the factory where she worked, she replied joyfully, 'We shan't need foremen any more.' While her entire ignoring of the fact that the foreman has other duties than keeping workers on their jobs was amusing, one wants to go beyond one's amusement and find out what this objection to being watched really means.

In a case in Scotland arising under the Minimum Wage Act, the overman was called in to testify whether or not a certain workman did his work properly. The examination was as follows:

MAGISTRATE: But isn't it your duty under the Mines Act to visit each working place twice a day?
OVERMAN: Yes.
MAGISTRATE: Don't you do it?
OVERMAN: Yes.
MAGISTRATE: Then why didn't you ever see him work?
OVERMAN: They always stop work when they see an overman coming and sit down and wait till he's gone – even take out their pipes, if it's a mine free from gas. They won't let anyone watch them.

An equally extreme standard was enforced for a part of the war period at a Clyde engineering works. The chairman of shop stewards was told one morning that there was a grievance at the smithy. He found one of the blacksmiths in a rage because the managing director in his ordinary morning's walk through the works had stopped for five minutes or so and watched this man's fire. After a shop meeting the chairman took up a deputation to the director and secured the promise that this should not happen again. At the next works meeting the chairman reported the incident to the body of workers, with the result that a similar demand was made throughout the works and practically acceded to, so that the director hardly dared to stop at all in his morning's walk.

I have seen similar instances cited. Many workmen feel that being watched is unbearable. What can we do about it? How can we get proper supervision without this watching which a worker resents? Supervision is necessary; supervision is resented, – how are we going to make the integration there? Some say, 'Let the workers elect the supervisors.' I do not believe in that.

There are three other points closely connected with the subject of this paper which I should like merely to point out. First, when and how do you point out mistakes, misconduct? One principle can surely guide us here; don't blame for the sake of blaming, make what you have to say accomplish something; say it in that form, at that time, under those circumstances, which will make it a real education to your subordinate. Secondly, since it is recognized that the one who gives the orders is not as a rule a very popular person, the management sometimes tries to offset this by allowing the person who has this onus upon him to give any pleasant news to the workers, to have the credit of any innovation which the workers very much desire. One manager told me that he always tried to do this. I suppose that this is good behaviouristic psychology, and yet I am not sure that it is a method I wholly like. It is quite different, however, in the case of a mistaken order having been given; then I think the one who made the mistake should certainly be the one to rectify it, not as a matter of strategy, but because it is better for him too. It is better for all of us not only to acknowledge our mistakes, but to do something about them. If a foreman discharges someone and it is decided to reinstate the man, it is obviously not only good tactics but a square deal to the foreman to allow him to do the reinstating.

There is, of course, a great deal more to this matter of giving orders than we have been able to touch on; far from exhausting the subject, I feel that I have only given hints. I have been told that the artillery men suffered more mentally in the war than others, and the reason assigned for this was that their work was directed from a distance. The combination of numbers by which they focused their fire was telephoned to them. The result was also at a distance. Their activity was not closely enough connected with the actual situation at either end.

One matter in regard to giving orders which seems to me of the utmost importance for business administration, I wish you would enlighten me about. When the numbers of employees are as large and as widely scattered as in the case of the Elevated and Telephone employees, how should the orders be conveyed? Someone said to me one day, 'How do you suppose the Elevated gives its orders?' I didn't know what she meant and asked her, and she replied, 'The uniform courtesy of the Elevated employees is such that I often wonder how the people at the top get their wishes across to so many widely scattered people.'

Our time is more than up, but let me, in order to indicate the scope of this subject, mention some of the things we have not touched on, or not adequately: the relation of orders to training; the effect of the emotions (hope, fear, etc.) in the obeying of orders; how to keep control and yet give control and responsibility to subordinates. Moreover, perhaps I have not said explicitly that the participation of employees in the planning of orders should take place before the order is given, not afterwards. After the order has been given the subordinate must obey. I certainly believe in authority – of the right kind. And I am sure that I have not emphasized sufficiently the careful, painstaking study that is necessary if we are to anticipate how orders will be received. A man grumbles at an order; this makes trouble and the one over him says: 'Why is that man kicking?' and he begins to study the situation. But perhaps by that time it is too late; the trouble has perhaps got too much headway. To anticipate the kicks, to learn the most successful methods of doing this, is an important part of the work of the order-giver.

I began this talk by saying that I was going to consider order-giving merely as an illustration of a method, the method of taking a conscious and responsible attitude toward our experience. I feel strongly on this point, on the necessity of taking a responsible attitude toward our experience. We students of social and industrial research are often lamentably vague. We sometimes do not even know what we know and what we do not know. We can avoid this vagueness only (1) by becoming conscious of what we believe in, (2) of what we do not believe in, and (3) by recognizing the large debatable ground in between those two fields and trying our experiments there. Don't let us try experiments where they are not needed, in regard to matters about which we have already made up our minds. For instance, there are certain things which people continue to urge about employee representation which are almost universally accepted. There is no need of saying these particular things any longer, there is no need of studying them; let us give our efforts to the things we don't know – there are plenty of them.

Another point: we should always know whether we are considering principles or methods. A confusion here is disastrous, as we often see in discussion. I have heard a discussion on whether shop-committee meetings should be held in company time, which seemed to me quite beside the mark because the distinction was not being made between the principles underlying the matter and the possible methods of carrying out the principles. Some were talking about one, and some about the other. Moreover, let us not confuse our methods one with the other; let us try out one until we have come to some conclusion about it. As a coach used to tell the

Harvard boat crew, 'It's better to have a method and stick to it, even if it's not the best possible method.'

This is all involved in what I spoke of as taking a conscious and responsible attitude toward experience. It is also taking a scientific attitude. The growing appreciation of the advantage of such an attitude is evidenced by the subject chosen for this course of conferences: *the scientific foundations of business administration*.

Reference

FOLLETT, M. P. (1924), *Creative Experience*, Longman.

9 C. I. Barnard

The Executive Functions

C. I. Barnard, 'The executive functions', *The Functions of the Executive*,
Harvard University Press, 1938, chapter 15, pp. 215–34.

The coordination of efforts essential to a system of cooperation
requires, as we have seen, an organization system of communication. Such a system of communication implies centers or points of
interconnection and can only operate as these centers are occupied by persons who are called executives. It might be said, then,
that the function of executives is to serve as channels of communication so far as communications must pass through central
positions. But since the object of the communication system is
coordination of all aspects of organization, it follows that the
functions of executives relate to all the work essential to the vitality
and endurance of an organization, so far, at least, as it must be
accomplished through formal coordination.

It is important to observe, however, that not all work done by
persons who occupy executive positions is in connection with the
executive functions, the coordination of activities of others. Some
of the work of such persons, though *organization* work, is not
executive. For example, if the president of a corporation goes out
personally to sell products of his company or engages in some of
the production work, these are not executive services. If the president of a university gives lectures to a class of students, this is not
executive work. If the head of a government department spends
time on complaints or disputes about services rendered by the
department, this is not necessarily executive work. Executive work
is not that *of* the organization, but the specialized work of *maintaining* the organization in operation.

Probably all executives do a considerable amount of non-
executive work. Sometimes this work is more valuable than the
executive work they do. This intermixture of functions is a matter
of convenience and often of economy, because of the scarcity of

abilities; or there may be other reasons for it. As a result of the combination of executive with non-executive functions, however, it is difficult in practice merely by comparison of titles or of nominal functions to determine the comparative methods of executive work in different organizations. If we mean by executive functions the specialized work of maintaining systems of cooperative effort, we may best proceed for general purposes to find out what work has to be done, and then, when desirable, to trace out who are doing that work in a particular organization.

This is especially true because executive work is itself often complexly organized. In an organization of moderate size there may be a hundred persons who are engaged part of the time in executive work; and some of them, for example clerks or stenographers, are not executives in any ordinary sense. Nevertheless, the activities of these persons constitute the executive organization. It is to the functions of this organization as a special unit that our attention should be given primarily, the distribution of work between persons or positions being for general purposes quite of secondary importance. This chapter will be devoted to the functions of the executive organization as a whole which exists exclusively for the coordination of the efforts of the entire organization.

The executive functions serve to maintain a system of cooperative effort. They are impersonal. The functions are not, as so frequently stated, to manage a group of persons. I do not think a correct understanding of executive work can be had if this narrower, convenient, but strictly speaking erroneous, conception obtains. It is not even quite correct to say that the executive functions are to manage the system of cooperative efforts. As a whole it is managed by itself, not by the executive organization, which is a part of it. The functions with which we are concerned are like those of the nervous system, including the brain, in relation to the rest of the body. It exists to maintain the bodily system by directing those actions which are necessary more effectively to adjust to the environment, but it can hardly be said to manage the body, a large part of whose functions are independent of it and upon which it in turn depends.

The essential executive functions, as I shall present them, correspond to the elements of organization as already stated in Chapter 7 and presented in some detail in Part 3 [not included]. They are, first, to provide the system of communication; second, to promote the securing of essential efforts; and, third, to formulate and define purpose. Since the elements of organization are interrelated and interdependent, the executive functions are so likewise; nevertheless they are subject to considerable specialization and as functions are to a substantial degree separable in practice. We shall deal with them only as found in complex, though not necessarily large, organizations.

1 The maintenance of organization communication

We have noticed in previous chapters that, when a complex of more than one unit is in question, centers of communication and corresponding executives are necessary. The need of a definite system of communication creates the first task of the organizer and is the immediate origin of executive organization. If the purpose of an organization is conceived initially in the mind of one person, he is likely very early to find necessary the selection of lieutenants; and if the organization is spontaneous its very first task is likely to be the selection of a leader. Since communication will be accomplished only through the agency of persons, the selection of persons for executive functions is the concrete method of establishing the *means* of communication, though it must be immediately followed by the creation of positions, that is, a *system* of communication; and, especially in established organizations, the positions will exist to be filled in the event of vacancies.

In other words, communication position and the 'locating' of the services of a person are complementary phases of the same thing. The center of communication is the organization service of a person at a place. Persons without positions cannot function as executives, they mean nothing but potentiality. Conversely, positions vacant are as defunct as dead nerve centers. This is why executives, when functioning strictly as executives, are unable to appraise men in the abstract, in an organization vacuum, as it were. Men are neither good nor bad, but only good or bad in this or that position. This is why they not infrequently 'change the organization', the arrangement of positions, if men suitable to fill them are not available. In fact, 'executive organization' in practice cannot be divorced from 'executive personnel'; and 'executive personnel' is without important meaning except in conjunction with a specific arrangement of positions.

Therefore, the problem of the establishment and maintenance of the system of communication, that is, the primary task of the executive organization, is perpetually that of obtaining the coalescence of the two phases, executive personnel and executive positions. Each phase in turn is the strategic factor of the executive problem – first one, then the other phase, must be adjusted. This is the central problem of the executive functions. Its solution is not in itself sufficient to accomplish the work of all these functions; but no others can be accomplished without it, and none well unless it is well done.

Although this communication function has two phases, it is usually necessary in practice to deal with one phase at a time, and the problems of each phase are of quite different kinds. The problems of positions are those of location and the geographical, temporal, social and functional specializations of unit and group organizations. The personnel problems are a special case of general personnel problems – the recruiting of contributors who have appropriate qualifications, and the development of the inducements, incentives, persuasion and objective authority that can make those qualifications effective executive services in the organization.

The scheme of organization

Let us call the first phase of the function – the definition of organization positions – the 'scheme of organization'. This is the aspect of organization which receives relatively excessive formal attention because it can apparently be reduced to organization charts, specifications of duties, and descriptions of divisions of labor, etc. It rests upon or represents a coordination chiefly of the work to be done by the organization, that is, its purposes broken up into subsidiary purposes, specializations, tasks, etc., which will be discussed in section 3 of this chapter; the kind and quantity of *services* of personnel that can be obtained; the kind and quantity of *persons* that must be included in the cooperative system for this purpose; the inducements that are required; and the places at which and the times when these factors can be combined, which will not be specifically discussed here.[1]

1. See chapter X, 'The Basis and Kinds of Specializations' [not included], and section 3 of the present chapter.

It is evident that these are mutually dependent factors, and that they all involve other executive functions which we shall discuss later. So far as the *scheme* of organization is separately attacked, it is always on the assumption that it is then the strategic factor, the other factors of organization remaining fixed for the time being; but since the underlying purpose of any change in a scheme of organization is to affect these other factors as a whole favorably, any scheme of organization at any given time represents necessarily a result of previous successive approximations through a period of time. It has always necessarily to be attacked on the basis of the present situation.

Personnel

The scheme of organization is dependent not only upon the general factors of the organization as a whole, but likewise, as we have indicated, on the availability of various kinds of services for the executive positions. This becomes in its turn the strategic factor. In general, the principles of the economy of incentives apply here as well as to other more general personnel problems. The balance of factors and the technical problems of this special class, however, are not only different from those generally to be found in other spheres of organization economy but are highly special in different types of organizations.

The most important single contribution required of the executive, certainly the most universal qualification, is loyalty, domination by the organization personality. This is the first necessity because the lines of communication cannot function at all unless the personal contributions of executives will be present at the required positions, at the times necessary, without default for ordinary personal reasons. This, as a personal qualification, is known in secular organizations as the quality of 'responsibility'; in political organizations as 'regularity'; in governmental organizations as fealty or loyalty; in religious organizations as 'complete submission' to the faith and to the hierarchy of objective religious authority.

The contribution of personal loyalty and submission is least susceptible to tangible inducements. It cannot be bought either by material inducements or by other positive incentives, except all other things be equal. This is as true of industrial organizations, I believe, as of any others. It is rather generally understood that although money or other material inducements must usually be paid to responsible persons, responsibility itself does not arise from such inducements.

However, love of prestige is, in general, a much more important inducement in the case of executives than with the rest of the personnel. Interest in work and pride in organization are other incentives that usually must be present. These facts are much obscured as respects commercial organizations, where material inducements appear to be the effective factors partly because such inducements are more readily offered in such organizations and partly because, since the other incentives are often equal as between such organizations, material inducements are the only available differential factor. It also becomes an important secondary factor to individuals in many cases, because prestige and official responsibilities impose heavy material burdens on them. Hence neither churches nor socialistic states have been able to escape the necessity of direct or indirect material inducements for high dignitaries or officials. But this is probably incidental and superficial in all organizations. It appears to be true that in all of them adequate incentives to executive services are difficult to offer. Those most available in the present age are tangible, materialistic; but on the whole they are both insufficient and often abortive.[2]

Following loyalty, responsibility and capacity to be dominated by organization personality, come the more specific personal abilities. They are roughly divided into two classes: relatively general abilities, involving general alertness, comprehensiveness of interest, flexibility, faculty of adjustment, poise, courage, etc.; and specialized abilities based on particular aptitudes and acquired techniques. The first kind is relatively difficult to appraise because

2. After much experience, I am convinced that the most ineffective services in a continuing effort are in one sense those of volunteers, or of semi-volunteers; for example, half-pay workers. What appears to be inexpensive is in fact very expensive, because non-material incentives – such as prestige, toleration of too great personal interest in the work with its accompanying fads and 'pet' projects, the yielding to exaggerated conceptions of individual importance – are causes of internal friction and many other undesirable consequences. Yet in many emergency situations, and in a large part of political, charitable, civic, educational and religious organization work, often indispensable services cannot be obtained by material incentives.

it depends upon innate characteristics developed through general experience. It is not greatly susceptible of immediate inculcation. The second kind may be less rare because the division of labor, that is, organization itself, fosters it automatically, and because it is susceptible to development (at a cost) by training and education. We deliberately and more and more turn out specialists; but we do not develop general executives well by specific efforts, and we know very little about how to do it.

The higher the positions in the line of authority, the more general the abilities required. The scarcity of such abilities, together with the necessity for keeping the lines of authority as short as feasible, controls the organization of executive work. It leads to the reduction of the number of formally executive positions to the minimum, a measure made possible by creating about the executives in many cases staffs of specialists who supplement them in time, energy and technical capacities. This is made feasible by elaborate and often delicate arrangements to correct error resulting from the faults of over-specialization and the paucity of line executives.

The operation of such systems of complex executive organization requires the highest development of the executive arts. Its various forms and techniques are most definitely exemplified in the armies and navies of the major powers, the Postal Administrations of several European countries, the Bell Telephone System, some of the great railway systems and the Catholic Church; and perhaps in the political organization of the British Empire.[3] One of the first limitations of world-wide or even a much more restricted international organization is the necessity for the development of these forms and techniques far beyond their present status.

Thus, jointly with the development of the scheme of organization, the selection, promotion, demotion and dismissal of men becomes the essence of maintaining the system of communication without which no organization can exist. The selection in part, but

3. From a structural point of view the organization of the United States of America is especially noteworthy, but from the viewpoint of the executive functions it is intended to be defective; that is, the system of States Rights or dual sovereignty and the separation of legislative, judicial and executive departments precludes a common center of authoritative communication in American government as a formal organization. It is intended or expected that the requirements will be met by informal organization.

especially the promotion, demotion, and dismissal of men, depend upon the exercise of supervision or what is often called 'control'.

Control relates directly, and in conscious application chiefly, to the work of the organization as a whole rather than to the work of executives as such. But so heavily dependent is the success of co-operation upon the functioning of the executive organization that practically the control is over executives for the most part. If the work of an organization is not successful, if it is inefficient, if it cannot maintain the services of its personnel, the conclusion is that its 'management' is wrong; that is, that the scheme of communication or the associated personnel or both, that is, the executive department directly related, are at fault. This is, sometimes at least, not true, but often it is. Moreover, for the correction of such faults the first reliance is upon executive organization. The methods by which control is exercised are, of course, numerous and largely technical to each organization, and need not be further discussed here.

Informal executive organizations

So far we have considered the first executive function only as it relates to the formal communication system. It has been emphasized several times in this treatise that informal organization is essential to formal organizations, particularly with reference to communication. This is true not only of the organization as a whole, or of its ultimate subordinate units, but also of that special part which we call the executive organization. The communication function of executives includes the maintenance of informal executive organization as an essential means of communication.

Although I have never heard it stated that this is an executive function or that such a thing as an informal executive organization exists, in all the good organizations I have observed the most careful attention is paid to it. In all of them informal organizations operate. This is usually not apparent except to those directly concerned.

The general method of maintaining an informal executive organization is so to operate and to select and promote executives that a general condition of compatibility of personnel is maintained. Perhaps often and certainly occasionally men cannot be promoted or selected, or even must be relieved, because they cannot function, because they 'do not fit', where there is no question of formal competence. This question of 'fitness' involves such matters as education, experience, age, sex, personal distinctions, prestige, race, nationality, faith, politics, sectional antecedents; and such very specific personal traits as manners, speech, personal appearance, etc. It goes by few if any rules, except those based at least nominally on other, formal, considerations. It represents in its best sense the political aspects of personal relationship in formal organization. I suspect it to be most highly developed in political, labor, church, and university organizations, for the very reason that the intangible types of personal services are relatively more important in them than in most other, especially industrial, organizations. But it is certainly of major importance in all organizations.

This compatibility is promoted by educational requirements (armies, navies, churches, schools); by requirement of certain background (European armies, navies, labor unions, Soviet and Fascist governments, political parties); by conferences and conventions; by specifically social activities; by class distinctions connected with privileges and 'authority' (in armies, navies, churches, universities). A certain conformity is required by unwritten understanding that can sometimes be formally enforced, expressed for its negative aspect by the phrase 'conduct unbecoming a gentleman and an officer'. There are, however, innumerable other processes, many of which are not consciously employed for this purpose.

It must not be understood that the desired degree of compatibility is always the same or is the maximum possible. On the contrary it seems to me to be often the case that excessive compatibility or harmony is deleterious, resulting in 'single track minds' and excessively crystallized attitudes and in the destruction of personal responsibility; but I know from experience in operating with new emergency organizations, in which there was no time and little immediate basis for the growth of an informal organization properly coordinated with formal organization that it is almost impossible to secure effective and efficient cooperation without it.

The functions of informal executive organizations are the communication of intangible facts, opinions, suggestions, suspicions, that cannot pass through formal channels without raising issues calling for decisions, without dissipating dignity and objective authority, and without overloading executive positions; also to minimize excessive cliques of political types arising from too great divergence of interests and views; to promote self-discipline of the group; and to make possible the development of important personal influences in the organization. There are probably other functions.

I shall comment on only two functions of informal executive organization. The necessity for avoiding formal issues, that is, for avoiding the issuance of numerous formal orders except on routine matters and except in emergencies, is important.[4] I know of major executives who issue an order or judgment settling an important issue rather seldom, although they are functioning all the time. The obvious desire of politicians to avoid important issues (and to impose them on their opponents) is based upon a thorough sense of organization. Neither authority nor cooperative disposition (largely the same things) will stand much overt division on formal issues in the present stage of human development. Hence most laws, executive orders, decisions, etc., are in effect formal notice that all is well – there is agreement, authority is not questioned.

The question of personal influence is very subtle. Probably most good organizations have somewhere a Colonel House; and many men not only exercise beneficent influence far beyond that implied by their formal status, but most of them, at the time, would lose their influence if they had corresponding formal status. The reason may be that many men have personal qualifications of high order that will not operate under the stress of commensurate official responsibility. By analogy I may mention the golfers of first skill who cannot 'stand up' in public tournaments.

To summarize: the first executive function is to develop and maintain a system of communication. This involves jointly a

4. When writing these lines I tried to recall an important general decision made by me on my initiative as a telephone executive within two years. I could recall none, although on reviewing the record I found several. On the other hand, I can still recall without any record many major decisions made by me 'out of hand' when I was a Relief Administrator. I probably averaged at least five a day for eighteen months. In the latter case I worked with a very noble group but a very poor informal organization under emergency conditions.

scheme of organization and an executive personnel. The processes by which the latter is accomplished include chiefly the selection of men and the offering of incentives; techniques of control permitting effectiveness in promoting, demoting and dismissing men; and finally the securing of an informal organization in which the essential property is compatibility of personnel. The chief functions of this informal organization are expansion of the means of communication with reduction in the necessity for formal decisions the minimizing of undesirable influences, and the promotion of desirable influences concordant with the scheme of formal responsibilities.

2 The securing of essential services from individuals

The second function of the executive organization is to promote the securing of the personal services that constitute the material of organizations.

The work divides into two main divisions: (*I*) the bringing of persons into cooperative relationship with the organization; (*II*) the eliciting of the services after such persons have been brought into that relationship.

I

The characteristic fact of the first division is that the organization is acting upon persons who are in every sense outside it. Such action is necessary not merely to secure the personnel of new organizations, or to supply the material for the growth of existing organizations, but also to replace the losses that continually take place by reason of death, resignation, 'backsliding', emigration, discharge, excommunication, ostracism. These factors of growth or replacement of contributors require bringing persons by organization effort within range of the consideration of the incentives available in order to induce some of these persons to attach themselves to the organization. Accordingly the task involves two parts: (a) bringing persons within reach of specific effort to secure services, and (b) the application of that effort when they have been brought near enough. Often both parts of the task occupy the efforts of the same persons or parts of an organization; but they are clearly distinct elements and considerable specialization is found with respect to them.

(a) Bringing persons within reach of recruiting or proselyting influence is a task which differs in practical emphasis among organizations in respect both to scope and to method. Some religious organizations – especially the Catholic Church, several Protestant Churches, the Mormon Church, for example – have as ideal goals the attachment of all persons to their organizations, and the wide world is the field of proselyting propaganda. During many decades the United States of America invited all who could reach its shores to become American citizens. Other organizations, having limits on the volume of their activities, restrict the field of propaganda. Thus many nations in effect now restrict substantial growth to those who acquire a national status by birth; the American Legion restricts its membership to those who have acquired a status by a certain type of previous service, etc. Others restrict their fields practically on the basis of proportions. Thus universities 'in principle' are open to all or to all with educational and character qualifications but may restrict their appeals to geographical, racial and class proportions, so as to preserve the cosmopolitan character of their bodies, or to preserve predominance of nationals, etc. Industrial and commercial organizations are theoretically limited usually by considerations of social compatibility and additionally by the costs of propaganda. They usually attempt no appeal when the geographic remoteness makes it ineffective.

Although the scope of the field of propaganda is for most organizations not clearly conceived or stated and as a problem only requires active consideration at intervals usually long, the question is nevertheless fundamental. This is best indicated by the methods practically employed in connection with it. In churches the organization of mission work and its territorial scope are the best indications of its importance. In most governments, at present, the accretion of members takes the form of stimulating reproduction by active promotional efforts, as in France and Italy, for example, or by the ease of acquiring citizenship and free land, as until recently in the United States. In many industrial organizations foreign recruiting was once an important aspect of their work, and directly or indirectly the appeal for contributors of capital or credit has been fundamentally international in scope until recent exchange restrictions. In fact, the most universal aspect of industrial organization appeal has been in respect to this type of contributor – for many practical purposes he is not usually regarded as the material of organization, though in the present study he is.

(b) The effort to induce specific persons who by the general appeal are brought into contact with an organization actually to become identified with it constitutes the more regular and routine work of securing contributors. This involves in its general aspects the method of persuasion which has already been described, the establishment of inducements and incentives, and direct negotiation. The methods required are indefinitely large in number and of very wide variety.[5] It would not be useful here to add to what has already been said in Chapter 11 [not included] on the economy of incentives. It is only necessary to emphasize again that fundamentally most persons potentially available are not susceptible at any given time of being induced to give service to any particular organization, large or small.

II

Although the work of recruiting is important in most organizations, and especially so in those which are new or rapidly expanding or which have high 'turnover', nevertheless in established and enduring organizations the eliciting of the quantity and quality of efforts from their adherents is usually more important and occupies the greater part of personnel effort. Because of the more tangible character of 'membership', being an 'employee', etc., recruiting is apt to receive more attention as a field of personnel work than the business of promoting the actual output of efforts and influences, which are the real material of organization.[6] Membership, nominal adherence, is merely the starting point; and the minimum contributions which can be conceived as enabling retention of such connection would generally be insufficient for the survival of active or productive organization. Hence every church, every govern-

5. I must repeat that although the emphasis is on the employee group of contributors, so far as industrial organizations are concerned, nevertheless 'customers' are equally included. The principles broadly discussed here relate to salesmanship as well as employing persons. See page 75 [not included].

6. As an instance, note the great attention in civil service regulations, and also in political appointments, to obtaining and retaining employment, and the relatively small attention to services.

ment, every other important organization, has to intensify or multiply the contributions which its members will make above the level or volume which would occur if no such effort were made. Thus churches must strengthen the faith, secure compliance by public and private acknowledgments of faith or devotion and secure material contributions from their members. Governments are concerned with increasing the quality of the citizenry – promoting national solidarity, loyalty, patriotism, discipline and competence. Other organizations are similarly occupied in securing loyalty, reliability, responsibility, enthusiasm, quality of efforts, output. In short, every organization to survive must deliberately attend to the maintenance and growth of its authority to do the things necessary for coordination, effectiveness, and efficiency. This, as we have seen, depends upon its appeal to persons who are already related to the organization.

The methods, the inducements and incentives, by which this is done have already been in general indicated in our discussion of incentives and authority. As executive functions they may be distinguished as the maintenance of morale, the maintenance of the scheme of inducements, the maintenance of schemes of deterrents, supervision and control, inspection, education and training.

3 The formulation of purpose and objectives

The third executive function is to formulate and define the purposes, objectives, ends, of the organization. It has already been made clear that, strictly speaking, purpose is defined more nearly by the aggregate of action taken than by any formulation in words; but that that aggregate of action is a residuum of the decisions relative to purpose and the environment, resulting in closer and closer approximations to the concrete acts. It has also been emphasized that purpose is something that must be accepted by all the contributors to the system of efforts. Again, it has been stated that purpose must be broken into fragments, specific objectives, not only ordered in time so that detailed purpose and detailed action follow in the series of progressive cooperation, but also ordered contemporaneously into the specializations – geographical, social and functional – that each unit organization implies. It is more apparent here than with other executive functions that it is an entire executive organization that formulates, redefines, breaks into details and decides on the innumerable simultaneous and progressive actions that are the stream of syntheses constituting purpose or action. No single executive can under any conditions accomplish this function alone, but only that part of it which relates to his position in the executive organization.

Hence the critical aspect of this function is the assignment of responsibility – the delegation of objective authority. Thus in one sense this function is that of the scheme of positions, the system of communication, already discussed. That is its potential aspect. Its other aspect is the actual decisions and conduct which make the scheme a working system. Accordingly, the general executive states that 'this is the purpose, this the objective, this the direction, in general terms, in which we wish to move, before next year'. His department heads, or the heads of his main territorial divisions, say to their departments or suborganizations: 'This means for us these things now, then others next month, then others later, to be better defined after experience.' Their subdepartment or division heads say: 'This means for us such and such operations now at these places, such others at those places, something today here, others tomorrow there.' Then district or bureau chiefs in turn become more and more specific, their sub-chiefs still more so as to place, group, time, until finally purpose is merely jobs, specific groups, definite men, definite times, accomplished results. But meanwhile, back and forth, up and down, the communications pass, reporting obstacles, difficulties, impossibilities, accomplishments; redefining, modifying purposes level after level.

Thus the organization for the definition of purpose is the organization for the specification of work to do; and the specifications are made in their final stage when and where the work is being done. I suspect that at least nine-tenths of all organization activity is on the responsibility, the authority, and the specifications of those who make the last contributions, who apply personal energies to the final objectives. There is no meaning to personal specialization, personal experience, personal training, personal location, personal ability, eyes and ears, arms and legs, brains and emotions, if this is not so. What must be added to the indispensable authority, responsibility and capability of each contributor is the indispensable coordination. This requires a pyramiding of the formulation of purpose that becomes more and more general as the number of units of basic organization becomes larger, and more and more remote in future time. Responsibility for abstract, generalizing, prospective, long-run decision is delegated *up* the line, responsibility for definition, action, remains always at the base where the authority for effort resides.

The formulation and definition of purpose is then a widely distributed function, only the more general part of which is executive. In this fact lies the most important inherent difficulty in the operation of cooperative systems – the necessity for indoctrinating those at the lower levels with general purposes, the major decisions, so that they remain cohesive and able to make the ultimate detailed decisions coherent; and the necessity, for those at the higher levels, of constantly understanding the concrete conditions and the specific decisions of the 'ultimate' contributors from which and from whom executives are often insulated. Without that up-and-down-the-line coordination of purposeful decisions, general decisions and general purposes are mere intellectual processes in an organization vacuum, insulated from realities by layers of misunderstanding. The function of formulating grand purposes and providing for their redefinition is one which needs sensitive systems of communication, experience in interpretation, imagination and delegation of responsibility.

Perhaps there are none who could consider even so extremely condensed and general a description of the executive functions as has here been presented without perceiving that these functions are merely elements in an organic whole. It is their combination in a working system that makes an organization.

This combination involves two opposite incitements to action. First, the concrete interaction and mutual adjustment of the executive functions are partly to be determined by the factors of the environment of the organization – the specific cooperative system as a whole and its environment. This involves fundamentally the logical processes of analysis and the discrimination of the strategic factors. We shall consider this aspect in the following chapter. Second, the combination equally depends upon the maintenance of the vitality of action – the will to effort. This is the moral aspect, the element of morale, the ultimate reason for cooperation, to which Chapter 17 [not included] will be given.

10 A. P. Sloan, Jr

The Management of General Motors

A. P. Sloan, Jr, 'The management: how it works', chapter 23 of *My Years with General Motors*, Doubleday, 1964.

It is not easy to say why one management is successful and another is not. The causes of success or failure are deep and complex, and chance plays a part. Experience has convinced me, however, that for those who are responsible for a business, two important factors are motivation and opportunity. The former is supplied in good part by incentive compensation, the latter by decentralization.

But the matter does not end there. It has been a thesis of this book that good management rests on a reconciliation of centralization and decentralization, or 'decentralization with coordinated control'.

Each of the conflicting elements brought together in this concept has its unique results in the operation of a business. From decentralization we get initiative, responsibility, development of personnel, decisions close to the facts, flexibility – in short, all the qualities necessary for an organization to adapt to new conditions. From coordination we get efficiencies and economies. It must be apparent that coordinated decentralization is not an easy concept to apply. There is no hard and fast rule for sorting out the various responsibilities and the best way to assign them. The balance which is struck between corporate and divisional responsibility varies according to what is being decided, the circumstances of the time, past experience, and the temperaments and skills of the executives involved.

The concept of coordinated decentralization evolved gradually at General Motors as we responded to tangible problems of management. As I have shown, at the time its development began, some four decades ago, it was clearly advisable to give each division a strong management which would be primarily responsible for the conduct of its business. But our experience in 1920–21 also demonstrated the need for a greater measure of control over the divisions than we had attained. Without adequate control from the central office, the divisions got out of hand, and failed to follow the policies set by corporation management, to the great detriment of the corporation. Meanwhile, the corporation management was in no position to set the best policies, since it was without appropriate and timely data from the divisions. A steady flow of operating data, for which procedures were later set up, finally made real coordination possible.

That still left us with the problem of finding the right combination of freedom for the divisions and control over them. The combination could not be set once and for all, of course. It varies with changing circumstances, and the responsibility for determining administrative organization is a continuing one. Thus, at one time, responsibility for the styling of the cars and other products was vested in the divisions. Since then it has been found desirable to place the responsibility for developing the general style characteristics of all our major products in the Styling Staff. This was suggested partly by the physical economies to be gained by coordinated styling. In addition, we learned from experience that work of higher quality could be obtained by utilizing, corporation-wide, the highly developed talents of the specialists. The adoption of any particular style is now a joint responsibility of the division concerned, the Styling Staff, and the central management.

Such continuing adjustments in the relative responsibility assumed by the division management and central management are permitted by the decentralized organization of General Motors whenever experience or changed circumstances present opportunities for improved or more economical performance. In my time as chief executive officer only a modest degree of supervision was actually exercised by general officers over division managers. I believe that basically the same is the case today, although changed circumstances and new and more complex problems have resulted in a somewhat closer degree of coordination than existed in my time.

In General Motors we do not follow the textbook definition of line and staff. Our distinction is between the central office (which includes staff) and the divisions. Broadly speaking, the staff officers – being primarily specialists – do not have line authority, yet in certain matters of established policy, they may communicate the application of such policy directly to a division.

The responsibility of the central management is to determine which decisions can be made more effectively and efficiently by the central office and which by the divisions. In order that such determinations be informed and knowledgeable, the central management depends heavily on the staff officers. Indeed, many of the important decisions of central management are first formulated in collaboration with the staff in the policy groups, and then adopted, after discussion, by the governing committees. Consequently, the staff is the real source of many decisions that are formally adopted by the committees. For example, the basic decision to participate in the manufacture of diesel locomotives was largely based on product research by the staff.

Some of the general staff activities, such as legal work, have no counterparts in the divisions. Other general staff activities correspond to activities in each of the divisions, among them engineering, manufacturing, and distribution activities. But there are some important distinctions between these staff and divisional activities: the general staffs are concerned with longer-range problems, and with problems of broader application, than their opposite numbers in the divisions. The corresponding divisional staffs are engaged largely in the application of policies and programs already developed. There have been exceptions to this, however, as when a project has been approved for development in a division. An example is the development of the Corvair, which is referred to in the next chapter [not included].

The economies that flow from central-office activities are considerable and the cost comes on the average to less than 1 per cent of the corporation's net sales. Through the general staff the divisions get their services cheaper than if they provided them or bought them on the outside, and they get better services. The latter feature is, in my opinion, by far the more important. The staff contributions in the fields of styling, finance, technical research, advanced engineering, personnel and labor relations, legal affairs, manufacturing and distribution are outstanding and certainly worth a large multiple of their cost.

Several kinds of economies are made possible by centralized staff operations. Among the most important are the economies that derive from the coordination of the divisions. These arise through the sharing of ideas and developments among general officers and divisional personnel. The divisions contribute ideas and techniques both to each other and to central management. Much of our managerial and engineering talent, and many of our general officers, have come out of the divisions. The development of high-compression engines and automatic transmissions, for example, was the work of both staff and divisions. Our progress in aviation engines and in diesel engines came out of the development work of both.

Under the decentralized operation of the divisions, problems of like kind are met in different ways by different division managers, subject to the advice of the central office of the corporation. Out of this process comes a winnowing of techniques and ideas, and a development of judgments and skills. The quality of General Motors' management as a whole derives in part from this shared experience with common goals and from divisional rivalry within the framework of these common goals.

There are also the economies of specialization possible under our decentralized system. It is an axiom of economics that costs are reduced and trade created by specialization and the division of labor. Applied to General Motors, this has meant that our internal supplying divisions which specialize in the production of components must be fully competitive in price, quality, and service; if they are not, the purchasing divisions are free to buy from outside sources. Even when we have decided to make an item rather than to buy it, and have established production of the item, it is by no means a closed decision that we will stay in that line of production. We try, wherever possible, to test our internal supplying divisions against external competitors and to make a continuing judgment on whether it is better to make or to buy.

The popular misconception that it always pays to make an item yourself rather than to buy it is based on the assumption of a cost saving. The argument runs that by making instead of buying, you can save the extra cost of your supplier's profit. But the fact is that if the suppliers' profit is a normal, competitive one, you must expect to make it on your own investment, or else there is no net saving. General Motors does not engage in the production of raw materials, as do some of its competitors, and we purchase a large proportion of the items that go into our end products, because there is no reason to believe that by producing them we could obtain better products or service, or a lower price.

Of the total cost of sales of our products, purchases of parts, materials, and services from outside sources account for 55 to 60 per cent.

The role of the division managers is an important one in our continuing efforts to maintain both efficiency and adaptability. These managers make almost all of the divisional operating decisions, subject, however, to some important qualifications. Their decisions must be consistent with the corporation's general policies; the results of the division's operations must be reported to the central management; and the division officers must 'sell' central management on any substantial changes in operating policies and be open to suggestions from the general officers.

The practice of selling major proposals is an important feature of General Motors' management. Any proposal must be sold to central management and if it affects other divisions it must be sold to them as well. Sound management also requires that the central office should in most cases sell its proposals to the divisions, which it does through the policy groups and group executives. The selling approach provides an important extra safeguard in General Motors against ill-considered decisions, over and above the safeguards normally implied in the responsibility of corporate officers to shareholders. It assures that any basic decision is made only after thorough consideration by all parties concerned.

Our decentralized organization and our tradition of selling ideas, rather than simply giving orders, impose the need upon all levels of management to make a good case for what they propose. The manager who would like to operate on a hunch will usually find it hard to sell his ideas to others on this basis. But, in general, whatever sacrifice might be entailed in ruling out a possibly brilliant hunch is compensated for by the better-than-average results which can be expected from a policy that can be strongly defended against well-informed and sympathetic criticism. In short, General Motors is not the appropriate organization for purely intuitive executives, but it provides a favorable environment for capable and rational men. In some organizations, in order to tap the potentialities of a genius, it is necessary to build around him and tailor the organization to his temperament. General Motors on the whole is not such an organization although Mr Kettering was an obvious exception.

Our management policy decisions are arrived at by discussions in the governing committees and policy groups. These were not the creation of a single inspired moment, but the result of a long process of development in dealing with a fundamental problem of management, that of placing responsibility for policy in the hands of those best able both to make the decisions and to assume the responsibility. To a certain extent this involves a contradiction. On the one hand, those best able to assume responsibility must have broad business perspective oriented toward the interest of the shareholder. On the other hand, those best qualified to make specific decisions must be close to the actual operation of the business. We have attempted to resolve this contradiction principally by dividing the policy-making responsibilities within central management between the Finance Committee and the Executive Committee, as I have shown.

Another source of policy recommendation is the Administration Committee, which is charged with the responsibility of making recommendations to the president with respect to the manufacturing and selling activities of the corporation, and on any other matters affecting the business and affairs of the corporation that may be referred to it by the president or the Executive Committee. The president is the chairman of the committee and, at the present time, its membership includes the members of the Executive Committee, two group executives who are not members of the Executive Committee, the general managers of the car and truck divisions, the general manager of Fisher Body Division, and the general manager of the Overseas Operations Division.

Under this separation of responsibility, policy development and recommendation are mainly the duty of the groups in central management made up of the men closest to operations. They work very closely, of course, with men from the divisions, and divisional men are on some policy groups. The Executive Committee, which views the corporation as a whole and at the same time is closely familiar with operating problems, has a somewhat judicial function. It makes the fundamental decisions on the basis of the work of the policy groups and the Administration Committee, plus the committee members' close knowledge of operating conditions.

The Finance Committee, which includes non-employee directors in its membership, exercises its responsibility and authority in the area of broader corporate policy.

Much of my life in General Motors was devoted to the development, organization and periodic reorganization of these governing groups in central management. This was required because of the paramount importance, in an organization like General Motors, of providing the right framework for decisions. There is a natural tendency to erode that framework unless it is consciously maintained. Group decisions do not always come easily. There is a strong temptation for the leading officers to make decisions themselves without the sometimes onerous process of discussion, which involves selling your ideas to others. The group will not always make a better decision than any particular member would make; there is even the possibility of some averaging down. But in General Motors I think the record shows that we have averaged up. Essentially this means that, through our form of organization, we have been able to adapt to the great changes that have taken place in the automobile market in each of the decades since 1920.

11 H. A. Simon

Decision Making and Organizational Design

H. A. Simon, 'The executive as decision maker' and 'Organizational design: man-machine systems for decision making', *The New Science of Management Decision*, Harper & Row, 1960, chapter 1, pp. 1–8, and chapter 5, pp. 35–50.

The executive as decision maker

What part does decision making play in managing? I shall find it convenient to take mild liberties with the English language by using 'decision making' as though it were synonymous with 'managing'.

What is our mental image of a decision maker? Is he a brooding man on horseback who suddenly rouses himself from thought and issues an order to a subordinate? Is he a happy-go-lucky fellow, a coin poised on his thumbnail, ready to risk his action on the toss? Is he an alert, gray-haired businessman, sitting at the board of directors' table with his associates, caught at the moment of saying 'aye' or 'nay'? Is he a bespectacled gentleman, bent over a docket of papers, his pen hovering over the line marked (X)?

All of these images have a significant point in common. In them, the decision maker is a man at the moment of choice, ready to plant his foot on one or another of the routes that lead from the crossroads. All the images falsify decision by focusing on its final moment. All of them ignore the whole lengthy, complex process of alerting, exploring and analysing that precede that final moment.

Intelligence, design and choice in decision making

In treating decision making as synonymous with managing, I shall be referring not merely to the final act of choice among alternatives, but rather to the whole process of decision. Decision making comprises three principal phases: finding occasions for making a decision; finding possible courses of action; and choosing among courses of action. These three activities account for quite different fractions of the time budgets of executives. The fractions vary greatly from one organization level to another and from one executive to another, but we can make some generalizations about them even from casual observation. Executives spend a large fraction of their time surveying the economic, technical, political and social environment to identify new conditions that call for new actions. They probably spend an even larger fraction of their time, individually or with their associates, seeking to invent, design and develop possible courses of action for handling situations where a decision is needed. They spend a small fraction of their time in choosing among alternative actions already developed to meet an identified problem and already analysed for their consequences. The three fractions, added together, account for most of what executives do.[1]

The first phase of the decision-making process – searching the environment for conditions calling for decision – I shall call *intelligence* activity (borrowing the military meaning of intelligence). The second phase – inventing, developing and analysing possible courses of action – I shall call *design* activity. The third phase – selecting a particular course of action from those available – I shall call *choice* activity.

Let me illustrate these three phases of decision. In the past five years, many companies have reorganized their accounting and other data-processing activities in order to make use of large electronic computers. How has this come about? Computers first became available commercially in the early 1950s. Although, in some vague and general sense, company managements were aware that computers existed, few managements had investigated their possible applications with any thoroughness before about 1955. For most companies, the use of computers required no decision before that time because it hadn't been placed on the agenda. (Cyert, Simon and Trow, 1956.)

The intelligence activity preceding the introduction of computers tended to come about in one of two ways. Some companies – for example, in the aircraft and atomic energy industries – were burdened with enormously complex computations for engineering design. Because efficiency in computation was a constant problem, and because the design departments were staffed with engineers

1. The way in which these activities take shape within an organization is described in some detail in March and Simon (1958), chapters 6 and 7.

who could understand, at least in general, the technology of computers, awareness of computers and their potentialities came early to these companies. After computers were already in extensive use for design calculations, businesses with a large number-processing load – insurance companies, accounting departments in large firms, banks – discovered these new devices and began to consider seriously their introduction.

Once it was recognized that computers might have a place in modern business, a major design task had to be carried out in each company before they could be introduced. It is now a commonplace that payrolls can be prepared by computers. Programs in both the general and computer senses for doing this are relatively easy to design in any given situation.[2] To develop the first computer programs for preparing payroll, however, was a major research and development project. Few companies having carried their investigations of computers to the point where they had definite plans for their use, failed to install them. Commitment to the new course of action took place gradually as the intelligence and design phases of the decision were going on. The final choice was, in many instances, almost *pro forma*.

Generally speaking, intelligence activity precedes design, and design activity precedes choice. The cycle of phases is, however, far more complex than this sequence suggests. Each phase in making a particular decision is itself a complex decision-making process. The design phase, for example, may call for new intelligence activities; problems at any given level generate subproblems that, in turn, have their intelligence, design, and choice phases, and so on. There are wheels within wheels within wheels. Nevertheless, the three large phases are often clearly discernible as the organizational decision process unfolds. They are closely related to the stages in problem solving first described by John Dewey (1910):

What is the problem?
What are the alternatives?
Which alternative is best?

It may be objected that I have ignored the task of carrying out

2. For a good discussion on the use of the computer for such purposes, see Gregory and Van Horn (1960).

decisions. I shall merely observe by the way that seeing that decisions are executed is again decision-making activity. A broad policy decision creates a new condition for the organization's executives that calls for the design and choice of a course of action for executing the policy. Executing policy, then, is indistinguishable from making more detailed policy. For this reason, I shall feel justified in taking my pattern for decision making as a paradigm for most executive activity.

Developing decision-making skills

It is an obvious step from the premise that managing is decision making to the conclusion that the important skills for an executive are decision-making skills. It is generally believed that good decision makers, like good athletes, are born, not made. The belief is about as true in the one case as it is in the other.

That human beings come into the world endowed unequally with biological potential for athletic prowess is undeniable. They also come endowed unequally with intelligence, cheerfulness and many other characteristics and potentialities. To a limited extent, we can measure some aspects of that endowment – height, weight, perhaps intelligence. Whenever we make such measurements and compare them with adult performance, we obtain significant, but low, correlations. A man who is not a natural athlete is unlikely to run the four-minute mile; but many men who are natural athletes have never come close to that goal. A man who is not 'naturally' intelligent is unlikely to star in science; but many intelligent scientists are not stars.

A good athlete is born when a man with some natural endowment, by dint of practice, learning and experience develops that natural endowment into a mature skill. A good executive is born when a man with some natural endowment (intelligence and some capacity for interacting with his fellow men) by dint of practice, learning and experience develops his endowment into a mature skill. The skills involved in intelligence, design and choosing activities are as learnable and trainable as the skills involved in driving, recovering and putting a golf ball. I hope to indicate some of the things a modern executive needs to learn about decision making.

Executive responsibility for organizational decision making

The executive's job involves not only making decisions himself, but also seeing that the organization, or part of an organization, that he directs makes decisions effectively. The vast bulk of the decision-making activity for which he is responsible is not his personal activity, but the activity of his subordinates.

Nowadays, with the advent of computers, we can think of information as something almost tangible; strings of symbols which, like strips of steel or plastic ribbons, can be processed – changed from one form to another. We can think of white-collar organizations as factories for processing information. The executive is the factory manager, with all the usual responsibilities for maintaining the factory operation, getting it back into operation when it breaks down, and proposing and carrying through improvements in its design.

There is no reason to expect that a man who has acquired a fairly high level of personal skill in decision-making activity will have a correspondingly high skill in designing efficient decision-making systems. To imagine that there is such a connection is like supposing that a man who is a good weight lifter can therefore design cranes. The skills of designing and maintaining the modern decision-making systems we call organizations are less intuitive skills. Hence, they are even more susceptible to training than the skills of personal decision making.

Programmed and nonprogrammed decisions

In discussing how executives now make decisions, and how they will make them in the future, let us distinguish two polar types of decisions. I shall call them *programmed decisions* and *nonprogrammed decisions*, respectively. Having christened them, I hasten to add that they are not really distinct types, but a whole continuum, with highly programmed decisions at one end of that continuum and highly unprogrammed decisions at the other end. We can find decisions of all shades of gray along the continuum, and I use the terms programmed and nonprogrammed simply as labels for the black and the white of the range.[3]

3. See March and Simon (1958), pp. 139–42 and 177–80 for further discussion of these types of decisions. The labels used there are slightly different.

Decisions are programmed to the extent that they are repetitive and routine, to the extent that a definite procedure has been worked out for handling them so that they don't have to be treated *de novo* each time they occur. The obvious reason why programmed decisions tend to be repetitive, and vice versa, is that if a particular problem recurs often enough, a routine procedure will usually be worked out for solving it. Numerous examples of programmed decisions in organizations will occur to you: pricing ordinary customers' orders; determining salary payments to employees who who have been ill; reordering office supplies.

Decisions are nonprogrammed to the extent that they are novel, unstructured and consequential. There is no cut-and-dried method for handling the problem because it hasn't arisen before, or because its precise nature and structure are elusive or complex, or because it is so important that it deserves a custom-tailored treatment. General Eisenhower's D-Day decision is a good example of a non-programmed decision. Remember, we are considering not merely the final act of ordering the attack, but the whole complex of intelligence and design activities that preceded it. Many of the components of the decisions were programmed – by standard techniques for military planning – but before these components could be designed they had to be provided with a broader framework of military and political policy.

I have borrowed the term program from the computer trade, and intend it in the sense in which it is used there. A *program* is a detailed prescription or strategy that governs the sequence of responses of a system to a complex task environment. Most of the programs that govern organizational response are not as detailed or as precise as computer programs. However, they all have the same intent: to permit an adaptive response of the system to the situation.

In what sense, then, can we say that the response of a system to a situation is nonprogrammed? Surely something determines the response. That something, that collection of rules of procedure, is by definition a program. By nonprogrammed I mean a response where the system has no specific procedures to deal with situations like the one at hand, but must fall back on whatever *general* capacity it has for intelligent, adaptive, problem-oriented action. In addition to his specific skills and specific knowledge, man has some general problem-solving capacities. Given almost any kind of situation, no matter how novel or perplexing, he can begin to reason about it in terms of ends and means.

This general problem-solving equipment is not always effective. Men often fail to solve problems, or they reach unsatisfactory solutions. But man is seldom completely helpless in a new situation. He possesses general problem-solving equipment which, however inefficient, fills some of the gaps in his special problem-solving skills. And organizations, as collections of men, have some of this same general adaptive capacity.

The cost of using general-purpose programs to solve problems is usually high. It is advantageous to reserve these programs for situations that are truly novel, where no alternative programs are available. If any particular class of situations recurs often enough, a special-purpose program can be developed which gives better solutions and gives them more cheaply than the general problem-solving apparatus.

My reason for distinguishing between programmed and nonprogrammed decisions is that different techniques are used for handling the programmed and the nonprogrammed aspects of our decision making. The distinction, then, will be a convenient one for classifying these techniques. I shall use it for that purpose, hoping that the reader will remind himself from time to time that the world is mostly gray with only a few spots of pure black or white.

The four-fold table below will provide a map of the territory I propose to cover. In the northern half of the map are some techniques related to programmed decision making, in the southern half, some techniques related to nonprogrammed decision making. In the western half of the map I placed the classical techniques used in decision making – the kit of tools that has been used by executives and organizations from the time of the earliest recorded history up to the present generation. In the eastern half of the map I placed the new techniques of decision making – tools that have been forged largely since the Second World War, and that are only now coming into extensive use in management in this country. I shall proceed across the map from west to east, and from north to south, taking up, in order, the north-west and the south-west quadrants (chapter II), the north-east quadrant (chapter III), and the south-east quadrant (chapter IV).

Table 1 Traditional and Modern Techniques of Decision Making

Types of decisions	Decision-making techniques	
	traditional	*modern*
Programmed: Routine, repetitive decisions Organization develops specific processes for handling them	1 Habit 2 Clerical routine: Standard operating procedures 3 Organization structure: Common expectations A system of subgoals Well-defined informational channels	1 Operations Research: Mathematical analysis Models Computer simulation 2 Electronic data processing
Nonprogrammed: One-shot, ill-structured novel, policy decisions Handled by general problem-solving processes	1 Judgement, intuition, and creativity 2 Rules of thumb 3 Selection and training of executives	Heuristic problem-solving techniques applied to: (a) training human decision makers (b) constructing heuristic computer programs

I can warn you now to what conclusion this journey is going to lead. We are in the midst of a major revolution in the art or science – whichever you prefer to call it – of management and organization. I shall try to describe the nature of this revolution and, in my final chapter, to discuss its implications.

Organizational design: man–machine systems for decision making

With operations research and electronic data processing we have acquired the technical capacity to automate programmed decision making and to bring into the programmed area some important classes of decisions that were formerly unprogrammed. Important innovations in decision-making processes in business are already resulting from these discoveries.

With heuristic programming, we are acquiring the technical capacity to automate nonprogrammed decision making. The next two decades will see changes in business decision making and business organization that will stem from this second phase in the revolution of our information technology. I should like now to explore, briefly, what the world of business will look like as these changes occur. (See Leavitt and Whisler, 1958, and Simon, 1960.)

Not all or, perhaps, most of the changes we may anticipate have to do with automation. As I pointed out earlier, the advance we may expect in the effectiveness of human decision-making processes is equally significant. Nevertheless, there has been so much public discussion about the automation and mechanization of data processing that I feel obliged to make some preliminary comments on this topic.

Some comments on automation

Although we always acknowledge our debt to machinery for the high productivity of Western industrial society, we almost always accompany that acknowledgment with warnings and head shakings about the unfortunate side effects that industrialization brings. Our concern about mechanization focuses on two points in particular: the hazard it creates of large-scale unemployment, and its supposed tendency to routinize work, draining it of the intrinsic satisfactions it might have possessed. Even management people, long accustomed to reassuring their blue-collar and clerical workers on these points, reveal exactly the same anxieties when the talk turns to the automation of decision making.

Automation and unemployment. In public discussion the danger of worker displacement through automation has been emphasized all out of proportion to its probable importance. The level of employment in a society is not related in any direct or necessary way to the level of automation in that society. There is absolutely no evidence that a society cannot and will not consume all the goods, services and leisure that the society can produce, provided that the social and economic institutions are even moderately well adapted to their functions of regulating production and distribution. If productivity increases especially rapidly in some sector of the economy (as, for example, productivity in agriculture has in the American economy), it may lead to significant temporary dislocation and technological unemployment of existing skills. There is no reason why the many should benefit from increases in productivity at the expense of the few who are displaced. Any society can and should devise means for eliminating most of the inequity associated with the displacement of skills.

I am aware that few societies in the past have done a good job of handling the undesirable transient effects of automation. This does not mean that it cannot be done, that we should blame our woes on automation, or that we should eschew the significant benefits resulting from productivity increases to avoid dealing with these transition problems. Fortunately, as past history shows, we will not, in fact, take the last-named course.

The pace of automation. How difficult it will be to take care of the transient effects of automation depends on the speed with which the automation occurs. A principal factor in regulating the rate of automation is the supply of capital for investment in the new equipment that is required. We can make a very rough estimate of what would be required for the complete automation of data processing and decision making.

Taking the respective income shares of capital and labor in total national income as the basis for our estimate, we may say that at the present time about four-fifths of the productive capacity of the American economy resides in its labor force, one-fifth in physical capital. Investment occurs at an annual rate of roughly ten per cent of the capital stock. Hence, it would take perhaps forty years – several generations – to accumulate capital equivalent in value to the capitalized value of the labor force.

If automated data-processing and decision-making devices just reached the break-even point where they were competitive with non-mechanized human data processing and decision making, it would still take several generations to bring about enough investment in the new automated systems to double the per capita productivity of the economy. Moreover, a 25 per cent increase in the technological efficiency of the *human* data processors and decision makers would produce as large an increase in productivity as this total investment in automated procedures.

I don't want to put more weight on these sorts of 'iffy' estimates than they will bear. Consideration of the quantities involved may have a useful sobering influence, however, on our prophecies of Utopia or of doom.

The composition of the labor force. We shall assume, then, that automation may affect the complexion of the labor force, but will not affect the employment level – except that general high incomes may lead to an increase in voluntary leisure. The division of labor between man and automatic devices will be determined by the doctrine of comparative advantage: those tasks in which machines have *relatively* the greatest advantage in productivity over men will be automated; those tasks in which machines have relatively the least advantage will remain manual.

I have done some armchair analysis of what this proposition means for predictions of the occupational profile twenty years hence. I do not have time to report this analysis in detail here, but I can summarize my conclusions briefly. Technologically, as I have argued earlier, machines will be capable, within twenty years, of doing any work that a man can do. Economically, men will retain their greatest comparative advantage in jobs that require flexible manipulation of those parts of the environment that are relatively rough – some forms of manual work, control of some kinds of machinery (e.g., operating earth-moving equipment), some kinds of nonprogrammed problem solving, and some kinds of service activities where face-to-face human interaction is of the essence. Man will be somewhat less involved in performing the day-to-day work of the organization, and somewhat more involved in maintaining the system that performs the work.[4]

4. What little evidence we have on recent factory automation suggests that

The routinization of work. We do not need to debate whether work was more creative and more enjoyable before the Industrial Revolution or after. A more fruitful question is whether the kinds of automation that are going on now in factories and in offices tend to increase or decrease work satisfactions, tend to enrich or impoverish the lives of the people who are employed there.

There are now in print some half-dozen studies that cast some light on the question.[5] The conclusion I have reached upon examining these is that there is no uniform tendency of mechanization or automation to make factory and office work either more routine or less routine. The introduction of the assembly line was generally an influence in the direction of routinization. But as the level of factory automation has risen – especially the automation of repetitive manipulative tasks – automation has probably tended to make work less, rather than more, routine, and has loosened the linkage between the pace of the man and the pace of the machine.

How do these generalizations, based largely on observations of factory automation, apply to the automation of data-processing tasks? I have already essayed an answer in the previous section: Men will retain their greatest comparative advantage in jobs that require flexible manipulation of those parts of the environment that are relatively rough. Applied to the present issue, this means, I think, that automation will result in somewhat less routine or at least less repetitiveness in the work of the inhabitants of clerical offices and executive suites.

Implicit in virtually all discussions of routine is the assumption that any increase in the routinization of work decreases work satisfaction and impairs the growth and self-realization of the worker. Not only is this assumption unbuttressed by empirical evidence, but casual observation of the world about us suggests that it is false. I mentioned earlier Gresham's Law of Planning –

---

it does not greatly change the distribution of skill levels. My own estimate is that the same will prove true of the automation of clerical and managerial work. This is so basically because humans will retain their comparative advantage in tasks that match their skills and abilities. Man will be, as always, the measure of what man can do relatively well. See H. A. Simon (1960) and H. A. Simon (1957), chapter 12, 'Productivity and Urban Rural Population Balance.'

5. Two good references are James R. Bright (1958) and S. Lilley (1957).

that routine drives out nonprogrammed activity. A completely unstructured situation, to which one can apply only the most general problem-solving skills, without specific rules or direction, is, if prolonged, painful for most people. Routine is a welcome refuge from the trackless forests of unfamiliar problem spaces (March and Simon, 1958, p.185).

The work on curiosity of Berlyne (1954) and others suggests that some kind of principle of moderation applies. People (and rats) find the most interest in situations that are neither completely strange nor entirely known – where there is novelty to be explored, but where similarities and programs remembered from past experience help guide the exploration. Nor does creativity flourish in completely unstructured situations. The almost unanimous testimony of creative artists and scientists is that the first task is to impose limits on the situation if the limits are not already given. The pleasure that the good professional experiences in his work is not simply a pleasure in handling difficult matters; it is a pleasure in using skillfully a well-stocked kit of well-designed tools to handle problems that are comprehensible in their deep structure but unfamiliar in their detail.

We must be cautious, then, in inferring, because managerial work will be more highly programmed in the future than it has been in the past – as it almost certainly will – that it will thereby be less satisfying or less creative.

Some fundamentals of organizational design

An organization can be pictured as a three-layered cake. In the bottom layer, we have the basic work processes – in the case of a manufacturing organization, the processes that procure raw materials, manufacture the physical product, warehouse it and ship it. In the middle layer, we have the programmed decision-making processes, the processes that govern the day-to-day operation of the manufacturing and distribution system. In the top layer, we have the nonprogrammed decision-making processes, the processes that are required to design and redesign the entire system, to provide it with its basic goals and objectives, and to monitor its performance.

Automation of data processing and decision making will not change this fundamental three-part structure. It may, by bringing about a more explicit description of the entire system, make the relations among the parts clear and more explicit.

The hierarchical structure of organizations.[6] Large organizations are almost universally hierarchical in structure. That is to say, they are divided into units which are subdivided into smaller units, which are, in turn, subdivided, and so on. They are also generally hierarchical in imposing on this system of successive partitionings a pyramidal authority structure. However, for the moment, I should like to consider the departmentalization rather than the authority structure.

Hierarchical subdivision is not a characteristic that is peculiar to human organizations. It is common to virtually all complex systems of which we have knowledge.

Complex biological organisms are made up of subsystems – digestive, circulatory and so on. These subsystems are composed of organs, organs of tissues, tissues of cells. The cell is, in turn, a hierarchically organized unit, with nucleus, cell wall, cytoplasm and other subparts.

The complex systems of chemistry and physics reveal the same picture of wheels within wheels within wheels. A protein molecule – one of the organismic building blocks – is constructed out of simpler structures, the amino acids. The simplest molecules are composed of atoms, the atoms of so-called elementary particles. Even in cosmological structures, we find the same hierarchical pattern: galaxies, planetary systems, stars and planets.

The near universality of hierarchy in the composition of complex systems suggests that there is something fundamental in this structural principle that goes beyond the peculiarities of human organization. I can suggest at least two reasons why complex systems should generally be hierarchical:

1. *Among possible systems of a given size and complexity, hierarchical systems, composed of subsystems, are the most likely to appear through evolutionary processes.* A metaphor will show why this is so. Suppose we have two watchmakers, each of whom is assembling watches of ten thousand parts. The watchmakers are

6. The speculations of the following paragraphs are products of my joint work over recent years with Allen Newell.

interrupted, from time to time by the telephone, and have to put down their work. Now watchmaker A finds that whenever he lays down a partially completed watch. it falls apart again, and when he returns to it, he has to start reassembling it from the beginning. Watchmaker B, however, has designed his watches in such a way that each watch is composed of ten subassemblies of one thousand parts each, the subassemblies being themselves stable components. The major subassemblies are composed, in turn, of ten stable subassemblies of one hundred parts each, and so on. Clearly, if interruptions are at all frequent, watchmaker B will assemble a great many watches before watchmaker A is able to complete a single one.

2. *Among systems of a given size and complexity, hierarchical systems require much less information transmission among their parts than do other types of systems.* As was pointed out many years ago, as the number of members of an organization grows, the number of *pairs* of members grows with the square (and the number of possible subsets of members even more rapidly). If each member, in order to act effectively, has to know in detail what each other member is doing, the total amount of information that has to be transmitted in the organization will grow at least proportionately with the square of its size. If the organization is subdivided into units, it may be possible to arrange matters so that an individual needs detailed information only about the behavior of individuals in his own unit, and aggregative summary information about average behavior in other units. If this is so, and if the organization continues to subdivide into suborganizations by cell division as it grows in size, keeping the size of the lowest level subdivisions constant, the total amount of information that has to be transmitted will grow only slightly more than proportionately with size.

These two statements are, of course, only the grossest sorts of generalization. They would have to be modified in detail before they could be applied to specific organizational situations. They do provide, however, strong reasons for believing that almost any system of sufficient complexity would have to have the rooms-within-rooms structure that we observe in actual human organizations. The reasons for hierarchy go far beyond the need for unity of command or other considerations relating to authority.

The conclusion I draw from this analysis is that the automation of decision making, irrespective of how far it goes and in what directions it proceeds, is unlikely to obliterate the basically hierarchical structure of organizations. The decision-making process will still call for departmentalization and sub-departmentalization of responsibilities. There is some support for this prediction in the last decade's experience with computer programming. Whenever highly complex programs have been written – whether for scientific computing, business data processing or heuristic problem solving – they have always turned out to have a clear-cut hierarchical structure. The over-all program is always subdivided into subprograms. In programs of any great complexity, the subprograms are further subdivided, and so on. Moreover, in some general sense, the higher-level programs control or govern the behavior of the lower-level programs, so that we find among these programs relations of authority among routines that are not dissimilar to those we are familiar with in human organizations.[7]

Since organizations are systems of behavior designed to enable humans and their machines to accomplish goals, organizational form must be a joint function of human characteristics and the nature of the task environment. It must reflect the capabilities and limitations of the people and tools that are to carry out the tasks. It must reflect the resistance and ductility of the materials to which the people and tools apply themselves. What I have been asserting, then, in the preceding paragraphs is that one of the near universal aspects of organizational form, hierarchy, reflects no very specific properties of man, but a very general one. An organization will tend to assume hierarchical form whenever the task environment is complex relative to the problem-solving and communicating powers of the organization members and their tools. Hierarchy is the adaptive form for finite intelligence to assume in the face of complexity.

The organizations of the future, then, will be hierarchies, no matter what the exact division of labor between men and computers. This is not to say that there will be no important differences between present and future organizations. Two points, in particular, will have to be re-examined at each stage of automation:

7. The exercise of authority by computer programs over others is not usually accompanied by affect. Routines do not resent or resist accepting orders from other routines.

1. What are the optimal sizes of the building blocks in the hierarchy? Will they become larger or smaller? This is the question of centralization and decentralization.

2. What will be the relations among the building blocks? In particular, how far will traditional authority and accountability relations persist, and how far will they be modified? What will be the effect of automation upon subgoal formation and subgoal identification?

Size of the building blocks: centralization and decentralization.
One of the major contemporary issues in organization design is the question of how centralized or decentralized the decision-making process will be – how much of the decision making should be done by the executives of the larger units, and how much should be delegated to lower levels. But centralizing and decentralizing are not genuine alternatives for organizing. The question is not whether we shall decentralize, but how far we shall decentralize. What we seek, again, is a golden mean: we want to find the proper level in the organization hierarchy – neither too high nor too low – for each important class of decisions.

Over the past twenty or more years there has been a movement toward decentralization in large American business organizations. This movement has probably been a sound development, but it does *not* signify that more decentralization is at all times and under all circumstances a good thing. It signifies that at a particular time in history, many American firms, which had experienced almost continuous long-term growth and diversification, discovered that they could operate more effectively if they brought together all the activities relating to individual products or groups of similar products and decentralized a great deal of decision making to the departments handling these products or product groups. At the very time this process was taking place there were many crosscurrents of centralization in the same companies – centralization, for example, of industrial relations activities. There is no contradiction here. Different decisions need to be made in different organizational locations, and the best location for a class of decisions may change as circumstances change.

There are usually two pressures toward greater decentralization in a business organization. First, it may help bring the profit motive to bear on a larger group of executives by allowing profit goals to be established for individual subdivisions of the company. Second, it may simplify the decision-making process by separating out groups of related activities – production, engineering, marketing and finance for particular products – and allowing decisions to be taken on these matters within the relevant organizational subdivisions. Advantages can be realized in either of these ways only if the units to which decision is delegated are natural subdivisions – if, in fact, the actions taken in one of them do not affect in too much detail or too strongly what happens in the others. Hierarchy always implies intrinsically some measure of decentralization. It always involves a balancing of the cost savings through direct local action against the losses through ignoring indirect consequences for the whole organization.

Organizational form, I said earlier, must be a joint function of the characteristics of humans and their tools and the nature of the task environment. When one or the other of these changes significantly, we may expect concurrent modifications to be required in organizational structure – for example, in the amount of centralization or decentralization that is desirable.

When the cable and the wireless were added to the world's techniques of communication, the organization of every nation's foreign office changed. The ambassador and minister who had exercised broad, discretionary decision-making functions in the previous decentralized system, were now brought under much closer central control. The balance between the costs in time and money of communication with the center, and the advantages of coordination by the center had been radically altered.

The automation of important parts of business data-processing and decision-making activity, and the trend toward a much higher degree of structure and programming of even the nonautomated part will radically alter the balance of advantage between centralization and decentralization. The main issue is not the economics of scale – not the question of whether a given data-processing job can better be done by one large computer at a central location or a number of smaller ones, geographically or departmentally decentralized. Rather, the main issue is how we shall take advantage of the greater analytic capacity, the larger ability to take into account the interrelations of things, that the new developments in decision making give us. A second issue is how we shall deal with the technological fact that the processing of information within a coordinated computing system is orders of magnitude faster than the input-output rates at which we can communicate from one such system to another, particularly where human links are involved.

Let us consider the first issue: the capacity of the decision-making system to handle intricate interrelations in a complex system. In many factories today, the extent to which the schedules of one department are coordinated in detail with the schedules of a second department, consuming, say, part of the output of the first, is limited by the computational complexity of the scheduling problem. Often the best we can do is to set up a reasonable scheduling scheme for each department and put a sizeable buffer inventory of semi-finished product between them to prevent fluctuations in the operation of the first from interfering with the operation of the second. We accept the cost of holding the inventory to avoid the cost of taking account of detailed scheduling interactions.

We pay large inventory costs, also, to permit factory and sales managements to make decisions in semi-independence of each other. The factory often stocks finished products so that it can deliver on demand to sales warehouses; the warehouses stock the same product so that the factory will have time to manufacture a new batch after an order is placed. Often, too, manufacturing and sales departments make their decisions on the basis of independent forecasts of orders.

With the development of operations research techniques for determining optimal production rates and inventory levels, and with the development of the technical means to maintain and adjust the data that are required, large savings are attainable through inventory reductions and the smoothing of production operations, but at the cost of centralizing to a greater extent than in the past the factory scheduling and warehouse ordering decisions. Since the source of the savings is in the coordination of the decisions, centralization is unavoidable if the savings are to be secured.

The mismatch – unlikely to be removed in the near future – between the kinds of records that humans produce readily and read readily and the kinds that automatic devices produce and read readily is a second technological factor pushing in the direction of centralization. Since processing steps in an automated data-processing system are executed in a thousandth or even millionth of a second, the whole system must be organized on a flow basis with infrequent intervention from outside. Intervention will take more and more the form of designing the system itself – programming – and less and less the form of participating in its minute-by-minute operation. Moreover, the parts of the system must mesh. Hence, the design of decision-making and data-processing systems will tend to be a relatively centralized function. It will be a little like ship design. There is no use in one group of experts producing the design for the hull, another the design for the power plant, a third the plans for the passenger quarters, and so on, unless great pains are taken at each step to see that all these parts will fit into a seaworthy ship.

It may be objected that the question of motivation has been overlooked in this whole discussion. If decision making is centralized how can the middle-level executive be induced to work hard and effectively? First, we should observe that the principle of decentralized profit-and-loss accounting has never been carried much below the level of product-group departments and cannot, in fact, be applied successfully to fragmented segments of highly interdependent activities. Second, we may question whether the conditions under which middle-management has in the past exercised its decision-making prerogatives were actually good conditions from a motivational standpoint.

Most existing decentralized organization structures have at least three weaknesses in motivating middle-management executives effectively. First, they encourage the formation of and loyalty to subgoals that are only partly parallel with the goals of the organization. Second, they require so much nonprogrammed problem solving in a setting of confusion that they do not provide the satisfactions which, we argued earlier, are valued by the true professional. Third, they realize none of the advantages, which by hindsight we find we have often gained in factory automation, of substituting machine-paced (or better, system-paced) for man-paced operation of the system.[8]

8. The general decline in the use of piece-rates is associated with the gradual spread of machine-paced operations through the factory with the advance of automation. In evaluating the human consequences of this

The question of motivation we have just raised has a broader relevance than the issue of decentralization and I will discuss it later, in the section on authority and responsibility relations. Meanwhile, we can summarize the present discussion by saying that the new developments in decision making will tend to induce more centralization in decision-making activities at middle-management levels.

Authority and responsibility. Let me draw a sketch of the factory manager's job today. How far it is a caricature, and how far a reasonably accurate portrait, I shall let you decide. What is the factory manager's authority? He can hire and fire. He can determine what shall be produced in his factory and how much. He can make minor improvements in equipment and recommend major ones. In doing all of these things, he is subject to all kinds of constraints and evaluations imposed by the rest of the organization. Moreover, the connection between what he decides and what actually happens in the factory is often highly tenuous. He proposes, and a complex administrative system disposes.

For what is the factory manager held accountable? He must keep his costs within the standards of the budget. He must not run out of items that are ordered. If he does, he must produce them in great haste. He must keep his inventory down. His men must not have accidents. And so on.

Subject to this whole range of conflicting pressures, controlling a complex system whose responses to instruction is often erratic and unpredictable, the environment of the typical middle-management executive – of which the factory manager is just one example – is not the kind of environment a psychologist would design to produce high motivation. The manager responds in understandable ways. He transmits to his subordinates the pressures imposed by his superiors – he becomes a work pusher, seeking to motivate by creating for his subordinates the same environment of pressure and constraint that he experiences. He and his subordinates become

---

development, we should not accept uncritically the common stereotypes that were incorporated so effectively in Charlie Chaplin's *Modern Times*. Frederick Taylor's sophisticated understanding of the relations between incentives and pace, expressed, for example, in his story of the pig-iron handler, is worth pondering.

expediters, dealing with the pressure that is felt at the moment by getting out a particular order, fixing a particular disabled machine, following up a particular tardy supplier.

I do not want to elaborate the picture further. The important point is that the task of middle managers today is very much taken up with pace setting, with work pushing and with expediting. As the automation and rationalization of the decision-making process progress, these aspects of the managerial job are likely to recede in importance.

If a couple of terms are desired to characterize the direction of change we may expect in the manager's job, I would propose rationalization and impersonalization. In terms of subjective feel the manager will find himself dealing more than in the past with a well-structured system whose problems have to be diagnosed and corrected objectively and analytically, and less with unpredictable and sometimes recalcitrant people who have to be persuaded, prodded, rewarded, and cajoled. For some managers, important satisfactions derived in the past from interpersonal relations with others will be lost. For other managers, important satisfactions from a feeling of the adequacy of professional skills will be gained.

My guess, and it is only a guess, is that the gains in satisfaction from the change will overbalance the losses. I have two reasons for making this guess: first, because this seems to be the general experience in factory automation as it affects supervisors and managers; second, because the kinds of interpersonal relations called for in the new environment seem to me generally less frustrating and more wholesome than many of those we encounter in present-day supervisory relations. Man does not generally work well with his fellow man in relations saturated with authority and dependence, with control and subordination, even though these have been the predominant human relations in the past. He works much better when he is teamed with his fellow man in coping with an objective, understandable, external environment. That will be more and more his situation as the new techniques of decision making come into wide use.

A final sketch of the new organization

Perhaps in the preceding paragraphs I have yielded to the temptation to paint a Utopian picture of the organization that the new decision-making techniques will create. If so, I have done so from an urge to calm the anxieties that are so often and so unnecessarily aroused by the stereotype of the robot. These anxieties are unnecessary because the existence in the world today of machines that think, and of theories that explain the processes of human thinking, subtracts not an inch, not a hair, from the stature of man. Man is always vulnerable when he rests his case for his worth and dignity on how he differs from the rest of the world, or on the special place he has in God's scheme or nature's. Man must rest his case on what he is. This is in no way changed when electronic systems can duplicate some of his functions or when some of the mystery of his processes of thought is taken away.

The changes I am predicting for the decision-making processes in organizations do not mean that workers and executives will find the organizations they will work in strange and unfamiliar. In concluding, I should like to emphasize the aspects in which the new organizations will much resemble those we know now.

1. Organizations will still be constructed in three layers; an underlying system of physical production and distribution processes, a layer of programmed (and probably largely automated) decision processes for governing the routine day-to-day operation of the physical system and a layer of nonprogrammed decision processes (carried out in a man-machine system) for monitoring the first-level processes, redesigning them and changing parameter values.

2. Organizations will still be hierarchical in form. The organization will be divided into major subparts, each of these into parts, and so on, in familiar forms of departmentalization. The exact bases for drawing departmental lines may change somewhat. Product divisions may become even more important than they are today, while the sharp lines of demarcation among purchasing, manufacturing, engineering and sales are likely to fade.

But there is a more fundamental way in which the organizations of the future will appear to those in them very much like the organizations of today. Man is a problem-solving, skill-using, social animal. Once he has satisfied his hunger, two main kinds of experiences are significant to him. One of his deepest needs is to apply his skills, whatever they be, to challenging tasks – to feel the exhilaration of the well-struck ball or the well-solved problem. The other need is to find meaningful and warm relations with a few other human beings – to love and be loved, to share experience, to respect and be respected, to work in common tasks.

Particular characteristics of the physical environment and the task environment are significant to man only as they affect these needs. The scientist satisfies them in one environment, the artist in another; but they are the same needs. A good business novel or business biography is not about business. It is about love, hate, pride, craftsmanship, jealousy, comradeship, ambition, pleasure. These have been, and will continue to be man's central concerns.

The automation and rationalization of decision making will, to be sure, alter the climate of organizations in ways important to these human concerns. I have indicated what some of the changes may be. On balance, they seem to me changes that will make it easier rather than harder for the executive's daily work to be a significant and satisfying part of his life.

References

BERLYNE, D. E. (1954), 'A theory of human curiosity', *British Journal of Psychology*, vol. 45, pp. 180–91.

BRIGHT, J. R. (1958), *Automation and Management*, Graduate School of Business Administration, Harvard University.

CYERT, R. M., SIMON, H. A., and TROW, D. B. (1956), 'Observation of a business decision', *Journal of Business*, vol. 29, pp. 237–48.

DEWEY, J. (1910), *How We Think*, Heath, chapter 8.

GREGORY, R. H., and VAN HORN, R. L. (1960), *Automatic Data-Processing Systems*, Wadsworth.

LEAVITT, H. J., and WHISLER, T. L. (1958), 'Management in the 1980s', *Harvard Business Review*, vol. 36, no. 6, November–December, pp. 41–8.

LILLEY, S. (1957), *Automation and Social Progress*, International Publishers.

MARCH, J. G., and SIMON, H. A. (1958), *Organizations*, Wiley.

SIMON, H. A. (1957), *Models of Man*, Wiley.

SIMON, H. A. (1960), 'The corporation: will it be managed by machines?', in M. Anshen and G. L. Bach (eds.), *Management and Corporations, 1985*, McGraw-Hill, pp. 17–55.

Part Three Behaviour in Organizations

Organizations are systems of interdependent human beings. From some points of view the members of an organization may be considered as a resource, but they are a special kind of resource in that they are directly involved in all the functioning processes of the organization, and they can affect its aims not merely the methods used to accomplish them. The contributors to this section are concerned to analyse the behaviour of people as they affect, and are affected by, organizational processes.

Elton Mayo (Reading 12) was the inspirer of the famous Hawthorne studies, and the 'founding father' of the Human Relations movement – the first major impact of social science on management thinking. He emphasized that workers must first be understood as people if they are to be understood as organization members. From his work have flowed a large number of studies which demonstrate the social processes which inevitably surround the formal management system; the informal organization which is part of every organization's infra-structure. Lewin was the inspiration of much research on group dynamics, attitude change and leadership styles. The reading included (Reading 13), written with his colleagues Lippitt and White, was the progenitor of almost all subsequent studies of leadership regarded as a social process rather than a personality trait. Although perhaps generally less well known than Mayo, Lewin had, if anything, an even greater impact within social science since he provided an approach to the explanation of social behaviour through his 'field theory' which many researchers have found exceedingly seminal.

Argyris (Reading 14) has conducted a series of studies devoted to presenting a model of organizational behaviour which is concerned to analyse and thus to limit the inevitable conflict between the needs of the individual and the needs of the organization of which he is a part. Likert (Reading 15) is at the head of a large group of social researchers who have been conducting field studies which suggest that the effective manager is one who can create a situation in which each member of his group feels that his relationships with others are 'supportive', that is that they satisfy *his* needs as well as those of others. The work of Likert and his colleagues is often referred to as 'neo-human relations'. It is more sophisticated and less sentimental than the original human relations work, but in terms of influence and achievement Likert may be regarded as the modern inheritor of Elton Mayo's mantle. McGregor (Reading 16) has had the most impact in presenting this approach to managers. His formulation of 'Theory X and Theory Y' has applied the neo-human relations approach throughout the whole organization and has been the vehicle of much work on 'organizational development' particularly when allied to such training methods as 'T-groups'.

Herzberg (Reading 17) challenges existing views on motivation, maintaining that as well as economic needs, human beings have psychological needs for autonomy, responsibility and development which have to be satisfied in work. He advocates the 'enrichment' of jobs through additional responsibility and authority in order to promote improved performance and increased mental health. Trist and his colleagues at the Tavistock Institute (Reading 18) have consistently developed a systems approach to organizations, in which the task requirements and individuals' needs are interrelated as an interdependent 'socio-technical system'. The present reading, with his colleague Bamforth, was an early and influential demonstration of this approach through the analysis of the behavioural disturbances caused by a major change in methods of coal mining.

12 E. Mayo

Hawthorne and the Western Electric Company

From E. Mayo, 'Hawthorne and the Western Electric Company', *The Social Problems of an Industrial Civilization*, Routledge, 1949, chapter 4, pp. 60–76.

A highly competent group of Western Electric engineers refused to accept defeat when experiments to demonstrate the effect of illumination on work seemed to lead nowhere. The conditions of scientific experiment had apparently been fulfilled – experimental room, control room; changes introduced one at a time; all other conditions held steady. And the results were perplexing: Roethlisberger gives two instances – lighting improved in the experimental room, production went up; but it rose also in the control room. The opposite of this: lighting diminished from 10 to 3 foot-candles in the experimental room and production again went up; simultaneously in the control room, with illumination constant, production also rose. [Roethlisberger, n.d.] Many other experiments, and all inconclusive; yet it had seemed so easy to determine the effect of illumination on work.

In matters of mechanics or chemistry the modern engineer knows how to set about the improvement of process or the redress of error. But the determination of optimum working conditions for the human being is left largely to dogma and tradition, guess, or quasi-philosophical argument. In modern large-scale industry the three persistent problems of management are:

1. The application of science and technical skill to some material good or product.
2. The systematic ordering of operations.
3. The organization of teamwork – that is, of sustained cooperation.

The last must take account of the need for continual reorganization of teamwork as operating conditions are changed in an *adaptive* society.

The first of these holds enormous prestige and interest and is the subject of continuous experiment. The second is well developed in practice. The third, by comparison with the other two, is almost wholly neglected. Yet it remains true that if these three are out of balance, the organization as a whole will not be successful. The first two operate to make an industry *effective*, in Chester Barnard's phrase, the third, to make it *efficient*. For the larger and more complex the institution, the more dependent is it upon the whole-hearted cooperation of every member of the group.

This was not altogether the attitude of Mr G. A. Pennock and his colleagues when they set up the experimental 'test room'. But the illumination fiasco had made them alert to the need that very careful records should be kept of everything that happened in the room in addition to the obvious engineering and industrial devices.[1] Their observations therefore included not only records of industrial and engineering changes but also records of physiological or medical changes, and, in a sense, of social and anthropological. This last took the form of a 'log' that gave as full an account as possible of the actual events of every day, a record that proved most useful to Whitehead when he was re-measuring the recording tapes and re-calculating the changes in productive output. He was able to relate eccentricities of the output curve to the actual situation at a given time – that is to say, to the events of a specific day or week.

First phase – the test room

The facts are by now well known. Briefly restated, the test room began its inquiry by first attempting to secure the active collaboration of the workers. This took some time but was gradually successful, especially after the retirement of the original first and second workers and after the new worker at the second bench had assumed informal leadership of the group. From this point on, the evidence presented by Whitehead or Roethlisberger and Dickson seems to show that the individual workers became a team, whole-heartedly committed to the project. Second, the conditions of work were changed one at a time: rest periods of different numbers and length, shorter working day, shorter working week, food with soup or coffee in the morning break. And the results seemed

1. For a full account of the experimental setup, see Roethlisberger and Dickson (1939), and T. North Whitehead, *The Industrial Worker*, vol. I.

satisfactory: slowly at first, but later with increasing certainty, the output record (used as an index of well-being) mounted. Simultaneously the girls claimed that they felt less fatigued, felt that they were not making any special effort. Whether these claims were accurate or no, they at least indicated increased contentment with the general situation in the test room by comparison with the department outside. At every point in the programme, the workers had been consulted with respect to proposed changes; they had arrived at the point of free expression of ideas and feelings to management. And it had been arranged thus that the twelfth experimental change should be a return to the original conditions of work – no rest periods, no mid-morning lunch, no shortened day or week. It had also been arranged that, after twelve weeks of this, the group should return to the conditions of Period 7, a fifteen-minute mid-morning break with lunch and a ten-minute mid-afternoon rest. The story is now well known: in Period 12 the daily and weekly output rose to a point higher than at any other time (the hourly rate adjusted itself downward by a small fraction), and in the whole twelve weeks 'there was no downward trend'. In the following period, the return to the conditions of work as in the seventh experimental change, the output curve soared to even greater heights: this thirteenth period lasted for thirty-one weeks.

These periods, 12 and 13, made it evident that increments of production could not be related point for point to the experimental changes introduced. Some major change was taking place that was chiefly responsible for the index of improved conditions – the steadily increasing output. Period 12 – but for minor qualifications, such as 'personal time out' – ignored the nominal return to original conditions of work and the output curve continued its upward passage. Put in other words, there was no actual return to original conditions. This served to bring another fact to the attention of the observers. Periods 7, 10 and 13 had nominally the same working conditions, as above described – fifteen-minute rest and lunch in mid-morning, ten-minute rest in the afternoon. But the average weekly output for each girl was:

Period 7 – 2500 units
Period 10 – 2800 units
Period 13 – 3000 units

Periods 3 and 12 resembled each other also in that both required a full day's work without rest periods. But here also the difference of average weekly output for each girl was:

Period 3 – less than 2500 units
Period 12 – more than 2900 units

Here then was a situation comparable perhaps with the illumination experiment, certainly suggestive of the Philadelphia experience where improved conditions for one team of mule spinners were reflected in improved morale not only in the experimental team but in the two other teams who had received no such benefit.

This interesting, and indeed amusing, result has been so often discussed that I need make no mystery of it now. I have often heard my colleague Roethlisberger declare that the major experimental change was introduced when those in charge sought to hold the situation humanly steady (in the interest of critical changes to be introduced) by getting the cooperation of the workers. What actually happened was that six individuals became a team and the team gave itself wholeheartedly and spontaneously to cooperation in the experiment. The consequence was that they felt themselves to be participating freely and without afterthought, and were happy in the knowledge that they were working without coercion from above or limitation from below. They were themselves astonished at the consequence, for they felt that they were working under less pressure than ever before: and in this, their feelings and performance echoed that of the mule spinners.

Here then are two topics which deserve the closest attention of all those engaged in administrative work – the organization of working teams and the free participation of such teams in the task and purpose of the organization as it directly affects them in their daily round.

Second phase – the interview programme

But such conclusions were not possible at the time: the major change, the question as to the exact difference between conditions of work in the test room and in the plant departments, remained something of a mystery. Officers of the company determined to 'take another look' at departments outside the test room – this, with the idea that something quite important was there to be observed, something to which the experiment should have made them alert. So the interview programme was introduced.

It was speedily discovered that the question-and-answer type of interview was useless in the situation. Workers wished to talk, and to talk freely under the seal of professional confidence (which was never abused) to someone who seemed representative of the company or who seemed, by his very attitude, to carry authority. The experience itself was unusual; there are few people in this world who have had the experience of finding someone intelligent, attentive and eager to listen without interruption to all that he or she has to say. But to arrive at this point it became necessary to train interviewers how to listen, how to avoid interruption or the giving of advice, how generally to avoid anything that might put an end to free expression in an individual instance. Some approximate rules to guide the interviewer in his work were therefore set down. These were, more or less, as follows:[2]

1. Give your whole attention to the person interviewed, and make it evident that you are doing so.

2. Listen – don't talk.

3. Never argue; never give advice.

4. Listen to:
(a) What he wants to say.
(b) What he does not want to say.
(c) What he cannot say without help.

5. As you listen, plot out tentatively and for subsequent correction the pattern (personal) that is being set before you. To test this, from time to time summarize what has been said and present for comment (e.g., 'Is this what you are telling me?'). Always do this with the greatest caution, that is, clarify but do not add or distort.

6. Remember that everything said must be considered a personal confidence and not divulged to anyone. (This does not prevent discussion of a situation between professional colleagues. Nor does it prevent some form of public report when due precaution has been taken.)

2. For a full discussion of this type of interview, see Roethlisberger and Dickson (1939), chapter XIII. For a more summary and perhaps less technical discussion, see Homans (1941).

It must not be thought that this type of interviewing is easily learned. It is true that some persons, men and women alike, have a natural flair for the work, but, even with them, there tends to be an early period of discouragement, a feeling of futility, through which the experience and coaching of a senior interviewer must carry them. The important rules in the interview (important, that is, for the development of high skill) are two. First, Rule 4 that indicates the need to help the individual interviewed to articulate expression of an idea or attitude that he has not before expressed; and, second, Rule 5 which indicates the need from time to time to summarize what has been said and to present it for comment. Once equipped to do this effectively, interviewers develop very considerable skill. But, let me say again, this skill is not easily acquired. It demands of the interviewer a real capacity to follow the contours of another person's thinking, to understand the meaning for him of what he says.

I do not believe that any member of the research group or its associates had anticipated the immediate response that would be forthcoming to the introduction of such an interview programme. Such comments as 'This is the best thing the Company has ever done', or 'The Company should have done this long ago', were frequently heard. It was as if workers had been awaiting an opportunity for expressing freely and without afterthought their feelings on a great variety of modern situations, not by any means limited to the various departments of the plant. To find an intelligent person who was not only eager to listen but also anxious to help to expression ideas and feelings but dimly understood – this, for many thousand persons, was an experience without precedent in the modern world.

In a former statement (Mayo, 1933, p. 114) I named two questions that inevitably presented themselves to the interviewing group in these early stages of the study:

1. Is some experience which might be described as an experience of personal futility a common incident of industrial organization for work?

2. Does life in a modern industrial city, in some unrealized way, predispose workers to obsessive response?

And I said that these two questions 'in some form' continued to preoccupy those in charge of the research until the conclusion of the study.

After twelve years of further study (not yet concluded), there are certain developments that demand attention. For example, I had not fully realized in 1932, when the above was written, how profoundly the social structure of civilization has been shaken by scientific, engineering and industrial development. This radical change – the passage from an *established* to an *adaptive* social order – has brought into being a host of new and unanticipated problems for management and for the individual worker. The management problem appears at its acutest in the work of the supervisor. No longer does the supervisor work with a team of persons that he has known for many years or perhaps a lifetime; he is a leader of a group of individuals that forms and disappears almost as he watches it. Now it is difficult, if not impossible, to relate oneself to a working group one by one; it is relatively easy to do so if they are already a fully constituted team. A communication from the supervisor, for example, in the latter instance has to be made to one person only with the appropriate instructions; the individual will pass it on and work it out with the team. In the former instance, it has to be repeated to every individual and may often be misunderstood.

But for the individual worker the problem is really much more serious. He has suffered a profound loss of security and certainty in his actual living and in the background of his thinking. For all of us the feeling of security and certainty derives always from assured membership of a group. If this is lost, no monetary gain, no job guarantee, can be sufficient compensation. Where groups change ceaselessly as jobs and mechanical processes change, the individual inevitably experiences a sense of void, of emptiness, where his fathers knew the joy of comradeship and security. And in such situation, his anxieties – many, no doubt, irrational or ill-founded – increase and he becomes more difficult both to fellow workers and to supervisor. The extreme of this is perhaps rarely encountered as yet, but increasingly we move in this direction as the tempo of industrial change is speeded by scientific and technical discovery.

In the first chapter of this book I have claimed that scientific method has a dual approach – represented in medicine by the clinic and the laboratory. In the clinic one studies the whole situation with two ends in view: first, to develop intimate knowledge of and skill in handling the facts, and, second, on the basis of such a skill to separate those aspects of the situation, that skill has shown to be closely related, for detailed laboratory study. When a study based upon laboratory method fails, or partially fails, because some essential factor has been unknowingly and arbitrarily excluded, the investigator, if he is wise, returns to clinical study of the entire situation to get some hint as to the nature of the excluded determinant. The members of the research division at Hawthorne, after the twelfth experimental period in the test room, were faced by just such a situation and knew it. The so-called interview programme represented for them a return from the laboratory to clinical study. And, as in all clinical study, there was no immediate and welcome revelation of a single discarded determinant: there was rather a slow progress from one observation to another, all of them important – but only gradually building up into a single complex finding. This slow development has been elsewhere described, in *Management and the Worker*; one can however attempt a succinct résumé of the various observations, more or less as they occurred.

Officers of the company had prepared a short statement, a few sentences, to be repeated to the individual interviewed before the conversation began. This statement was designed to assure the worker that nothing he said would be repeated to his supervisors or to any company official outside the interviewing group. In many instances, the worker waved this aside and began to talk freely and at once. What doubts there were seemed to be resident in the interviewers rather than in those interviewed. Many workers, I cannot say the majority for we have no statistics, seemed to have something 'on their minds', in ordinary phrase, about which they wished to talk freely to a competent listener. And these topics were by no means confined to matters affecting the company. This was, I think, the first observation that emerged from the mass of interviews reported daily. The research group began to talk about the need for *emotional release* and the great advantage that accrued to the individual when he had 'talked off' his problem. The topics varied greatly. One worker two years before had been sharply reprimanded by his supervisor for not working as usual: in interview he wished to explain that on the night preceding the day of the incident his wife and child had both died, apparently unexpectedly. At the time he was unable to explain; afterwards he had no opportunity to do so. He told the story dramatically and in great detail; there was no doubt whatever that telling it thus benefited him greatly. But this story naturally was exceptional; more often a worker would speak of his family and domestic situation, of his church, of his relations with other members of the working group – quite usually the topic of which he spoke presented itself to him as a problem difficult for him to resolve. This led to the next successive illumination for the inquiry. It became manifest that, whatever the problem, it was partly, and sometimes wholly, determined by the attitude of the individual worker. And this defect or distortion of attitude was consequent on his past experience or his present situation, or, more usually, on both at once. One woman worker, for example, discovered for herself during an interview that her dislike of a certain supervisor was based upon a fancied resemblance to a detested stepfather. Small wonder that the same supervisor had warned the interviewer that she was 'difficult to handle'. But the discovery by the worker that her dislike was wholly irrational eased the situation considerably (Roethlisberger and Dickson, 1939, pp. 307–10). This type of case led the interviewing group to study carefully each worker's *personal situation* and attitude. These two phrases 'emotional release' and 'personal situation' became convenient titles for the first phases of observation and seemed to resume for the interviewers the effective work that they were doing. It was at this point that a change began to show itself in the study and in the conception of the study.

The original interviewers, in these days, after sixteen years of industrial experience, are emphatic on the point that the first cases singled out for report were special cases – individuals – and not representative either of the working group or of the interviews generally. It is estimated that such cases did not number more than an approximate 2 per cent. of the twenty thousand persons originally interviewed. Probably this error of emphasis was inevitable and for two reasons: first, the dramatic changes that occur in such instances seemed good evidence of the efficacy of the method, and, second, this type of interviewing had to be insisted upon as *necessary to the training of a skilled interviewer*. This last still holds good; a skilled interviewer must have passed through the stage of careful and observant listening to what an individual says and to all that he says. This stage of an interviewing programme closely resembles the therapeutic method and its triumphs are apt to be therapeutic. And I do not believe that the study would have been equipped to advance further if it had failed to observe the great benefit of emotional release and the extent to which every individual's problems are conditioned by his personal history and situation. Indeed, even when one has advanced beyond the merely psychotherapeutic study of individuals to study of industrial groups, one has to beware of distortions similar in kind to those named; one has to know how to deal with such problems. The first phase of the interview programme cannot therefore be discarded; it still retains its original importance. But industrial studies must nevertheless move beyond the individual in need of therapy. And this is the more true when the change from established routines to adaptive changes of routine seems generally to carry a consequence of loss of security for many persons.

A change of attitude in the research group came gradually. The close study of individuals continued, but in combination with an equally close study of groups. An early incident did much to set the new pattern for inquiry. One of the earliest questions proposed before the original test-room experiment began was a question as to the fatigue involved in this or that type of work. Later a foreman of high reputation, no doubt with this in mind, came to the research group, now for the most part engaged in interviewing, and asserted that the girls in his department worked hard all day at their machines and must be considerably fatigued by the evening; he wanted an inquiry. Now the interviewers had discovered that this working group claimed a habit of doing most of their work in the morning period and 'taking things easy' during the afternoon. The foreman obviously realized nothing of this, and it was therefore fortunate that the two possibilities could be directly tested. The officer in charge of the research made a quiet arrangement with the engineers to measure during a period the amount of electric current used by the group to operate its machines; this quantity indicated the overall amount of work being done. The results of this test wholly supported the statements made by the girls in interview; far more current was used in the morning period than during the afternoon.

And the attention of the research group was, by this and other incidents, thus redirected to a fact already known to them, namely, that the working group as a whole actually determined the output of individual workers by reference to a standard, pre-determined but never clearly stated, that represented the group conception of a fair day's work. This standard was rarely, if ever, in accord with the standards of the efficiency engineers.

The final experiment, reported under the title of the Bank Wiring Observation Room, was set up to extend and confirm these observations (Roethlisberger and Dickson, 1939, Part 4, pp. 379 ff.). Simultaneously it was realized that these facts did not in any way imply low working morale as suggested by such phrases as 'restriction of output'. On the contrary, the failure of free communication between management and workers in modern large-scale industry leads inevitably to the exercise of caution by the working group until such time as it knows clearly the range and meaning of changes imposed from above. The enthusiasm of the efficiency engineer for the organization of operations is excellent; his attempt to resume problems of cooperation under this heading is not. At the moment, he attempts to solve the many human difficulties involved in whole-hearted cooperation by organizing the organization of organization without any reference whatever to workers themselves. This procedure inevitably blocks communication and defeats his own admirable purpose.[3]

This observation, important as it is, was not however the leading point for the interviewers. The existence and influence of the group – those in active daily relationship with one another – became the important fact. The industrial interviewer must learn to distinguish and specify, as he listens to what a worker says, references to 'personal' or group situations. More often than not, the special case, the individual who talks himself out of a gross distortion, is a solitary – one who has not 'made the team'. The usual interview, on the other hand, though not by any means free from distortion, is speaking as much for the working group as for the person. The influence of the communication in the interview, therefore, is not limited to the individual but extends to the group.

Two girl workers in a large industry were recently offered

3. For further evidence on this point, see Mathewson (1969) and also Mayo (1933), pp. 119–21.

'upgrading'; to accept would mean leaving their group and taking a job in another department: they refused. Then representatives of the union put some pressure on them, claiming that, if they continued to refuse, the union organizers 'might just as well give up' their efforts. With reluctance the girls reversed their decision and accepted the upgrading. Both girls at once needed the attention of an interviewer: they had liked the former group in which they had earned informal membership. Both felt adjustment to a new group and a novel situation as involving effort and private discontent. From both much was learned of the intimate organization and common practices of their groups, and their adjustments to their new groups were eased, thereby effectively helping to reconstitute the teamwork in those groups.

In another recent interview a girl of eighteen protested to an interviewer that her mother was continually urging her to ask Mr X, her supervisor, for a 'raise'. She had refused, but her loyalty to her mother and the pressure the latter exerted were affecting her work and her relations at work. She talked her situation out with an interviewer, and it became clear to her a 'raise' would mean departure from her daily companions and associates. Although not immediately relevant, it is interesting to note that, after explaining the situation at length to the interviewer, she was able to present her case dispassionately to her mother – without exaggeration or protest. The mother immediately understood and abandoned pressure for advancement, and the girl returned to effective work. This last instance illustrates one way in which the interview clears lines of communication of emotional blockage – within as without the plant. But this is not my immediate topic; my point is rather that the age-old human desire for persistence of human association will seriously complicate the development of an adaptive society if we cannot devise systematic methods of easing individuals from one group of associates into another.

But such an observation was not possible in the earliest inquiry. The important fact brought to the attention of the research division was that the ordinary conception of management-worker relation as existing between company officials, on the one hand, and an unspecified number of individuals, on the other, is utterly mistaken. Management, in any continuously successful plant, is not related to single workers, but always to working groups. In every department that continues to operate, the workers have – whether aware of it or not – formed themselves into a group with appropriate customs, duties, routines, even rituals; and management succeeds (or fails) in proportion as it is accepted without reservation by the group as authority and leader. This, for example, occurred in the relay-assembly test room at Hawthorne. Management, by consultation with the girl workers, by clear explanation of the proposed experiments and the reasons for them, by accepting the workers' verdict in special instances, unwittingly scored a success in two most important human matters – the girls became a self-governing team, and a team that cooperated whole-heartedly with management. The test room was responsible for many important findings – rest periods, hours of work, food, and the like: but the most important finding of all was unquestionably in the general area of teamwork and cooperation.

It was at this time that the research division published, for private circulation within the company, a monograph entitled 'Complaints and Grievances'. Careful description of many varied situations within the interviewers' experience showed that an articulate complaint only rarely, if ever, gave any logical clue to the grievance in which it had origin; this applied at least as strongly to groups as to individuals. Whereas economists and industry generally *tend to concentrate upon the complaint and upon logical inferences from its articulate statement* as an appropriate procedure, the interviewing group had learned almost to ignore, except as symptom, the – sometimes noisy – manifestation of discomfort and to study the situation anew to gain knowledge of its source. Diagnosis rather than argument became the proper method of procedure.

It is possible to quote an illustration from a recently published book, *China Enters the Machine Age* (Shih Kuo-heng, 1944). When industries had to be moved, during this war, from Shanghai and the Chinese coast to Kunming in the interior of China, the actual operation of an industry still depended for the most part on skilled workers who were refugees from Shanghai and elsewhere. These skilled workers knew their importance to the work and gained considerable prestige from it; nevertheless discontent was rife among them. Evidence of this was manifested by the continual, deliberate breaking of crockery in the company mess hall and complaints about the quality of the food provided. Yet this food was much better than could have been obtained outside the plant – especially at the prices charged. And in interview the individual workers admitted freely that the food was good and could not rightly be made the subject of complaint. But the relationship between the skilled workers as a group and the *Chih Yuan* – the executive and supervisory officers – was exceedingly unsatisfactory.

Many of these officers – the *Chih Yuan* – have been trained in the United States – enough at least to set a pattern for the whole group. Now in America we have learned in actual practice to accept the rabble hypothesis with reservations. But the logical Chinese student of engineering or economics, knowing nothing of these practical reservations, returns to his own country convinced that the workman who is not wholly responsive to the 'financial incentive' is a troublemaker and a nuisance. And the Chinese worker lives up to this conviction by breaking plates.[4] Acceptance of the complaint about the food and collective bargaining of a logical type conducted at that level would surely have been useless.

Yet this is what industry, not only in China, does every day, with the high sanction of State authority and the alleged aid of lawyers and economists. In their behaviour and their statements, economists indicate that they accept the rabble hypothesis and its dismal corollary of financial incentive as the only effective human motive. They substitute a logical hypothesis of small practical value for the actual facts.

The insight gained by the interviewing group, on the other hand, cannot be described as substituting irrational for rational motive, emotion for logic. On the contrary, it implies a need for competent study of complaints and the grievances that provoke them, a need for knowledge of the actual facts rather than acceptance of an out-dated theory. It is amusing that certain industrialists, rigidly disciplined in economic theory, attempt to shrug off the Hawthorne studies as 'theoretic'. Actually the shoe is on the other foot; Hawthorne has re-studied the facts without prejudice, whereas the critics have unquestioningly accepted that theory of man which had its vogue in the nineteenth century and has already outlived its usefulness.

4. Shih Kuo-heng (1944), chapter 8, pp. 111–27; also chapter 10, pp. 151–3.

The Hawthorne interview programme has moved far since its beginning in 1929. Originally designed to study the comfort of workers in their work as a mass of individuals, it has come to clear specification of the relation of working groups to management as one of the fundamental problems of large-scale industry. It was indeed this study that first enabled us to assert that the third major preoccupation of management must be that of organizing teamwork, that is to say, of developing and sustaining cooperation.

References

BARNARD, C. (1938), 'The executive functions', *The Functions of the Executive*, Harvard University Press, chapter 15, pp. 215–34.

HOMANS, G. C. (1941), *Fatigue of Workers*, Reinhold.

MATHEWSON, S. B. (1931), *Restriction of Output among Unorganized Workers*, Viking.

MAYO, E. (1933), *The Human Problems of an Industrial Civilization*, Macmillan Co.

ROETHLISBERGER, F. J. (n.d.), *Management and Morale*, Harvard University Press, pp. 9–10.

ROETHLISBERGER, F. J., and DICKSON, W. J. (1939), *Management and the Worker*, Harvard University Press, pp. 379–510.

SHIH KUO-HENG (1944), *China Enters the Machine Age*, Harvard University Press.

13 K. Lewin, R. Lippitt and R. K. White

Patterns of Aggressive Behaviour in Experimentally
Created 'Social Climates'

K. Lewin, R. Lippitt, and R. K. White, 'Patterns of aggressive
behavior in experimentally created "social climates"', *Journal of Social
Psychology*, 1939, no. 10, pp. 271–99.

A Problems and methods

The present report is a preliminary summary on one phase of a
series of experimental studies of group life which has as its aim a
scientific approach to such questions as the following: What under-
lies such differing patterns of group behavior as rebellion against
authority, persecution of a scapegoat, apathetic submissiveness to
authoritarian domination, or attack upon an outgroup? How
may differences in subgroup structure, group stratification and
potency of ego-centred and group-centred goals be utilized as
criteria for predicting the social resultants of different group
atmospheres? Is not democratic group life more pleasant, but
authoritarianism more efficient? These are the sorts of questions to
which 'opinionated' answers are many and varied today, and to
which scientific answers, are, on that account, all the more
necessary. An experimental approach to the phenomena of group
life obviously raises many difficulties of creation and scientific
control, but the fruitfulness of the method seems to compensate
for the added experimental problems.

In the first experiment Lippitt organized two clubs of ten-year-
old children, who engaged in the activity of theatrical mask-making
for a period of three months. The same adult leader, changing his
philosophy of leadership, led one club in an authoritarian manner
and the other club in accordance with democratic techniques,
while detailed observations were made by four observers. This
study, reported in detail elsewhere (Lippitt, 1939b), suggested more
hypotheses than answers and led to a second and more extensive
series of experiments by White and Lippitt. Four new clubs of ten-
year-old boys were organized on a voluntary basis as before, the
variety of club activities was extended, while four different adult

leaders participated. To the variables of authoritarian and democratic procedure was added a third, *laissez-faire* or group life without adult participation. Also the behavior of each club was studied in different 'social climates'. Every six weeks each group had a new leader with a different technique of leadership, each club having three leaders during the course of the five months of the experimental series. The data on aggressive behavior summarized in this paper are drawn from both series of experiments.

Some of the techniques used for the equating of groups have been described previously (Lewin and Lippitt, 1938), but will be summarized here with the improvements in method of the second experiment. Before the clubs were organized the schoolroom group as a whole was studied. Using the sociometric technique developed by Moreno (1934) the interpersonal relations of the children, in terms of rejections, friendships and leadership, were ascertained. Teacher ratings on relevant items of social behavior (e.g., teasing, showing off, obedience, physical energy) were secured, and observations were made on the playground and in the schoolroom by the investigators. The school records supplied information on intellectual status, physical status and socio-economic background. From the larger number of eager volunteers in each room it was then possible to select from each schoolroom two five-member clubs, which were carefully equated on patterns of interpersonal relationships, intellectual, physical and socio-economic status, in addition to personality characteristics. The attempt was not to equate the boys within a particular club, but to ensure the same pattern in each group as a whole.

In spite of the methods described above to control by selection some of the more elusive social variables, it was essential to use a number of experimental controls which would help to make the results more clear-cut. First of all, to check on the 'individuality' of the club as a whole, each group was studied in different social atmospheres so that it could be compared with itself. A second question raised by the first experiment was that concerning the personality of the leader as a factor in the creating of social atmospheres. The second experiment, with four leaders, makes possible a comparison of the authoritarianism and democracy of four different leaders, and the *laissez-faire* method of two different leaders.

Table 1

Authoritarian	Democratic	Laissez-faire
1. All determination of policy by the leader.	1. All policies a matter of group discussion and decision, encouraged and assisted by the leader.	1. Complete freedom for group or individual decision, without any leader participation.
2. Techniques and activity steps dictated by the authority, one at a time, so that future steps were always uncertain to a large degree.	2. Activity perspective gained during first discussion period. General steps to goal sketched, and where technical advice was needed the leader suggested two or three alternative procedures from which choice could be made.	2. Various materials supplied by the leader, who made it clear that he would supply information when asked. He took no other part in work discussions.
3. The leader usually dictated the particular work task and work companions of each member.	3. The members were free to work with whomever they chose, and the division of tasks was left up to the group.	3. Complete nonparticipation by leader.
4. The dominator was 'personal' in his praise and criticism of the work of each member, but remained aloof from active group participation except when demonstrating. He was friendly or impersonal rather than openly hostile.	4. The leader was 'objective' or 'fact-minded' in his praise and criticism, and tried to be a regular group member in spirit without doing too much of the work.	4. Very infrequent comments on member activities unless questioned, and no attempt to participate or interfere with the course of events.

In two cases it is also possible to compare the same atmosphere, created by two different leaders with the same club.

One other type of control seemed very important, the nature of the club activity, and the physical setting. Using the same club-rooms (two clubs met at the same time in adjacent but distinctly separate areas of the same large room) seemed to answer the latter problem, but the question of activity was more complex. The following technique was developed: a list of activities which were of interest to all the children was assembled (e.g., mask making, mural painting, soap carving, model airplane construction, etc.). Meeting first, in chronological time, the democratic groups used these possibilities as the basis for discussion and voted upon their club activity. The authoritarian leaders were then ready, as their clubs met, to launch the same activity without choice by the members. The *laissez-faire* groups were acquainted with the variety of materials which were available, but they were not otherwise influenced in their choice of activity; in their case, consequently, the activity factor could not be completely controlled.

The contrasting methods of the leaders in creating the three types of group atmospheres may be briefly summarized as in Table 1.

It should be clear that due to the voluntary nature of the group participation, and the cooperation of the parents and school systems, no radically autocratic methods (e.g. use of threats, instilling fear, etc.) were used. Fairly congenial extra-club relationships were maintained with each member by the leader.

The kinds of data collected during the course of the experiments may be classed roughly as: 1. pre-club data, described above in relation to the problem of equating the groups; 2. observations of behavior in the experimental situation; and 3. extra-club information.

Observations of club behavior consisted of:

1. A quantitative running account of the social interactions of the five children and the leader, in terms of symbols for directive, compliant and objective (fact-minded) approaches and responses, including a category of purposeful refusal to respond to a social approach.

2. A minute-by-minute group-structure analysis giving a record of:

activity subgroupings, the activity goal of each sub-group was initiated by the leader or spontaneously formed by the children, and ratings on degree of unity of each sub-grouping.

3. An interpretive running account of significant member actions, and changes in dynamics of the group as a whole.

4. Continuous stenographic records of all conversation.

5. An interpretive running account of inter-club relationships.

6. An 'impressionistic' write-up by the leader as to what he saw and felt from within the group atmosphere during each meeting.

7. Comments by guest observers.

8. Movie records of several segments of club life.

All of these observations (except 6, 7 and 8) were synchronized at minute intervals so that side by side they furnish a rather complete cross-sectional picture of the ongoing life of the group. The major purpose of this experiment in methodology of observation was to record as fully and with as much insight as possible the total behavior of the group, a distinct break away from the usual procedure of recording only certain pre-determined symptoms of behavior. The second aim was to ascertain whether data collected by this method could be fruitfully analyzed from both a sociological and psychological point of view (Lewin, 1939b, and Lippitt, 1939a).

Extra-club information is of the following types:

1. Interviews with each child by a friendly 'non-club' person during each transition period (from one kind of group atmosphere and leader to another) and at the end of the experiment, concerning such items as comparison of present club leader with previous ones, with the teacher, and with parents; opinions on club activities; how the club could be run better; who were the best and poorest club members; what an ideal club leader would be like, etc.

2. Interviews with the parents by the investigators, concentrating on kinds of discipline used in the home, status of the child in the family group (relations with siblings, etc.), personality ratings on the same scale used by the teachers, discussion of child's attitude toward the club, school and other group activities.

3. Talks with the teachers concerning the transfer to the schoolroom, of behavior patterns acquired in the club.

4. Administration of a Rorschach test to each club member.

5. Conversations with the children during two summer hikes arranged after the experiment was over.

These data were gathered with a view to correlating the individual pattern of behavior in the club situation with the types of group membership which exitsed outside the experiment, and with the more or less stable individual personality structure. The individual differences in 'social plasticity' seem to be rather striking.

Two other points of experimental technique seem of interest. The first concerns the introduction of observers into the club situation. In Lippitt's first experiment it was found that four observers grouped around a table in a physically separated part of the club room attracted virtually no attention if it was explained at the first meeting that 'those are some people interested in learning how a mask-making club goes; they have plenty to do so they won't bother us and we won't bother them.' In the second experiment the arrangement was even more advantageous and seemed to make for equally unselfconscious behavior on the part of the clubs. In this set-up the lighting arrangement was such that the observers were grouped behind a low burlap wall in a darkly shaded area, and seemed 'not to exist at all' as far as the children and leaders were concerned.

The second point of interest is the development of a number of 'group-test' situations, which aided greatly in getting at the actual social dynamics of a given group atmosphere. One test used systematically was for the leader to leave the room on business during the course of the club meeting, so that the 'social-pressure' factor could be analyzed more realistically. Another practice was for the leader to arrive a few minutes late so that the observers could record the individual and 'atmospheric' differences in spontaneous work initiation and work perspective. A third fruitful technique was that of having a stranger (a graduate student who played the role of a janitor or electrician) enter the club situation and criticize the group's work efforts. A rather dramatic picture of the results of this type of situation may be seen in Figures 5 and 6. Further variations of such experimental manipulations are being utilized in a research now in progress.

B Results

The analysis of the results from the second experiment is now proceeding in various directions, following two main trends: 1. interpretation of sociological or 'group-centered' data; 2. interpretation of psychological or 'individual-centered' data. The sociological approach includes such analyses as differences in volume of social interaction related to social atmosphere, nature of club activity, out-group relationship, differences in pattern of interaction related to outgroup and ingroup orientation, atmosphere differences in leader-group relationship, effect upon group structure pattern of social atmosphere and types of activity, group differences in language behavior, etc. The psychological approach includes such analyses as relation of home background to pattern of club behavior, range of variation of member behavior in different types of social atmosphere, patterns of individual reaction to atmosphere transitions in relation to case history data, correlation between position in group stratification and pattern of social action, etc. In this paper will be presented only certain data from the partially completed general analysis which are relevant to the dynamics of individual and group aggression.

We might first recall one or two of the most striking results of the first experiment (Lippitt, 1939b). As the club meetings progressed the authoritarian club members developed a pattern of aggressive domination toward one another, and their relation to the leader was one of submission or of persistent demands for attention. The interactions in the democratic club were more spontaneous, more fact-minded and friendly. Relations to the leader were free and on an 'equality basis'. Comparing the two groups on the one item of overt hostility the authoritarian group was surprisingly more aggressive, the ratio being 40 to 1. Comparing a constellation of 'ego-involved' types of language behavior (e.g., hostile, resistant, demands for attention, hostile criticism, expression of competition) with a group of objective or 'nonemotive' behaviors, it was found that in the authoritarian group 73 per cent of the analyzed language behavior was of the 'ego-involved' type as compared to 31 per cent in the democratic club. Into the objective category went 69 per cent of the behavior of the democratic group as compared to 37 per cent of the language activities of the authoritarian group.

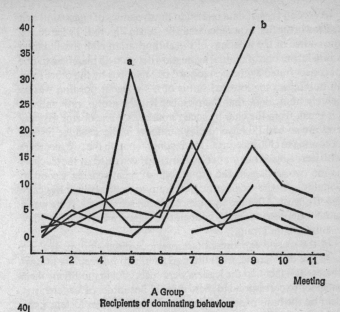

A Group
Recipients of dominating behaviour

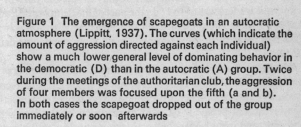

Figure 1 The emergence of scapegoats in an autocratic
atmosphere (Lippitt, 1937). The curves (which indicate the
amount of aggression directed against each individual)
show a much lower general level of dominating behavior in
the democratic (D) than in the autocratic (A) group. Twice
during the meetings of the authoritarian club, the aggression
of four members was focused upon the fifth (a and b).
In both cases the scapegoat dropped out of the group
immediately or soon afterwards

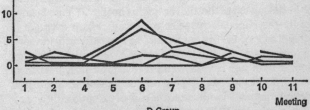

D Group
Recipients of dominating behaviour

A second type of data related to the dynamics of aggression as it existed in the first experiment may be seen in Figure 1. Twice during the course of the meetings of the authoritarian club the situation shifted from one of mutual aggression between all members to one of concentrated aggression toward one member by the other four. In both cases the lowered status of a scapegoat position was so acutely unpleasant that the member left the group, rationalizing his break from the club by such remarks as, 'The doctor says my eyes are so bad I'll have to play outdoors in the sunshine instead of coming to club meetings.' Interestingly enough the two members who were singled out for persecution had been rated by the teachers as the two leaders in the group, one of them scoring second in popularity by the sociometric technique, as well as being physically the strongest. After the emergence of both scapegoats, there was a rather brief rise in friendly cooperative behavior between the other members of the group.

In the second experiment (see previous discussion, p. 4) there were five democratic, five autocratic and two *laissez-faire* atmospheres. The fact that the leaders were successful in modifying their behavior to correspond to these three philosophies of leadership is clear on the basis of several quantitative indices. For instance, the ratio of 'directive' to 'compliant' behavior on the part of the autocratic leaders was 63 to 1; on the part of the democratic leaders it was 1·1 to 1. The total amount of leader participation was less than half as great in *laissez-faire* as in either autocracy or democracy.

The data on aggression averages in these three atmospheres are summarized in Figures 2, 3, and 4. All of them indicate average amounts of aggression per fifty-minute, five-member club meeting. They represent behavior records, as recorded by the interaction observer, and include all social actions, both verbal and physical, which he designated as 'hostile' or 'joking hostile'. Figure 2 shows especially the bimodal character of the aggression averages in autocracy; four of the five autocracies had an extremely low level of aggression, and the fifth had an extremely high one. For comparison, a sixth bar has been added to represent aggression in Lippitt's 1937 experiment, computed on the same basis. It is obviously comparable with the single case of exceptionally aggressive behavior in the 1938 experiment. For comparison also, four

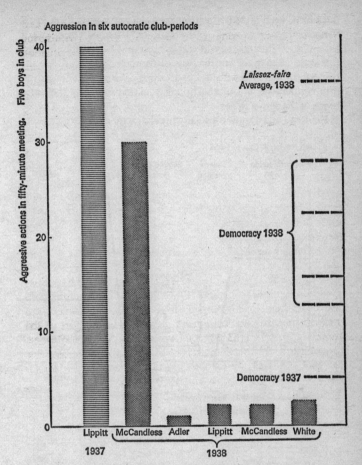

Figure 2 Aggression in autocracy. The amount of aggression is either very great or very small compared with aggression in democracy

lines have been added which indicate the aggression level in the two *laissez-faire* groups, in the four 1938 democracies, and in Lippitt's 1937 democracy. It can be seen that two of the six autocracies are above the entire range of democracies, and are in this respect comparable with the two *laissez-faire* groups. The other four autocracies are at the opposite extreme, below the entire range of the democracies.

Figures 3 and 4 show especially the character of the experimental

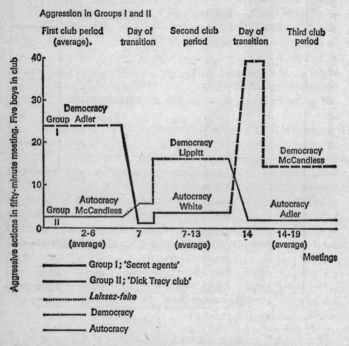

Figure 3 The same group in different atmospheres. In each group, suggestion was at a medium level in democracy and at a very low level in autocracy. Note that the leaders in the third period were the same as in the first, but reversed. Note also the sharp rise of aggression in one group of the day of transition to democracy. Group I shows release of tension on the first day of freedom (14) after apathetic autocracy. The name of the leader is indicated below that of the atmosphere

controls. Together, they show how each of four groups was carried through three different periods with three different adult leaders. The relative importance of the deliberately created social atmosphere, as compared with either the personality make-up of the group or the personality of the adult leader, can be estimated from the character of these curves. It is clear that the same group usually changes markedly, and sometimes to an extreme degree, when it is changed to a new atmosphere under a different leader. In such transitions the factor of group personnel is held relatively constant, while the factors of leader personality and social atmosphere are varied. In addition, the factor of leader personality was systematically varied, as can be seen if the four curves are compared with each other. Each of the four leaders played the role of a democratic leader at least once; also each played the role of an autocrat at least once; two of them (Adler and White) played in addition the role of bystander in a *laissez-faire* group. One leader (Lippitt) was democratic with two different groups; and one (McCandless) was autocratic with two different groups. Through this systematic variation of both club personnel and leader's personality, the effects of the deliberately created social atmosphere (autocracy, democracy, *laissez-faire*) stand out more clearly and more reliably than would otherwise be possible.

In Figure 3, for instance, the two curves both tell the same story: a moderate amount of aggression in democracy and an abnormally small amount in autocracy, regardless of the personality of the leader (note that the roles of Lippitt and McCandless were reversed, with each playing once the role of autocrat and once the role of democratic leader), and regardless of the personnel of the group itself (note that the curves cross once when the atmospheres are reversed, and cross back again when the atmospheres return to what they were at the beginning). In Figure 4, the two *laissez-faire* atmospheres give very high levels of aggression although different groups and different leaders are involved. The most extreme change of behavior recorded in any group occurred when Group IV was changed from autocracy (in which it had shown the apathetic reaction) to *laissez-faire*. One of the autocratic groups (Figure 4) reacted apathetically, the other very aggressively. The aggressiveness of Group III may be due to the personalities of the boys, or to the fact that they had just previously 'run wild' in *laissez-faire*.

The average number of aggressive actions per meeting in the different atmospheres was as follows:

Laissez-faire	38
Autocracy (aggressive reaction)	30
Democracy	20
Autocracy (apathetic reaction)	2

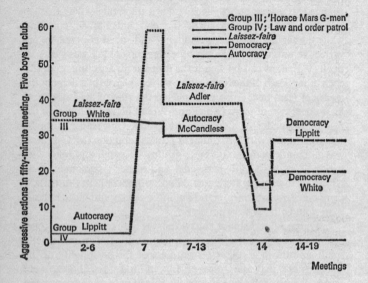

Figure 4 The same group in different atmospheres. Group IV shows changes to the levels typical for each atmosphere. It shows also the 'release of tension' on the first day of freedom (7) after apathetic autocracy. Group III seemed resistant to change; it was relatively aggressive even in democracy

Critical ratios for these comparisons have not yet been computed. The data are comparable, however, with Lippitt's 1937 data, in which the critical ratios for the more important indices ranged between 4·5 and 7·5.

In the interpretation of these data it is natural to ask: Why are the results for autocracy paradoxical? Why is the reaction to autocracy sometimes very aggressive, with much rebellion or persecution of scapegoats, and sometimes very non-aggressive? Are the underlying dynamics in these two cases as different as the surface behavior? The high level of aggression in some autocracies has often been interpreted mainly in terms of tension, which presumably results from frustration of individual goals. Is it, then, an indication of non-frustration when the aggression level in some other autocracies is found to be extremely low?

Four lines of evidence in our experiments indicate that this is not the case, and that the low level of aggression in the apathetic autocracies is not due to lack of frustration.

First of all, there are the sudden outbursts of aggression which occurred on the days of transition from a repressed autocratic atmosphere to the much freer atmosphere of democracy or *laissez-faire*. Two of these are well illustrated in Figure 4. The boys behaved just as if they had previously been in a state of bottled-up tension, which could not show itself overtly as long as the repressive influence of the autocrat was felt, but which burst out unmistakably when that pressure was removed.

A second and very similar type of evidence can be obtained from the records on the days when the leader left the room for ten or fifteen minutes. In the three other atmospheres (*laissez-faire*, aggressive autocracy and democracy) the aggression level did not rise when the leader left the room. In the apathetic autocracies, however, the level of aggression rises very rapidly to ten times its former level. These data should not be overstressed, because aggression even then does not rise to a level significantly above that of the other atmospheres. It is so extremely low in the apathetic atmosphere that even multiplication by ten does not produce what could be called a high level of aggression. (The effect of the leader's absence is shown more significantly in a deterioration of work than in an outburst of aggression.) Nevertheless, the rapid disappearance of apathy when the leader goes out shows clearly that it was due to the repressive influence of the leader rather than to any particular absence of frustration. In this connection it should be added that the autocratic leader never forbade aggression. His 'repressive influence' was not a prohibition created by explicit command but a sort of generalized inhibition or restraining force.

In the third place, there are the judgments of observers who found themselves using such terms as 'dull', 'lifeless', 'submissive', 'repressed' and 'apathetic' in describing the non-aggressive reaction to autocracy. There was little smiling, joking, freedom of movement, freedom of initiating new projects, etc.; talk was largely confined to the immediate activity in progress, and bodily tension was often manifested. Moving pictures tell the same story. The impression created was not one of acute discontent, by any means, and the activities themselves were apparently enjoyable enough so that the net result for most of the boys was more pleasant than unpleasant. Nevertheless, they could not be described as genuinely contented.

The fourth and perhaps the most convincing indication of the existence of frustration in these atmospheres is the testimony of the boys themselves. They were individually interviewed, just before each day of transition to a new atmosphere, and again at the end of the whole experiment. The interviewing was done by an adult who had not served as a leader in the boy's own group. On the whole good rapport was achieved, and the boys talked rather freely, comparing the three leaders under whom their club had been conducted. (For them it was a question of comparing leaders they liked or did not like, as they were unaware of the deliberate change in the behavior of the same leader from one atmosphere to another or of the nature of the experiment.) With surprising unanimity the boys agreed in a relative dislike for their autocratic leader regardless of his individual personality. Nineteen of the twenty boys liked their leader in democracy better than their leader in autocracy. The twentieth boy, as it happened, was the son of an army officer (the only one in the group), and consciously put a high value upon strict discipline. As he expressed it, the autocratic leader 'Was the strictest, and I like that a lot'. The other two leaders 'Let us go ahead and fight, and that isn't good.' For the other nineteen, strictness was not necessarily a virtue, their description of the autocrat being that he was 'too strict'. Typical comments about the autocrat were: 'He didn't let us do what we wanted to do'; 'He wouldn't let us go behind the burlap'; 'He was all right mostly – sort of dictator-like'; 'We just had to do things; he wanted us to get it done in a hurry'; 'He made us make masks, and the boys didn't like that'; 'The other two guys suggested and we could do it or not, but not with him'; 'We didn't have any fun with him – we didn't have any fights'. Typical comments about the democratic leader were: 'He was a good sport, worked along with us and thinks of things just like we do'; 'He never did try to be the boss, but we always had plenty to do'; 'Just the right combination – nothing I didn't like about him'; 'We all liked him; he let us tear down the burlap and everything'. These comments were almost uniformly dependent upon the role played by the leader, and were exactly reversed when he played a different role.

As between the leaders in autocracy and *laissez-faire*, the preference was for the *laissez-faire* leader in seven cases out of ten. The three boys who preferred the autocrat made such comments about the *laissez-faire* leader as: 'He was too easy-going'; 'He had too

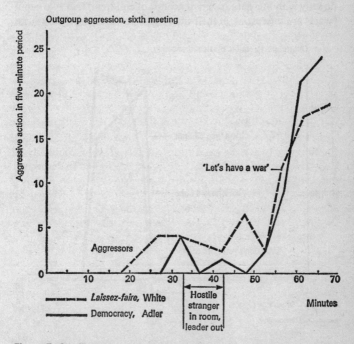

Figure 5 Conflict between groups after intrusion of hostile stranger. After the stranger left, strong hostility developed between the two groups. Before the major conflict, minor hostilities had already occurred, with one or two members of the laissez-faire group playing the role of aggressors

K. Lewin, R. Lippitt and R. K. White 245

few things for us to do'; 'He let us figure things out too much'; in contrast the autocrat 'Told us what to do, and we had something to do all the time'. For the other seven, even disorder was preferable to rigidity: 'We could do what we pleased with him'; 'He wasn't strict at all'.

Another form of aggression was outgroup hostility, as manifested especially in two 'wars' between clubs meeting in the same large room at the same time. Both wars seemed to be mainly in a spirit of play. They were much more like snowball fights than serious conflicts. (This is one more reason why in this case one should be cautious in comparing adult political phenomena directly with our data on small groups of children.) Our two small 'wars' are interesting in their own right, however, especially since

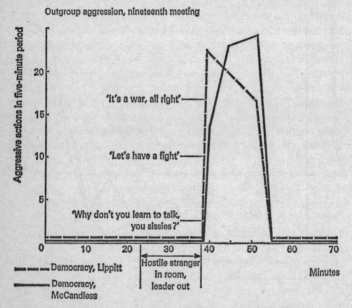

Figure 6 Conflict between groups after intrusion of hostile stranger. The intrusion of a hostile stranger was followed by inter-group conflict (as in Figure 5). In this case the hostilities began suddenly, rising within four minutes almost to their maximum level

246 Behaviour in Organizations

the same general constellation of factors seemed to be operating in both cases.

The curves of rising hostility, computed for five-minute intervals, are shown in Figures 5 and 6. From these curves it can be seen that the first 'war' started gradually, with a long period of minor bickering and name calling, followed by a much steeper gradient of increasing hostility. The overt hostilities consisted of throwing water, small pieces of clay (which nearly always missed their mark) and sometimes water color paint, flicked from the end of a long paint brush. No one was hurt. The second conflict (Figure 6) began much more suddenly. Name calling began in the first minute after the 'hostile stranger' left the room, and almost immediately the boys seemed to remember their previous conflict and to wish a repetition of it. Beginning with verbal aggression such as, 'Why don't you learn to talk, you sissies?' they passed within three minutes to throwing small pieces of soap (small pieces of soap statuettes, which they had carved, were lying about), and within five minutes nearly all the boys on both sides were wholeheartedly participating. This difference in steepness of the hostility gradient was perhaps due in part to a higher level of tension or to weaker restraining forces on the later occasion, but it seemed to be due also to a cognitive difference. On the later occasion the pattern of inter-group conflict had been established; it was, by that time, a part of the boys' 'cognitive structure' – a clearly defined region which they could enter or not as they chose; and since they had found the first 'war' to be very pleasantly exciting, they readily and quickly entered the same region again when the general psychological situation was conducive to conflict. In this connection it may be noted that the second conflict was labelled verbally almost immediately, while the first one was not labelled until it was already well under way. On the first occasion the shout, 'Let's have a war' went up long after the minor hostilities had begun; on the second occasion, one boy shouted, 'Let's have a fight,' only two minutes after the name calling began, and another one legalized it two minutes later with the words, 'It's a war all right.'

Certain similarities between the two days of conflict suggest some very tentative hypotheses as to the psychological factors conducive to this sort of conflict. In the first place, both occurred on days when, with the adult leader absent, a hostile stranger had been in the room and had criticized the work which the boys were doing. This had been deliberately planned as a 'test situation'; a graduate student, playing the role of a janitor or an electrician, was the hostile stranger. It may be doubtful whether or not the term 'substitute hate object' is an appropriate one here; but there was no question in the observers' minds that in both cases the intrusion of the stranger tended to disorganize the regular play activities of the clubs and to build up a tense, restless psychological condition which was conducive to intergroup conflict. In the second place, both conflicts started when no respected adult was present. In the first one the main aggressors were unquestionably the *laissez-faire* group (see Figure 5). Their leader was physically present at the time, but he was psychologically unimportant. The second conflict began when the leaders on both sides were out of the room, and by the time the leaders returned, it had gathered great momentum. In the third place, both conflicts occurred at a time when there was no absorbing group activity as an alternative. The first one began at a time when the members of the *laissez-faire* group seemed unusually bored and dissatisfied with their own lack of solid accomplishment. The second one began after the boys had become somewhat bored with their soap carving, and after this individualistic activity had been further disrupted by the criticisms of the stranger.

The free direct expression of aggression by the 'wars' following frustration in the *laissez-faire* and democratic situations offers a contrast to several other patterns of expression which were observed in some of the authoritarian situations. These types of behavior might be briefly labelled: 1. a 'strike'; 2. rebellious acts; 3. reciprocal aggression among all members; 4. scapegoat attack; 5. release behavior after a decrease in leader pressure; 6. aggression against impersonal 'substitute hate objects'.

Both the 'strike' and symptoms of rebellious action occurred in the aggressive type of autocracy. About the middle of the series of six meetings the club members went to their teacher with a letter of resignation signed by four of them. They asked their teacher to give this to the leader when he came to get them after school. The teacher refused to act as a go-between, suggesting that the boys go to the leader directly, but when he appeared after school, courage seemed to wane and they all went to the meeting as usual. Overt rebellious acts were of the following nature: breaking a rule by carving on the posts in the clubroom (while casting sidelong glances at the leader), deliberately walking behind the burlap walls of the clubroom without permission (mentioned to an interviewer), leaving the club meeting early, and pretending not to hear when spoken to by the leader. The third and fourth kinds of behavior were also typical of aggressive authoritarianism and have been mentioned in describing the first experiment during which two scapegoats emerged. As has been mentioned, changes in amount of aggression while the leader was out, and days of transition to a freer atmosphere were especially good indicators of the existence of unexpressed tension in the apathetic autocracies.

Two very interesting examples of what we have tentatively called 'release behavior through an impersonal substitute hate object' are worthy of description. During the eleventh meeting of the first experiment the authoritarian group was given a chance to indicate by secret ballot whether they would like the club to stop or continue for several more meetings. We may go to an observer's record for further comments:

Peculiar actions follow the leader's announcement that because of the vote there will be no more meetings after today. The leader asks RO and J to put the paper on the floor as usual. They put it down and then run and jump on it time and again in a wild manner. The group masks are divided among the members and J immediately begins to throw his around violently, pretending to jump on it. He throws it down again and again, laughing. R wants to know if it won't break, then starts to throw his down too. Later J and RO chase each other around the room wildly with streamers of towelling. . . .

Rather clearly the work products of this authoritarian atmosphere seemed to be the objects of aggressive attack rather than prideful ownership.

During a last meeting of the second experiment a rather similar burst of behavior occurred in one of the democratic groups. The group was highly involved in an activity of making an oil painting on glass. While the leader was out for a short time (by arrangement) a student in the janitor role came in to sweep. From the running accountist's record of the twenty-second minute we find,

He is making dirt fly and sweeping it toward the group. They all begin to cough but don't move from their work.

Several minutes later we find the comment,

Janitor has almost swept them away, but still no hostile response. The project seems to have a very high valance.

Five minutes later the janitor had gotten them out of their chairs in order to sweep, then

the janitor accidentally knocks a piece of their glass on the floor. They all yell and R makes as if to throw something at him. F says that if the leader were here he would beat up the janitor.

Five minutes later, after a number of comments criticizing the art work of the club, the janitor left. The members dropped their work completely, climbed the rafters and made considerable noise. On the thirty-sixth minute we find,

R comes down from the rafter and begins to complain about the janitor, L joins him and they all complain bitterly and loudly.

Within three minutes the group began to destroy a large wooden sign upon which they had painted the club name. Such comments as this appear in the running account,

F is wielding two hammers at once. . . . R is busy pulling out all the nails. . . . They are excited. . . . F knocks the first hole through it. . . . R tries to caution F for a minute, and then gets busy himself . . . their unexpressed aggression toward the janitor is taking a violent outlet . . . they are all very serious and vicious about the destruction of the sign . . . they seem to be getting a great deal of 'pure animal pleasure' out of the pillage.

The meeting ended with three or four minutes of pleasant conversation.

C Interpretive comments

From the many theoretical problems involved we should like to discuss but one, namely, the problem of aggression and apathy. Even here we wish to show the complexity of the problem and its possible attack from a field theoretical point of view rather than to set forth a definite theory.

It is not easy to say what aggression is, that is, if one is not satisfied with mere verbal definition. One important aspect obviously is that one group or an individual within a group turns against another group (or individual). In case these groups are subgroups of one original group, it can be called aggression *within a group*, otherwise aggression *against an outgroup*.

Both kinds of aggression occurred in our experiments. All of these aggressions were spontaneous in character. In other words, it was not a situation where a group of people are ordered by a politically dominating power (like the state) to indulge in a certain type of directed activity called war. On the whole the aggression was the outcome of the momentary emotional situation, although in two cases the aggressions had definitely the character of a fight of one group against another group and showed a certain amount of cooperative organization within each group.

It is necessary to mention four points which seem to play a dominant role in the spontaneous aggressions: tension, the space of free movement, rigidity of group structure, and the style of living (culture).

Tension

An instance where tension was created by *annoying* experiences occurred when the group work was criticized by a stranger (janitor). There were two cases where fighting broke out immediately afterwards.

In the autocratic atmosphere the behavior of the leader probably annoyed the children considerably (to judge from the interviews reported above).

In addition, there were six times as many directing approaches to an individual by the leader in autocracy than in democracy (Figure 7). It is probably fair to assume that the bombardment with such frequent ascendant approaches is equivalent to higher *pressure* and that this pressure created a higher tension.

Narrow space of free movement as a source of tension

On the whole, even more important than this single annoying experience was the general atmosphere of the situation. Experiments in individual psychology (Lewin, 1935) seemed to indicate that lack of space of free movement is equivalent to higher pressure; both conditions seem to create tension. This seemed particularly true if an originally larger space was narrowed down (one is

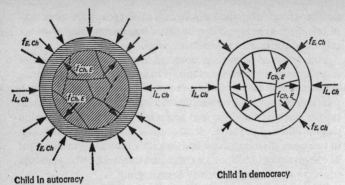

Child in autocracy

Child in democracy

Figure 7 Leader pressure and child tension. In the authoritarian situation the leader makes six times as many directing approaches ($l_{L, Ch}$) to the child member as in the democratic situation. This creates social pressure (equivalent to forces $f_{E, Ch}$ of the environment on the child) and therefore a higher state of tension in the child in the autocratic group; this tension demands some sort of outlet toward the environment (equivalent to forces $f_{Ch, E}$)

reminded here of the physical tension created by decreasing volume, although one should not overstress the analogy).

Our experiments seemed to indicate that a similar relation between the narrow space of free movement and high tension holds also in regard to groups. The space of free movement in autocracy was smaller in relation to the activities permitted and the social status which could be reached (Figures 8 and 9). In *laissez-faire*, contrary to expectations, the space of free movement was not larger but smaller than in democracy, partly because of the lack of time perspective and partly because of the interference of the work of one individual with the activities of his fellows.

Aggression as the effect of tension

The annoying occurrences, the pressure applied by the leader, and the lack of space of free movement, are three basic facts which brought up a higher tension. Our experiments indicate that this higher tension might suffice to create aggression. This seems to be of theoretical importance; obviously some aggressive facts can be viewed mainly as a kind of 'purposive' action (for instance, to destroy a danger), and one might ask whether or not this

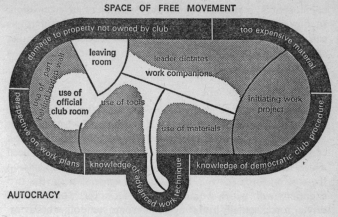

SPACE OF FREE MOVEMENT

AUTOCRACY

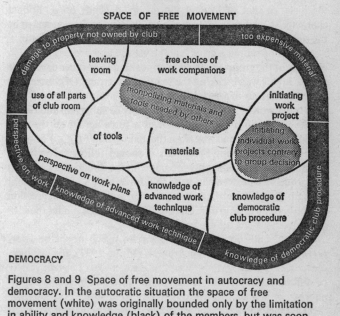

SPACE OF FREE MOVEMENT

DEMOCRACY

Figures 8 and 9 Space of free movement in autocracy and democracy. In the autocratic situation the space of free movement (white) was originally bounded only by the limitation in ability and knowledge (black) of the members, but was soon limited much further by the social influence of the leader (grey). In democracy the space was increased with the help of the leader component is an essential part in the causation of any aggression. In our experiments, the two wars between the two outgroups can hardly be classified in this way. They seemed to be rather clear cases where aggression was 'emotional expression' of an underlying tension.

Rigidity of group structure

However, to understand aggression one will have to realize that tension is only one of the factors which determine whether or not an aggressive action will take place. The building up of tension can be said to be equivalent to the creation of a certain type of need which might express itself in aggressive action. Tension sets up the driving force (Lewin, 1938) for the aggression (in the two situations with which we are dealing). However, whether these driving forces actually lead to aggression or to some other behavior, for instance that of leaving the group, depends on additional characteristics of the situation as a whole. One of these seems to be the rigidity of the social position of the person within the group.

Aggression within a group can be viewed as a process by which one part of the group sets itself in opposition to another part of the group, in this way breaking the unity of the group. Of course, this separation is only of a certain degree.

In other words, if M indicates a member or subgroup and Gr the whole group, an aggression involves a force acting on the subgroup in the direction away from the main group ($f_{M,-Gr}$) or other part of the subgroup. From this it should follow theoretically that if a subgroup can easily locomote in the direction away from the group it will do so in case this force shows any significant strength. In other words, a strong tension and an actual aggression will be built up only in case there exist forces which hinder the subgroup from leaving the group (Figure 10).

Cultural anthropology gives examples which might be interpreted from this angle. The Arapesh (Mead, 1937), for instance, are living in a society where everyone is a member of a great variety of different groups and seems to shift easily from one group to another; it is a society without rigidly fixed social position. The fact that they show extremely little aggression might well be linked with this lack of rigid social structure.

Another example might be seen in the fact that adolescents who

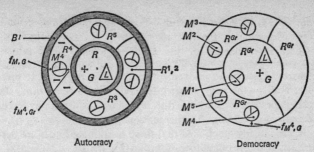

Autocracy   Democracy

Figure 10 Rigidity of group structure as a tension factor. In autocracy where each member or subgroup (M^1, M^2, ..., M^5) has a circumscribed region of activity (R^1, R^2, ..., R^5), and especially where the central regions of group life (policy formation R^p) are inaccessible to most members, rigid barriers B to own goals G continually frustrate members' efforts. The member's own position in the group structure R^4 therefore acquires a negative valence, usually creating a force away from group membership ($f_{M^4, -Gr}$). But in rigid group structures a restraining barrier (B^1) keeps members or subgroups from leaving until a very state of tension develops. In democracy where all group regions (R^{Gr}) are accessible to all members (M^1, M^2, ..., M^5), their own goals (G) are more easily attained and no such frustrating situation develops

have been kept within the family probably show more aggression; in other words, the more rigid the family structure the more difficult it is for them to move from childhood to adulthood.

An additional example is the well-known fact that narrow family ties which serve to make it difficult for husband and wife to leave each other may make aggression between them particularly violent.

In our experiment, autocracy provided a much more rigid social group than democracy. It was particularly difficult for the members of an autocracy to change their social status (Lewin, 1939a). On the other hand, in both groups the member did not like to leave the group as a whole because of the interest in the work project and the feeling of responsibility to the adult leader.

On the whole, then, the rigidity of the group will function as a restraining force (Lewin, 1938) against locomotion away from the group, or from the position within the group. Sufficient strength of this restraining force seems to be one of the conditions for the building up of a tension which is sufficiently high to lead to aggression.

It can be seen easily that the barriers limiting the space of free movement may have a similar function. We mentioned above, that a narrow space of free movement seems to be equivalent to pressure, and, in this way, creates tension. At the same time, the barriers prevent locomotion, thus providing the restraining forces necessary for building up higher tension.

It was already mentioned that these restraining forces are particularly strong in our autocratic group (Figure 10).

Style of living (culture)

Whether or not a given amount of tension and given restraining forces will cause a person to become aggressive depends finally upon the particular patterns of action which are customarily used in the culture in which he lives. The different styles of living can be viewed as different ways a given problem is usually solved. A person living in a culture where a show of dominance is 'the thing to do' under certain conditions will hardly think of any other way in which the solution of this problem may be approached. Such social patterns are comparable to 'habits'. Indeed, individual habits as well as cultural patterns have dynamically the character of restraining forces against leaving the paths determined by these patterns. In addition, they determine the cognitive structure which a given situation is likely to have for a given individual.

For the problem of aggression, this cultural pattern, determined by the group in which an individual lives and by his past history, is of great importance. It determines under what conditions aggression will be, for the individual concerned, the 'distinguished path' to the goal (Lewin, 1938). It determines, furthermore, how easily a situation will show for him a cognitive structure where aggression appears to be one possible path for his action (Figure 11).

The factors named are sufficient to warn against any 'one-factor' theory of aggression. Here, as in regard to any other behavior, it is the specific constellation of the field as a whole that determines whether or not aggression will occur. In every case one has to consider both the driving and the restraining forces and the cognitive structure of the field. Such a field theoretical approach seems to be rather arduous. On the other hand, only in this way will

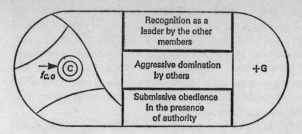

Figure 11 Different styles of living as represented by different distinguished paths (aggressive autocracy). The goal G of maximum social status and space of free movement can be reached by one or more of the several procedures depending on actual possibilities and the prevailing mode of behavior in that group. In our 'experimentally created cultures', the distinguished path to G was for a child C in aggressive autocracy that of aggressive domination of other members. In a similar situation the distinguished path for a member of democratic groups seemed to be that of gaining voluntary recognition of the other members, as a leader through work and social efforts. In the situation of apathetic authoritarianism the path seemed to be that of submissive obedience to authority, which might win praise from the leader

one be able to understand for instance the paradox of behavior that autocracy may lead either to aggression or to apathy. It was stated that aggression is partly to be viewed as an emotional outbreak due to tension and that this tension, in turn, is due to pressure and restraining forces (lack of space of free movement). We have apathy when the pressure and the restraining forces from without are kept stronger than the forces ($f_{Ch,E}$ in Figure 7) within the person which lead to the emotional expression, and are due to the tension. Whether or not the forces from without or those from within are stronger depends upon the absolute amount of pressure and also on the 'willingness' of the person to 'accept' the pressure.

The field theoretical approach also provides indications for the circumstances under which one might generalize the results of such experimental group studies. One must be careful of making too hasty generalization, perhaps especially in the field of political science. The varieties of democracies, autocracies, or *laissez-faire* atmospheres are, of course, very numerous. Besides, there are always individual differences of character and background to consider. On the other hand, it would be wrong to minimize the possibility of generalization. The answer in social psychology and sociology has to be the same as in an experiment in any science. The essence of an experiment is to create a situation which shows a certain pattern. What happens depends by and large upon this pattern and is largely although not completely independent of the absolute size of the field. This is one of the reasons why experiments are possible and worthwhile.

The generalization from an experimental situation should, therefore, go always to those life situations which show the same or sufficiently similar general patterns. This statement includes both the rights and the limitations of generalization.

D Summary

1. In a first experiment, Lippitt compared one group of five ten-year-old children, under autocratic leadership, with a comparable group under democratic leadership. In a second experiment, Lippitt and White studied four comparable clubs of ten-year-old boys, each of which passed successively through three club periods in such a way that there were altogether five democratic periods, five autocratic periods, and two *laissez-faire* periods.

2. In the second experiment, the factor of personality differences in the boys was controlled by having each group pass through autocracy and then democracy, or vice versa. The factor of leader's personality was controlled by having each of four leaders play the role of autocrat and the role of democratic leader at least once.

3. Records on each club meeting include stenographic records of conversation, quantitative symbolic records of group structure, quantitative symbolic records of all social interactions and a continuous interpretive running account. Parents and teachers were interviewed; each boy was given the Rorschach ink blots, a Moreno-type questionnaire, and was interviewed three times. Analysis of casual relationships between these various types of data is still far from complete. As a preliminary report we are giving here a part of the data bearing upon one specific problem, that of aggression.

4. In the first experiment, hostility was thirty times as frequent in the autocratic as in the democratic group. Aggression (including

both 'hostility' and 'joking hostility') was eight times as frequent. Much of this aggression was directed toward two successive scape-goats within the group; none of it was directed toward the autocrat.

5. In the second experiment, one of the five autocracies showed the same aggressive reaction as was found in the first experiment. In the other four autocracies, the boys showed an extremely non-aggressive, 'apathetic' pattern of behavior.

6. Four types of evidence indicate that this lack of aggression was probably not caused by lack of frustration, but by the repressive influence of the autocrat: (a) outbursts of aggression on the days of transition to a freer atmosphere; (b) a sharp rise of aggression when the autocrat left the room; (c) other indications of generalized apathy, such as an absence of smiling and joking; and (d) the fact that nineteen out of twenty boys liked their democratic leader better than their autocratic leader, and seven out of ten also liked their *laissez-faire* leader better.

7. There were two wars, more or less playful, and without bodily damage, between clubs meeting in the same room at the same time. The first of these began gradually, the second suddenly. Three factors, present in both cases, seemed conducive to group conflict: (a) irritation and tension produced by a hostile stranger, (b) absence of a respected adult, and (c) lack of any absorbing alternative activity.

8. There were two striking instances of aggression against impersonal objects.

9. A general interpretation of the above data on aggression can be made in terms of four underlying factors: tension, restricted space of free movement, rigidity of group structure, and style of living (culture).

References

LEWIN, K. (1935), *A Dynamic Theory of Personality: Selected papers*, translated by D. K. Adams and K. E. Zener, McGraw-Hill.

LEWIN, K. (1938), 'The conceptual representation and the measurement of psychological forces', *The Duke University Contribution to Psychology*, vol. 1, no. 4, p. 247.

LEWIN, K. (1939a), 'Experiments in social space', *Harvard Educational Review*, vol. 9, no. 1.

LEWIN, K. (1939b), 'Field theory and experiment in social phychology; concepts and methods', *American Journal of Sociology*, vol. 44, no. 6.

LEWIN, K., and LIPPITT, R. (1938), 'An experimental approach to the study of autocracy and democracy: A preliminary note', *Sociometry*, vol. 1, pp. 292–300.

LIPPITT, R. (1939a), 'Field theory and experiment in social psychology: autocratic and democratic group atmosphere', *American Journal of Sociology*, vol. 45, no. 1.

LIPPITT, R. (1939b), 'An experimental study of authoritarian and democratic group atmospheres', *University of Iowa Studies: Studies in Child Welfare*, vol. 16, no. 3.

MEAD, M. (ed.) (1937), *Cooperation and Competition among Primitive Peoples*, Macmillan.

MORENO, J. L. (1934), *Who Shall Survive? A new approach to the problem of human interrelations*, Nervous and Mental Disease Monograph Series No. 58, Nervous and Mental Disease Publishing Co.

14 C. Argyris

The Impact of the Formal Organization upon the Individual

From C. Argyris, *Understanding Organizational Behavior*, Tavistock, 1960, pp. 7–24.

One may summarize our position as follows. Theoretical explanations may be classified as genetic or dynamic. Genetic explanations are those which attempt to explain how an organism becomes what it is. Dynamic explanations focus on how the organism behaves at the present time (Janis, 1959). Our strategy is to begin by developing a genetic model which, once completed will also provide dynamic explanations.

If we accept this strategy then the first step is to select a small number of variables with which to begin weaving the genetic theory. Formal organizations and human beings (both conceived as dynamic, goal-directed unities) may be chosen to be two basic variables. The next step is clear. What is known about the properties of each of these two unities? From this knowledge we should be able to predict the resultants when these two variables are 'fused'.[1] In this manner, we may be able (1) to enumerate the relevant variables, (2) to reconstruct the mechanisms by which they are created, and (3) to show how the parts are related to one another to create the whole.

A first approximation

The writer has already attempted such a step. The results are reported in detail elsewhere. What follows *is only an outline*. By beginning with the research literature on the nature of personality and formal organization, he was able to evolve the beginnings of a theoretical framework which defines some of the relevant variables and their interrelationships (i.e., the processes by which they influence one another).

[1]. At this point the approach is similar to that which E. W. Bakke (1953) discusses as the 'fusion process'.

In order to provide the reader with an acquaintance of the framework, some of the basic propositions are outlined below. It must be emphasized again that what follows is a *summary outline* and much has been omitted in order to conserve space.[2]

The development of the individual in our culture

The development of the human personality can be hypothesized to follow the directions and dimensions outlined in the following model.

It is hypothesized that human beings in our culture:

1. Tend to develop from a state of passivity as infants to a state of increasing activity as adults. (This is what Erikson[3] has called self-initiative and Bronfenbrenner (1951) has called self-determination.)

2. Tend to develop from a state of dependence upon others as infants to a state of relative independence as adults. Relative independence is the ability to 'stand on one's own two feet' and simultaneously to acknowledge healthy dependencies.[4] It is characterized by the liberation of the individual from his childhood determiners of behavior (e.g., family) and developing his own set of behavioral determiners. This individual does not tend to react to others (e.g., the boss) in terms of patterns learned during childhood. (White, 1952, p. 339.)

3. Tend to develop from being capable of behaving only in a few ways as an infant to being capable of behaving in many different ways as an adult.[5]

4. Tend to develop from having erratic, casual, shallow, quickly dropped interests as an infant to having deeper interests as an adult. The mature state is characterized by an endless series of challenges, where the reward comes from doing something for its

2. The interested reader is referred to Argyris (1957).

3. Erikson (1950). See also Witner and Kotinsky (1952).

4. This is similar to Erikson's 'sense of autonomy' and Bronfenbrenner's 'state of creative interdependence'.

5. Lewin and Kounin believe that, as the individual develops needs and abilities, the boundaries between them become more rigid. This explains why an adult is better able than a child to be frustrated in one activity and behave constructively in another. See Lewin (1935), and Kounin (1943).

own sake. The tendency is to analyze and study phenomena in their full-blown wholeness, complexity and depth (White, 1952, p. 347).

5. Tend to develop from having a short time perspective (i.e., the present largely determines behavior) as an infant to a much longer time perspective as an adult (i.e., where the behavior is more affected by the past and the future)[6]. Bakke (1940) cogently describes the importance of time perspective in the lives of workers and their families and the variety of foresight practices by means of which they seek to secure the future.

6. Tend to develop from being in a subordinate position in the family and society as an infant to aspiring to occupy an equal and/or superordinate position relative to their peers.

7. Tend to develop from a lack of awareness of self as an infant to an awareness of and control over self as an adult. The adult who tends to experience adequate and successful control over his own behavior tends to develop a sense of integrity (Erikson, 1950) and feelings of self-work (Rogers, 1952). Bakke (1940, pp. 29 and 247) shows that one of the most important needs of workers is to enlarge those areas of their lives in which their own decisions determine the outcome of their efforts.

A word about the concept of growth. Growth is not a black or white, mature or immature phenomenon. Rather it is a matter of degree. Thus each dimension is conceptualized to be a continuum upon which the development of any given human being can be plotted at a given time. In real life, the exact location of any given individual along the continua will differ and may also differ with the same individual at different times. We do not assume that all individuals need to be or are at the right ends of the continua. We are presenting this as simply a model by which we can plot the individual differences of individual's growth pattern.

Keeping these qualifications in mind, we define *one* characteristic of a mature individual in *our* culture, as an individual who is predisposed toward the right ends (mature ends) of the continua *and* who while striving toward growth behaves in such a way so that he *simultaneously permits others to do the same*. It is important to emphasize that our definition does not assume that a mature

6. Lewin (1948) also cites the billions of dollars that are invested in insurance policies.

individual is a self-centered individual who is interested only in his own growth. Basic to our model is the assumption that all human beings are incomplete by themselves. They gain their wholeness through interaction with others. There is nothing new or startling about this position. We are simply following the ideas of men like Sullivan, Lewin, Fromm, McDougal, May, Rogers, Maslow, Rank, Horney, etc., that man is fundamentally an interpersonal organism. Self-actualization in the eyes of these scientists cannot occur in isolation. It can only occur in relationship with others. A mature individual therefore never assumes that he will be maximally independent, have complete control, and be completely active without inhibiting others' growth. To put it another way, one characteristic of a mature individual is hypothesized to be an individual who can give 'of' himself without giving 'up' himself; an individual who sees himself as constantly being 'in relationship' with his fellow man. 'Self-actualization', as used here, does not mean 'happiness', if by 'happiness' we mean a relatively tension-less state where 'everything is going my way'. Tension *per se* may be quite healthy and provide motivation for growth.[7]

Organization is a strategy

Next we turn to the organization and begin by hypothesizing that organizations are intricate human strategies designed to achieve certain objectives. What are the organization's objectives? The objectives are postulated to be achieving its goals (intended consequences), maintaining itself internally and adapting to its external environment.

Who chooses the strategy that the organization will follow? In order to answer the question properly, the time dimension must be considered. *At the outset*, those who sign the legal charter to create the organization have much to say as to how it shall be organized. They plan an organizational structure which they assume represents the best strategy for the organization. Because of historical reasons too complex to discuss here, the basic characteristics of the structure are usually defined by generalizations from economics, scientific management, public administration

7. Allport (1953), Barker, Dembo and Lewin (1941) found that a mild frustration could increase children's degree of constructiveness of play.

and traditional formal organization theory. This strategy is crystalized, 'photographed' and represented as a typical organizational chart.

Let us look more closely at the nature of the phenomena depicted by the organizational chart.

The intended rationality of formal organization

The first requirement (or the first characteristic of the strategy) is for the organization to be rational and to make rational demands upon the employees. Thus the initial or formal structure represents the intended rational strategy of the organization. Urwick (1953), one of the pioneers in formal organizational theory, describes the property of intended rationality eloquently. He insists that the creation of a formal organization requires a logical 'drawing-office' approach. Although he admits that 'nine times out of ten it is impossible to start with a clean sheet', the organizer should sit down and in a 'cold-blooded, detached spirit . . . draw an ideal structure'.

The task of the organizer, therefore, is to create a logically ordered world where Fayol suggests there is a 'proper order' and in which there is a 'place for everything (everyone)' (Koontz and O'Donnell, 1955).

The possibility that the formal organization can be altered by personalities, as found by McGregor and Arensberg (1942) and Stodgill and Koehler (1952), is not denied by formal organizational experts. Urwick, for example, states that the planner must take into account the human element. But not that he perceives these adjustments as 'temporary deviations from the pattern in order to deal with idiosyncrasy of personality'. If possible, these deviations should be minimized by careful prior planning.

Some basic principles of formal organization[8]

Along with the emphasis upon rationality is the specialization of tasks, the emphasis upon power, conformity to and loyalty for company objectives. These emphases are embodied in four principles (more accurately assumptions) of scientific management theories.

8. Some illustrative names are Urwick, Mooney, Holden *et al*, Fayol, Dennison, Brown, Gulick, White, Gauss, Steve Hopf and Taylor. For a more detailed discussion see Argyris (1957), chapter iii.

Briefly these principles may be stated as follows:

1. *Task (work) specialization.* If concentrating effort on a limited field of endeavor increases the quality and quantity of output, organizational and administrative efficiency is increased by specialization of tasks assigned to the participants of the organization.

2. *Chain of command.* The principle of task specialization creates a plurality of parts, each performing a highly specialized task. However, a plurality of parts busily performing their particular objective does not form an organization. A pattern of parts must be formed so that the interrelationships among the parts create the organization. Following the logic of specialization the planners create a new function (leadership) whose primary responsibility shall be the control, direction and coordination of the interrelationships of the parts and to make certain that each part performs its objectives adequately. Thus the assumption is made that administrative and organizational efficiency is increased by arranging the parts in a determinate hierarchy of authority where the part on top can direct and control the part on the bottom.

If the parts being considered are individuals, then they must be motivated to accept direction, control and coordination of their behavior. The leader is therefore assigned formal power to hire, discharge, reward and penalize the individuals in order that their behavior be molded toward the organization's objectives.

3. *Unity of direction.* If the tasks of every person in a unit are specialized, the objective or purpose of the unit must be specialized. The principle of unity of direction states that administrative and organizational efficiency increases if each unity has a single activity (or homogeneous set of activities) that is planned and directed by the leader.

4. *Span of control.* The principle of control states that administration efficiency is increased by limiting the span of control of a leader to no more than five or six subordinates whose work interlocks.

The impact of the formal organization upon the individual[9]

What is the impact of the formal organization upon the individual? Clearly, the answer is that it depends upon the individual, the

9. For a detailed discussion of these principles plus their impact upon the individuals see Argyris (1957), chapter iii.

organization and the context in which these are studied. Thus, as in our discussion of the human personality, we cannot state *a priori* what will happen in an individual case.

However, some position must be taken if generalizations are to be evolved. We must state the generalizations in such a way that when it comes time to use them in a particular organization, the uniqueness of the particular case will not be violated.

In developing our generalizations, therefore, we must assume a certain individual and a certain organization. *For the sake of illustration only* we will take as our example the case of a relatively mature individual and a formal organization that maximizes the principles of scientific management (e.g., an organization with an assembly line). We select this case in order to make our point clearly and unambiguously and *not* because we want to imply that formal organizations are bad. On the contrary. In the example we have chosen we assume that the individual *and* the formal organization have a right to optimize their own expression.

The impact of the principles above is to place employees in work situations where (1) they are provided minimal control over their workaday world, (2) they are expected to be passive, dependent and subordinate, (3) they are expected to have the frequent use of a few skin-surface shallow abilities, and (5) they are expected to produce under conditions leading to psychological failure.

All these characteristics are incongruent to the ones that relatively mature human beings in our culture are postulated to desire. They are much more congruent with the needs of infants in our culture. In effect, therefore, organizations adapt an initial strategy where they are willing to pay wages and provide adequate seniority if mature adults will, for eight hours a day, behave in a less than mature manner.

Stating the findings up to this point about the nature of organization in terms of propositions they are:

Proposition 1: There is a lack of congruency between the needs of healthy individuals and the demands of the (initial) formal organization. If one uses the traditional formal principles of organization (i.e., traditional chain of command, task specialization, etc.) to create a social organization, and if one uses as input, agents who tend toward a mature state of psychological development (i.e., they are predisposed toward relative independence, activeness, use of their important abilities, control over their immediate work world) then a disturbance is created because the needs of healthy individuals listed above are not congruent with the requirements of formal organization, which tends to require the agents to work in situations where they are dependent, passive, use few and unimportant abilities, etc.

Corollary 1. The disturbance will vary in proportion to the degree of incongruency between the needs of the individuals and the requirements of the formal organization. An administrator is, therefore, always faced with an inherent tendency toward continual disturbance. Drawing on the existing knowledge of the human personality, a second proposition can be stated.

Proposition 2: The resultants of this disturbance are frustration, failure, short time perspective and conflict. If the participants in the organization desire a healthy, more mature self-actualization:

1. They will tend to experience frustration because their self-expression will be blocked.

2. They will tend to experience failure because they will not be permitted to define their own goals in relation to central needs, the paths to these goals, etc.

3. They will tend to experience short time perspective because they have no control over the clarity and stability of their future.

4. They will tend to experience conflict because, as healthy agents, they will dislike frustration, failure and short time perspective which is characteristic of the present job. However, if they leave they may not find a new job easily, and/or even if a new job is found, it may not be different.

Based upon the analysis of the nature of formal organization, one may state a third proposition.

Proposition 3: Under certain conditions the degree of frustration, failure, short time perspective and conflict will tend to increase. The resultants of the disturbance in the organization will tend to increase in degree:

1. As the individual agents increase in degree of maturity and/or

2. As the degree of dependence, subordination, passivity, etc., increases, this tends to occur:

(a) As one goes down the chain of command
(b) As directive leadership increases
(c) As management controls are increased
(d) As human relations programs are undertaken but improperly implemented and/or

3. As the jobs become more specialized, and/or

4. As the exactness with which the traditional formal principles are used increases.

Proposition 4: The nature of the formal principles of organization cause the subordinates, at any given level, to experience competition, rivalry, intersubordinate hostility and to develop a focus toward the parts rather than the whole.

1. Because of the degree of dependence, subordination, etc., of the subordinates, upon the leader, and because the number of positions above any given level always tend to decrease, the subordinates aspiring to perform effectively[10] and to advance will tend to find themselves in competition with, and receiving hostility from each other.

2. Because according to the formal principles, the subordinates are directed toward and rewarded for, performing their own task well, the subordinates tend to develop an orientation toward their own particular part rather than toward the whole.

3. This part-orientation increases the need for the leader to co-ordinate the activity among the parts in order to maintain the whole. This need for the leader, in turn, increases the subordinates' degree of dependence, subordination, which creates a circular process whose impact is to maintain and/or increase the degree of dependence, subordination, etc., plus the rivalry and competition for the leader's favor.

Proposition 5: Employees react to the formal organization by creating informal activities. Continuing from Proposition 2, it can be shown that under conflict, frustration, failure and short time

10. These problems may not arise for the subordinate who decides to become apathetic, disinterested, etc.

perspective, the employees will tend to maintain self-integration by creating specific adaptive (informal) behavior such as:[11]

1. Leaving the organization.

2. Climbing the organizational ladder.

3. Manifesting defense reactions such as daydreaming, aggression, ambivalence, regression, projection, etc.

4. Becoming apathetic and disinterested toward the organization, its make-up and goals. This leads to such phenomena as:
(a) Employees reduce the number and potency of the needs they expect to fulfill while at work.
(b) Employees goldbrick, set rates, restrict quotas, make errors, cheat, slow down, etc.

5. Creating informal groups to sanction the defense reactions and apathy, disinterest and the lack of self-involvement.

6. Formalizing the informal groups.

7. Evolving group norms that perpetuate the behavior outlined in 3, 4, 5 and 6 above.

8. Evolving a psychological set that human or nonmaterial factors are becoming increasingly unimportant while material factors become increasingly important.

9. Acculturating the youth to accept the norms discussed in 7 and 8. Comparing the informal organization, we may state:
Proposition 6: The employee adaptive behavior maintains individual self-integration and simultaneously facilitates integration with the formal organization.
Proposition 7: The adaptive behavior of the employees has a cumulative effect, feeds back into the formal organization, and reinforces itself.

1. All these adaptive reactions reinforce each other so that they not only have their individual impact on the system, but they also have a cumulative impact. Their total impact is to increase the degree of dependence, submissiveness, etc., and increase the resulting turnover, apathy, disinterest, etc. Thus a feedback process exists where the adaptive mechanisms become self-maintaining.

11. Adaptive activities numbered one to nine become major categories under which much empirical research can be included.

2. The continual existence of these adaptive mechanisms tend to make these norms or codes which, in turn, act to maintain the adaptive behavior and to make it the proper behavior for the system.

3. If the above is valid, then employees who may desire to behave differently from the norms will tend to feel deviant, different, not part of the work community (e.g. rate busters).

The individual and cumulative impact of the defense mechanisms is to influence the output-input ratio in such a way that a greater input (energy, money, machines) will be required to maintain a constant output.

Proposition 8: Certain management reactions tend to increase the antagonisms underlying the adaptive behavior. Those managements that base their judgment on the logics of the formal organization will tend to dislike the employee adaptive behavior. It follows, therefore, for these managements that they should tend to take those 'corrective' actions that are congruent with the logics of formal organization. These actions tend to be: 1. increasing the degree of directive leadership; 2. increasing the degree of management controls; 3. increasing the number of pseudohuman relations programs.

The first two modes of reaction tend to compound, reinforce and help to maintain the basic disturbance outlined in Proposition 1. It follows, therefore, that the behavior included in Propositions 4, 6 and 7 will also be reinforced. (This is the behavior management desires to change in the first place.) The third mode of reaction tends to increase the distance and mistrust between employee and management because it does not jibe with the realities of the system within which the employees work.

One must conclude that the management behavior described in Proposition 8 primarily acts to influence the output–input ratio so that a much greater input is required to obtain the same constant output, or that a disproportionately higher input will be necessary for a given increment of increased output.

A clarifying comment about the propositions

A word about the propositions outlined above. It is possible for a physical scientist to make such predictions as, if one passes electricity through wire, heat will result. However, he cannot predict *a priori how much* heat will result. The amount of heat can be predicted only by ascertaining the values of such variables as the length and type of wire, the capacity of the battery, the milieu in which the experiment is conducted, etc.

The propositions presented above are on a similar level of generalization. They make such predictions as the dependence, submissiveness, etc., that people will experience will tend to be caused by the formal organization, directive leadership, and managerial controls (to list three major variables). They predict that the dependence and submissiveness will frustrate the people and place them in conflict *if* the people aspire toward the mature ends of the continua listed above. They predict further that the people will tend to react by creating informal activities (e.g., apathy, indifference, goldbricking, rate-setting, etc.). Nothing is said however about *how much* dependence, submissiveness; *how much* conflict, frustration; *how much* apathy, indifference, etc. This is a matter of empirical research. The value of the theoretical propositions is that they guide the researcher in his choice of relevant variables and the probable relationships among these variables.

For example, one can predict that the conflict, frustration, etc., will tend to be high when the formal organizational structure, the directive leadership, and the controls require (1) 'maturity-directed' people to be directed toward infancy[12] and (2) 'infancy directed' people to be directed toward maturity. One can predict, therefore, that absenteeism, turnover, apathy, etc., will be as high when 'mature' people are frustrated by being required to be immature as when 'immature' people are frustrated by being required to be mature. Furthermore, one can predict that the conflict, frustration, etc. will tend to be minimal when (3) 'infancy-directed' employees are required to behave immaturely and (4) 'maturity-directed' employees are required to behave maturely.[13]

12. The 'amount' of conflict, frustration, etc. must be empirically ascertained by measuring the 'maturity-directiveness' of the employees and the degree to which the organization requires that they be 'infancy-directed'.

13. Case (a) was chosen to be illustrated in *Personality and Organization* because most of the research literature that the writer is aware of supports the view. This does *not* imply that *all* organizations can be so categorized.

It is therefore readily admitted that an organization may provide the institutional arrangements whereby individuals may express their needs no matter how mature or immature they may be. Organizations may be quite 'functional' for individuals with varying degrees of maturity and vice versa.[14] The theoretical framework predicts that as the degree of congruency increases between the individual's needs and the organizational demands, the need for the informal activities will tend to decrease and as the degree of congruency decreases the need for the informal activities will tend to increase.

However, nothing is stated *a priori* about the *amount* of dependence, submissiveness, etc., an individual will tend to experience in a specific case. This is a matter for empirical research. The only *a priori* prediction is that the amount of dependence, etc. will tend to increase as one goes 'down the line' of a formal organization as the organization takes on the characteristics of mass production, and as managerial controls are used to control the participant's behavior.

One might find, for example, that the directive leadership, in a given organization, causes more dependence, etc. than do the formal organizational structure or the controls. In another organization, the controls may be the major cause of dependence. In short, in the actual world many different combinations are possible. The theoretical framework, therefore, hypothesizes that the *direction* of impact of the formal organizational structure, the directive leadership, and the managerial controls are the same. The hypothesis is that *if* the formal structure is defined according to such principles as unity of command, task specialization, etc., and *if* the leadership is directive, and *if* the controls are defined as they are in scientific management, then employees will tend to experience dependence, submissiveness, etc.[15]

Organizations will differ and the same organization may differ at different periods of time. In *Personality and Organization* I cite job enlargement, role enlargement as two activities that inveigh against the trend predicted above.

14. The role concept may be a useful one to study this particular problem. For a systematic discussion, see Levinson (1959).

15. May I again remind the readers (especially the practitioner) that the model purports to understand all organizations who use (at the outset) a pyramidal structure and people. Thus churches, families, schools, and scout troops (to use a few examples) coerce dependency, etc. long before people become employees of industrial organizations.

There are two other related problems raised by the framework that require explanation. One of the basic assumptions of the approach is that the individual and the organization are not separable. They interact, fuse with (Bakke, 1953), or interpenetrate (Parsons, 1958), one another. The personality is highly influenced by the organization and vice versa. Thus no assumption is made that one is necessarily more important than the other. Nor do we assume as Dubin (1959) implies that the motivation of the participant in the organization resides 'in' the participant. From our viewpoint it is simply impossible to say that the motivation resides 'in' the individual or 'in' the organization. Our viewpoint suggests the motivation of the participant is best understood as a resultant of the *transactions* between the individual and the organization.[16] It is therefore equally inaccurate to assume that the motivation of the individual lies 'within' the individual or as Dubin (1959) suggests 'within' the organization.

It may be possible that for certain problems and under certain conditions one of these variables may have greater potency than the other. If such problems and conditions exist (and we believe they do), then they are to be discovered through empirical research. Our hypothesis is that they will vary with different organizational studies.

The second point is related to the failure of some to understand the interactional nature of the framework. There are some who imply that the approach assumes that employees must be 'happy' (whatever that means). Happiness should be the objective of management practice. Nothing could be further from the position of the writer. First, the writer is not attempting to tell any administrator what his objectives ought to be. The writer's aim is to try to understand the causes of human problems within organizations. True, he has chosen a theoretical framework that has as one of its basic concepts the development of the individual in our culture. But, *this concept was chosen because with it and the concept of formal organization the writer was able to integrate much of the behavioral science research within organizations of which he was aware.*

The fact that the concept of self-actualization turns out to be important is *not* because the writer wishes to require administrators to emphasize it. The concept is crucial *because it helps to*

16. For an excellent discussion, see Levinson (1959).

create a scheme that integrates much of the existing research. It is true, however, that if the administrator decides to use this scheme then self-actualization would be a crucial variable. However, it also follows from the discussion of the interaction of the individual and the organization above that organizational actualization is equally important. *Each needs the other.* The exact degree of this need varies with the problem and the situation.

Perhaps some examples may be helpful to suggest in what type of cases self-actualization may be crucial for organizational survival. Let us postulate that human beings manifest psychological (as well as physiological) energy of one form or another. This is a postulate many personality theorists accept because energy concepts are the pillars of most personality theories.[17] Psychological energy may be postulated to vary with the state of mind, to be indestructible, and to be unblockable (Ruesch and Bateson, 1952). If these properties of psychological energy are valid, then the administrator may not ignore individual self-actualization. If the individual's actualization is low, then the amount of psychological energy that he has available to produce will be less than if his self-actualization is higher. Another example may be related to tension. If we may hypothesize that coping with tension (the source of which an individual reports is beyond his control) requires much energy in the form of maintaining defenses, then it follows that uncontrolled tension can draw upon the energy that an individual will tend to have available to be productive.

Turning to another example, if the vast field of perceptual psychological research is valid, we may hypothesize that what a person 'sees' or is able to consider in his awareness is partially a function of his needs (Asch, Bruener, Postman, etc.). This means that decision making can be critically affected by the self-actualization of an individual (Holt and Salveson, 1959). If the individual's 'needs' at work are related to defense mechanisms, then he may tend to narrow his range of tolerance to new ideas so that threatening ideas will not arise. Still another example may be found in the work of Schutz (1958) and others. They show evidence that the individual personality plays an important role in the effective functioning of groups. These results have important implications

17. George Kelly (Kelly, 1955) provides a most interesting discussion of the difficulties of the motivational or 'energy' approach.

in terms of the impact of self-actualization on such activities as decision making, planning, etc.[18] In still another crucial area of interest for the administrator, Gardner Murphy points out in his classic and sweeping analysis of human potentialities, the individual's degree of creativity and productivity (intellectual and emotional) is highly influenced by his self-actualization.[19]

Summary

Let us summarize the main ideas of the discussions up to this point.

1. Organizations are grand strategies individuals create to achieve objectives that require the effort of many. For historical reasons, most social organizations follow a particular initial or formal strategy whose roots may be found in military theory, industrial economics, scientific management and public administration.

2. The strategy derived from these roots leads to a pyramid-shaped, formal organization defined by such principles as chain of command, unity of direction, span of control, and task specialization. If this formal strategy works as it is intended, then the analysis could end here. Unfortunately, the formal organizational strategy hits some snags – the primary one being the individual human being.

3. Mutual adaptations take place where the organization modifies the individual's personality and the individual, through the informal activities, modifies the formal organization. These modifications become part of the organization.

4. A total organization therefore is more than the formal organization. Conceptualizing it as a behavioral system we may conclude that an organization is a composite of four different but interrelated subsystems resulting in the following kinds of behavior:

(a) The behavior that results from the formal organizational demands.

(b) The behavior that results from the demands of the informal activities.

18. Some interesting studies which make explicit the importance of self-actualization are reported by Flanagan (1959).

19. Murphy (1958), see especially parts iii and iv.

(c) The behavior that results from each individual's attempt to fulfill his idiosyncratic needs.

(d) The behavior that is a resultant of the unique patterning for each organization of the three levels above.

References

ALLPORT, G. W. (1953), 'The trend in motivational theory', *American Journal of Orthopsychiatry*, vol. 23, no. 1, pp. 107–19.

ARGYRIS, C. (1957), *Personality and Organisation*, Harper & Row.

ARENSBERG, C. M., and MCGREGOR, D. (1942), 'Determination of morale in an industrial company', *Applied Anthropology*, vol. 1, chapter 2, January–March, pp. 12–34.

BAKKE, E. W. (1940), *The Unemployed Worker*, Yale University Press.

BAKKE, E. W. (1953), *The Fusion Process*, Yale University Press.

BARKER, R., DEMBO, T., and LEWIN, K. (1941), *Frustration and Regression*, University of Iowa Studies in Child Welfare.

BRONFENBRENNER, U. (1951), 'Toward an integrated theory of personality', in Blake, R. R., and Ramsey, G. B. (eds.), *Perception*, Ronald, pp. 206–57.

DUBIN, R. (1959), 'Industrial research and the discipline of sociology', *Proceedings*, Industrial Relations Research Association, 11th Annual Meeting.

ERIKSON, E. H. (1950), *Childhood and Society*, Norton.

FLANAGAN, J. C. (1959), 'Leadership skills: Their identification, development and evaluation', Paper presented at the ONR–LSU Symposium on Leadership and Interpersonal Behavior, 3–5 March.

HOLT, H., and SALVESON, M. E. (1959), 'A psychoanalytic study of management', Mgt. Report, no. 10, Center for Advanced Management.

JANIS, I. L., and HOVLAND, C. I. (eds.) (1959), *Personality and Persuasibility*, Yale University Press, p. 22.

KELLY, G. (1955), *The Psychology of Personal Constructs*, vol. 1, Norton.

KOONTZ, H., and O'DONNELL, C. (1955), *Principles of Management*, McGraw-Hill, p. 24.

KOUNIN, J. S. (1943), 'Intellectual Development and Rigidity', in Barker, R., Kounin, J., and Wright, H. R. (eds.), *Child Behavior and Development*, McGraw-Hill, pp. 179–98.

LEVINSON, D. J. (1959), 'Role, Personality and Social Structure in the Organizational Setting', *Journal of Abnormal and Social Psychology*, vol. 63, March, pp. 170–80.

LEWIN, K. (1935), *A Dynamic Theory of Personality*, McGraw-Hill.

LEWIN, K. (1948), 'Time perspective and morale', in Lewin, K. (ed.), *Resolving Social Conflicts*, Harper & Row, p. 105.

MURPHY, G. (1958), *Human Potentialities*, Basic Books.

PARSONS, T. (58),19 'Social structure and the development of personality trends: Construction to the integration of psychology and sociology', *Psychiatry*, vol. 21, no. 4, November, pp. 321–40.

ROGERS, C. R. (1952), *Client-Centered Therapy*, Houghton Mifflin.

RUESCH, J., and BATESON, G. (1952), *Communication: The Social Matrix of Psychiatry*, Norton.

SCHUTZ, W. C. (1958), *A Theory of Interpersonal Relations*, Holt, Rinehart & Winston.

STODGILL, R. M., and KOEHLER, K. (1952), *Measures of Leadership Structure and Organization Change*, Personal Research Board, Ohio State.

URWICK, L. (1953), *The Elements of Administration*, Harper & Row.

WHITE, R. W. (1952), *Lives in Progress*, Dryden.

WITMER, H. L., and KOTINSKY, R. (1952), *Personality in the Making*, Harper & Row, pp. 8–25.

15 R. Likert

The Principle of Supportive Relationships

R. Likert, 'An integrating principle and an overview', *New Patterns of Management*, McGraw-Hill, 1961, chapter 8, pp. 97–118.

The managers whose performance is impressive appear to be fashioning a better system of management. At the end of Chapter 4 two generalizations were stated based on the available research findings:

1. The supervisors and managers in American industry and government who are achieving the highest productivity, lowest costs, least turnover and absence, and the highest levels of employee motivation and satisfaction display, on the average, a different pattern of leadership from those managers who are achieving less impressive results. The principles and practices of these high-producing managers are deviating in important ways from those called for by present-day management theories.

2. The high-producing managers whose deviations from existing theory and practice are creating improved procedures have not yet integrated their deviant principles into a theory of management. Individually, they are often clearly aware of how a particular practice of theirs differs from generally accepted methods, but the magnitude, importance, and systematic nature of the differences when the total pattern is examined do not appear to be recognized.

Based upon the principles and practices of the managers who are achieving the best results, a newer theory of organization and management can be stated. An attempt will be made in this chapter to present briefly some of the overall characteristics of such a theory and to formulate a general integrating principle which can be useful in attempts to apply it.

There is no doubt that further research and experimental testing of the theory in pilot operations will yield evidence pointing to modifications of many aspects of the newer theory suggested in this volume. Consequently, in reading this and subsequent chapters it will be well not to quarrel with the specific aspects of the newer theory as presented. These specifics are intended as stimulants for discussion and as encouragement for experimental field tests of the theory. It will be more profitable to seek to understand the newer theory's general basic character and, whenever a specific aspect or derivation appears to be in error, to formulate more valid derivations and propositions.

Research findings indicate that the general pattern of operations of the highest-producing managers tends to differ from that of the managers of mediocre and low-producing units by more often showing the following characteristics:

1. A preponderance of favorable attitudes on the part of each member of the organization toward all the other members, toward superiors, toward the work, toward the organization – toward all aspects of the job. These favorable attitudes toward others reflect a high level of mutual confidence and trust throughout the organization. The favorable attitudes toward the organization and the work are not those of easy complacency, but are the attitudes of identification with the organization and its objectives and a high sense of involvement in achieving them. As a consequence, the performance goals are high and dissatisfaction may occur whenever achievement falls short of the goals set.

2. This highly motivated, cooperative orientation toward the organization and its objectives is achieved by harnessing effectively all the major motivational forces which can exercise significant influence in an organizational setting and which, potentially, can be accompanied by cooperative and favorable attitudes. Reliance is not placed solely or fundamentally on the economic motive of buying a man's time and using control and authority as the organizing and coordinating principle of the organization. On the contrary, the following motives are all used fully and in such a way that they function in a cumulative and reinforcing manner and yield favorable attitudes:

(a) The ego motives. These are referred to throughout this volume as the desire to achieve and maintain a sense of personal worth and importance. This desire manifests itself in many forms, depending upon the norms and values of the persons and groups involved. Thus, it is responsible for such motivational forces as the desire for growth and significant achievement in terms of one's own values and goals, i.e., self-fulfillment, as well as the desire for status, recognition, approval, acceptance and power and the desire to undertake significant and important tasks.

(b) The security motives.
(c) Curiosity, creativity, and the desire for new experiences.
(d) The economic motives.

By tapping all the motives which yield favorable and co-operative attitudes, maximum motivation oriented toward realizing the organization's goals as well as the needs of each member of the organization is achieved. The substantial decrements in motivational forces which occur when powerful motives are pulling in opposite directions are thereby avoided. These conflicting forces exist, of course, when hostile and resentful attitudes are present.

3. The organization consists of a tightly knit, effectively functioning social system. This social system is made up of interlocking work groups with a high degree of group loyalty among the members and favorable attitudes and trust between superiors and subordinates. Sensitivity to others and relatively high levels of skill in personal interaction and the functioning of groups are also present. These skills permit effective participation in decisions on common problems. Participation is used, for example, to establish organizational objectives which are a satisfactory integration of the needs and desires of all members of the organization and of persons functionally related to it. High levels of reciprocal influence occur, and high levels of total coordinated influence are achieved in the organization. Communication is efficient and effective. There is a flow from one part of the organization to another of all the relevant information important for each decision and action. The leadership in the organization has developed what might well be called a highly effective social system for interaction and mutual influence.

4. Measurements of organizational performance are used primarily for self-guidance rather than for superimposed control. To tap the motives which bring cooperative and favorable rather than hostile

attitudes, participation and involvement in decisions is a habitual part of the leadership processes. This kind of decision-making, of course, calls for the full sharing of available measurements and information. Moreover, as it becomes evident in the decision-making process that additional information or measurements are needed, steps are taken to obtain them.

In achieving operations which are more often characterized by the above pattern of highly cooperative, well-coordinated activity, the highest-producing managers use all the technical resources of the classical theories of management, such as time-and-motion study, budgeting and financial controls. They use these resources at least as completely as do the low-producing managers, but in quite different ways. This difference in use arises from the differences in the motives which the high-producing, in contrast to the low-producing, managers believe are important in influencing human behavior.

The low-producing managers, in keeping with traditional practice, feel that the way to motivate and direct behavior is to exercise control through authority. Jobs are organized, methods are prescribed, standards are set, performance goals and budgets are established. Compliance with them is sought through the use of hierarchical and economic pressures.

The highest-producing managers feel, generally, that this manner of functioning does not produce the best results, that the resentment created by direct exercise of authority tends to limit its effectiveness. They have learned that better results can be achieved when a different motivational process is employed. As suggested above, they strive to use all those major motives which have the potentiality of yielding favorable and cooperative attitudes in such a way that favorable attitudes are, in fact, elicited and the motivational forces are mutually reinforcing. Motivational forces stemming from the economic motive are not then blunted by such other motivations as group goals which restrict the quantity or quality of output. The full strength of all economic, ego and other motives is generated and put to use.

Widespread use of participation is one of the more important approaches employed by the high-producing managers in their efforts to get full benefit from the technical resources of the classical theories of management coupled with high levels of reinforcing motivation. This use of participation applies to all aspects of the job and work, as, for example, in setting work goals and budgets, controlling costs, organizing the work, etc.

In these and comparable ways, the high-producing managers make full use of the technical resources of the classical theories of management. They use these resources in such a manner, however, that favorable and cooperative attitudes are created and all members of the organization endeavor to pull concertedly toward commonly accepted goals which they have helped to establish.

This brief description of the pattern of management which is more often characteristic of the high-producing than of the low-producing managers points to what appears to be a critical difference. The high-producing managers have developed their organizations into highly coordinated, highly motivated, cooperative social systems. Under their leadership, the different motivational forces in each member of the organization have coalesced into a strong force aimed at accomplishing the mutually established objectives of the organization. This general pattern of highly motivated, cooperative members seems to be a central characteristic of the newer management system being developed by the highest-producing managers.

How do these high-producing managers build organizations which display this central characteristic? Is there any general approach or underlying principle which they rely upon in building highly motivated organizations? There seems to be, and clues as to the nature of the principle can be obtained by re-examining some of the materials in Chapters 2 to 4. The research findings show, for example, that those supervisors and managers whose pattern of leadership yields consistently favorable attitudes more often think of employees as 'human beings rather than just as persons to get the work done'. Consistently, in study after study, the data show that treating people as 'human beings' rather than as 'cogs in a machine' is a variable highly related to the attitudes and motivation of the subordinate at every level in the organization.

The superiors who have the most favorable and cooperative attitudes in their work groups display the following characteristics.

1. The attitude and behavior of the superior toward the sub-

ordinate as a person, *as perceived by the subordinate*, is as follows:

(a) He is supportive, friendly and helpful rather than hostile. He is kind but firm, never threatening, genuinely interested in the well-being of subordinates and endeavors to treat people in a sensitive, considerate way. He is just, if not generous. He endeavors to serve the best interests of his employees as well as of the company.

(b) He shows confidence in the integrity, ability and motivations of subordinates rather than suspicion and distrust.

(c) His confidence in subordinates leads him to have high expectations as to their level of performance. With confidence that he will not be disappointed, he expects much, not little. (This, again, is fundamentally a supportive rather than a critical or hostile relationship.)

(d) He sees that each subordinate is well trained for his particular job. He endeavors also to help subordinates be promoted by training them for jobs at the next level. This involves giving them relevant experience and coaching whenever the opportunity offers.

(e) He coaches and assists employees whose performance is below standard. In the case of a subordinate who is clearly misplaced and unable to do his job satisfactorily, he endeavors to find a position well suited to that employee's abilities and arranges to have the employee transferred to it.

2. The behavior of the superior in directing the work is characterized by such activity as:

(a) Planning and scheduling the work to be done, training subordinates, supplying them with material and tools, initiating work activity, etc.

(b) Providing adequate technical competence, particularly in those situations where the work has not been highly standardized.

3. The leader develops his subordinates into a working team with high group loyalty by using participation and the other kinds of group-leadership practices summarized in Chapter 3.

The integrating principle

These results and similar data from other studies (Argyris, 1957c; March and Simon, 1958; Viteles, 1953) show that subordinates react favorably to experiences which they feel are supportive and contribute to their sense of importance and personal worth. Similarly, persons react unfavorably to experiences which are threatening and decrease or minimize their sense of dignity and personal worth. These findings are supported also by substantial research on personality development (Argyris, 1957c; Rogers, 1942; Rogers, 1951) and group behavior (Cartwright and Zander, 1960). Each of us wants appreciation, recognition, influence, a feeling of accomplishment, and a feeling that people who are important to us believe in us and respect us. We want to feel that we have a place in the world.

This pattern of reaction appears to be universal and seems to be the basis for the general principle used by the high-producing managers in developing their highly motivated, cooperative organizations. These managers have discovered that the motivational forces acting in each member of an organization are most likely to be cumulative and reinforcing when the interactions between each individual and the others in the organization are of such a character that they convey to the individual a feeling of support and recognition for his importance and worth as a person. These managers, therefore, strive to have the interactions between the members of their organizations of such a character that each member of the organization feels confident in his potentialities and believes that his abilities are being well used.

A second factor, however, is also important. As we have seen in Chapter 7, an individual's reaction to any situation is always a function not of the absolute character of the interaction, but of his perception of it. It is how he sees things that counts, not objective reality. Consequently, an individual member of an organization will always interpret an interaction between himself and the organization in terms of his background and culture, his experience and expectations. The pattern of supervision and the language used that might be effective with a railroad's maintenance-of-way crew, for example, would not be suitable in an office full of young women. A subordinate tends also to expect his superior to behave in ways consistent with the personality of the superior. All this means that each of us, as a subordinate or as a peer or as a superior, reacts in terms of his own particular background, experience, and expectations. In order, therefore, to have an interaction viewed as supportive, it is essential that it be of such a character that the individual himself, in the light of his experience and expectations, sees it as supportive. This provides the basis for stating the general principle which the high-producing managers seem to be using and which will be referred to as the *principle of supportive relationships*. This principle, which provides an invaluable guide in any attempt to apply the newer theory of management in a specific plant or organization, can be briefly stated: *The leadership and other processes of the organization must be such as to ensure a maximum probability that in all interactions and all relationships with the organization each member will, in the light of his background, values and expectations, view the experience as supportive and one which builds and maintains his sense of personal worth and importance.*

The principle of supportive relationships as an organizing concept

This general principle provides a fundamental formula for obtaining the full potential of every major motive which can be constructively harnessed in a working situation. There is impressive evidence, for example, that economic motivations will be tapped more effectively when the conditions specified by the principle of supportive relationships are met (Katz and Kahn, 1951; Krulee, 1955). In addition, as motives are used in the ways called for by this general principle, the attitudes accompanying the motives will be favorable and the different motivational forces will be cumulative and reinforcing. Under these circumstances, the full power from each of the available motives will be added to that from the others to yield a maximum of coordinated, enthusiastic effort.

The principle of supportive relationships points to a dimension essential for the success of every organization, namely, that the mission of the organization be seen by its members as genuinely important. To be highly motivated, each member of the organization must feel that the organization's objectives are of significance and that his own particular task contributes in an indispensable manner to the organization's achievement of its objectives. He should see his role as difficult, important and meaningful. This is necessary if the individual is to achieve and maintain a sense of personal worth and importance. When jobs do not meet this specification they should be reorganized so that they do. This is likely to require the participation of those involved in the work in a manner suggested in subsequent chapters.

The term 'supportive' is used frequently in subsequent chapters and also is a key word in the principle of supportive relationships. Experiences, relationships, etc., are considered to be supportive when the individual involved sees the experience (in terms of his values, goals, expectations and aspirations) as contributing to or maintaining his sense of personal worth and importance.

The principle of supportive relationships contains within it an important clue to its effective use. To apply this general principle, a superior must take into consideration the experience and expectations of each of his subordinates. In determining what these expectations are, he cannot rely solely on his observations and impressions. It helps the superior to try to put himself in his subordinate's shoes and endeavor to see things as the subordinate sees them, but this is not enough. Too often, the superior's estimates are wrong. He needs direct evidence if he is to know how the subordinate views things and to estimate the kinds of behavior and interaction which will be seen by the subordinate as supportive. The superior needs accurate information as to how his behavior is actually seen by the subordinate. Does the subordinate, in fact, perceive the superior's behavior as supportive?

There are two major ways to obtain this evidence. In a complex organization it can be found by the use of measurements of the intervening variables, as suggested in Chapter 5 and discussed at greater length in Chapter 13. It can also be obtained by the development of work-group relationships, which not only facilitate but actually require, as part of the group building and maintenance functions, candid expressions by group members of their perceptions and reactions to the behavior of others (see Chapter 11).

The central role of the work group

An important theoretical derivation can be made from the principle of supportive relationships. This derivation is based directly on the desire to achieve and maintain a sense of personal worth, which is a central concept of the principle. The most important source of satisfaction for this desire is the response we get from the people we are close to, in whom we are interested, and whose approval and support we are eager to have. The face-to-face groups with whom we spend the bulk of our time are, consequently, the most important to us. Our work group is one in which we spend much of our time and one in which we are particularly eager to achieve and maintain a sense of personal worth. As a consequence, most persons are highly motivated to behave in ways consistent with the goals and values of their work group in order to obtain recognition, support, security, and favorable reactions from this group. It can be concluded, therefore, that *management will make full use of the potential capacities of its human resources only when each person in an organization is a member of one or more effectively functioning work groups that have a high degree of group loyalty, effective skills of interaction and high-performance goals.*

The full significance of this derivation becomes more evident when we examine the research findings that show how groups function when they are well knit and have effective interaction skills. Research shows, for example, that the greater the attraction and loyalty to the group, the more the individual is motivated (1) to accept the goals and decisions of the group; (2) to seek to influence the goals and decisions of the group so that they are consistent with his own experience and his own goals; (3) to communicate fully to the members of the group; (4) to welcome communication and influence attempts from the other members; (5) to behave so as to help implement the goals and decisions that are seen as most important to the group; and (6) to behave in ways calculated to receive support and favorable recognition from members of the group and especially from those who the individual feels are the more powerful and higher-status members (Cartwright and Zander, 1960). Groups which display a high level of member attraction to the group and high levels of the above characteristics will be referred to in this volume as *highly effective groups.* These groups are described more fully in Chapter 11.

As our theoretical derivation has indicated, an organization will function best when its personnel function not as individuals but as members of highly effective work groups with high-performance goals. Consequently, management should deliberately endeavor to build these effective groups, linking them into an overall organization by means of people who hold overlapping group membership (Figure 1). The superior in one group is a subordinate in the next group, and so on through the organization. If the work groups at each hierarchical level are well knit and effective, the linking process will be accomplished well. Staff as well as line should be characterized by this pattern of operation.

The dark lines in Figure 1 are intended to show that interaction occurs between individuals as well as in groups. The dark lines are omitted at the lowest level in the chart in order to avoid complexity. Interaction between individuals occurs there, of course, just as it does at higher levels in the organization.

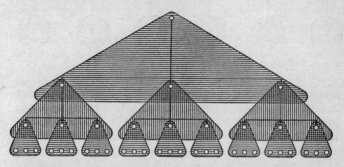

Figure 1 The overlapping group form of organization. Work groups vary in size as circumstances require although shown here as consisting of four persons

In most organizations, there are also various continuing and *ad hoc* committees, committees related to staff functions, etc., which should also become highly effective groups and thereby help further to tie the many parts of the organization together. These links are in addition to the linking provided by the overlapping members in the line organization. Throughout the organization, the supervisory process should develop and strengthen group functioning. This theoretically ideal organizational structure provides the framework for the management system called for by the newer theory.

The traditional company organization

Let us examine the way an organization would function were it to apply this one derivation and establish highly effective groups with high performance goals, instead of adhering to the traditional man-to-man pattern. First, let us look briefly at how the traditional man-to-man pattern usually functions. Figure 2 shows the top of an ordinary organization chart. Such an organization ordinarily

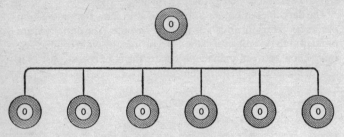

Figure 2 Typical organization chart

functions on a man-to-man basis as shown in Figure 3a. In Figure 3a, the president, vice presidents, and others reporting to the president are represented by 0s. The solid lines in Figure 3a indicate the boundaries of well-defined areas of responsibility.

The president of such a man-to-man organization has said to us, 'I have been made president of this company by the board of directors because they believe I am more intelligent or better trained or have more relevant experience than my fellow managers. Therefore, it is my responsibility to make the top-level decisions.' He regularly holds meetings of the people who report to him for purposes of sharing information, but *not* for decision-making.

What happens? The vice president in charge of manufacturing, for example, may go to the president with a problem and a recommendation. Because it involves a model change, the vice president in charge of sales is called in. On the basis of the discussion with the two vice presidents and the recommendations they make, the president arrives at a decision. However, in any organization larger than a few hundred employees, that decision usually will affect other vice presidents and subordinates whose interests were not represented in it. Under the circumstances, they are not likely to accept this decision wholeheartedly nor strive hard to implement it. Instead, they usually begin to plan how they can get decisions from the president which are going to be beneficial to them but not necessarily to sales and manufacturing.

And what happens to the communication process? This presi-

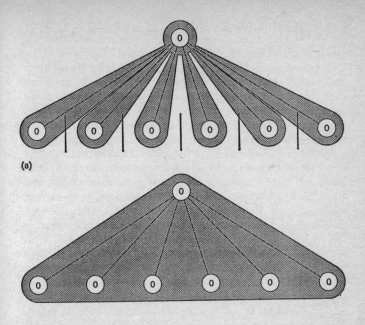

Figure 3 Man-to-man and group patterns of organization.
(a) Man-to-man pattern of organization. (b) Group pattern of organization

dent, it will be recalled, holds meetings for the primary purpose of sharing information. But if the manufacturing vice president, for example, has some important facts bearing on an action which he wants the president to approve, does he reveal them at these meetings? No, he does not. He waits until he is alone with the president and can use the information to obtain the decision he seeks. Each vice president is careful to share in these communication meetings only trivial information. The motivational pressures are against sharing anything of importance.

The man-to-man pattern of operation enables a vice president or manager to benefit by keeping as much information as possible to himself. Not only can he obtain decisions from his superior beneficial to himself, but he can use his knowledge secretly to connive with peers or subordinates or to pit one peer or subordinate against the other. In these ways, he often is able to increase his own power and influence. He does this, however, at the expense of the total organization. The distrust and fear created by his behavior adversely affect the amount of influence which the organization can exert in coordinating the activities of its members. Measures of the amount of influence an organization can exert on its members show that distrust of superiors, colleagues, and subordinates adversely affects the amount of influence that can be exercised.

Another serious weakness of the communication process in the man-to-man method of operating is that communications upward are highly filtered and correspondingly inaccurate. Orders and instructions flow down through the organization, at times with some distortion. But when management asks for information on the execution of orders and on difficulties encountered, incomplete and partially inaccurate information is often forthcoming. With these items and with other kinds of communication as well, those below the boss study him carefully to discover what he is interested in, what he approves and disapproves of, and what he wants to hear and does not want to hear. They then tend to feed him the material he wants. It is difficult and often hazardous for an individual subordinate in man-to-man discussion to tell the boss something which he needs to know but which runs counter to the boss's desires, convictions, or prejudices. A subordinate's future in an organization often is influenced appreciably by how well he senses and communicates to his boss material which fits the latter's orientation.

Another characteristic of the man-to-man pattern concerns the point of view from which problems are solved. When a problem is brought to the president, each vice president usually states and discusses the problem from a departmental orientation, despite efforts by the president to deal with it from a company-wide point of view. This operates to the disadvantage of the entire organization. Problems tend to be solved in terms of what is best for a department, not what is best for the company as a whole.

Effect of competition between functions

In the man-to-man situation it is clear that sharply defined lines of responsibility are necessary (Figure 3a) because of the nature of the promotion process and because the men involved are able people who want promotion.

Now, what are the chances of having one's competence so visible that one moves up in such an organization or receives offers elsewhere? Two factors are important: the magnitude of one's responsibility and the definition of one's functions so as to assure successful performance. For example, if you are head of sales and can get the president to order the manufacturing department to make a product or to price it in such a way that it is highly competitive, that will be to your advantage, even though it imposes excessive difficulties and cost problems on the manufacturing operation.

Each man, in short, is trying to enlarge his area of responsibility, thereby encroaching on the other's territory. He is also trying to get decisions from the president which set easily attained goals for him and enable him to achieve excellent performance. Thus, the sales vice president may get prices set which make his job easy but which put undue pressure on the manufacturing vice president to cut production costs.

One consequence of this struggle for power is that each department or operation has to be staffed for peak loads, and job responsibilities and boundaries have to be precisely defined. No one dares let anybody else take over any part of his activity temporarily for fear that the line of responsibility will be moved over permanently.

The tighter the hierarchical control in an organization, in the sense that decisions are made at the top and orders flow down, the greater tends to be the hostility among subordinates. In autocratic organizations, subordinates bow down to superiors and fight among themselves for power and status. Consequently, the greater the extent to which the president makes the decisions, the greater is the probability that competition, hostility, and conflict will exist between his vice presidents and staff members.

The group system of operation

Figure 3b represents a company patterned on the group system of organization. One of the presidents we interviewed follows this pattern. He will not permit an organization chart to be drawn because he does not want people to think in terms of man-to-man hierarchy. He wants to build working groups. He holds meetings of his top staff regularly to solve problems and make decisions. Any member of his staff can propose problems for consideration, but each problem is viewed from a company-wide point of view. It is virtually impossible for one department to force a decision beneficial to it but detrimental to other departments if the group, as a whole, makes the decisions.

An effectively functioning group pressing for solutions in the best interest of *all* the members and refusing to accept solutions which unduly favor a particular member or segment of the group is an important characteristic of the group pattern of organization. It also provides the president, or the superior at any level in an organization, with a powerful managerial tool for dealing with special requests or favors from subordinates. Often the subordinate may feel that the request is legitimate even though it may not be in the best interest of the organization. In the man-to-man operation (Figure 3a), the chief sometimes finds it difficult to turn down such requests. With the group pattern of operation, however, the superior can suggest that the subordinate submit his proposal to the group at their next staff meeting. If the request is legitimate and in the best interest of the organization, the group will grant the request. If the request is unreasonable, an effectively functioning group can skillfully turn it down by analyzing it in relation to what is best for the entire organization. Subordinates in this situation soon find they cannot get special favors or preferred treatment from the chief. This leads to a tradition that one does not ask for any treatment or decision which is recognized as unfair to one's colleagues.

The capacity of effective groups to press for decisions and action in the best interest of all members can be applied in other ways. An example is provided by the president of a subsidiary of a large corporation. He was younger (age forty-two) than most of his staff and much younger than two of his vice presidents (ages sixty-one and sixty-two). The subsidiary had done quite well under its previous president, but the young president was eager to have it do still better. In his first two years as president, his company showed substantial improvement. He found, however, that the two older vice presidents were not effectively handling their responsibilities. Better results were needed from them if the company was to achieve the record performance which the president and the other vice presidents sought.

The president met the situation by using his regular staff meetings to analyze the company's present position, evaluate its potential, and decide on goals and on the action required to reach them. The president had no need to put pressure on his coasting vice presidents. The other vice presidents did it for him. One vice president, in particular, slightly younger but with more years of experience than the two who were dragging their feet, gently but effectively pushed them to commit themselves to higher performance goals. In the regular staff meetings, progress toward objectives was watched and new short-term goals were set as needed. Using this group process, steady progress was made. The two oldest vice presidents became as much involved and worked as enthusiastically as did the rest of the staff.

Group decision-making

With the model of organization shown in Figure 3b, persons reporting to the president, such as vice presidents for sales, research and manufacturing, contribute their technical knowledge in the decision-making process. They also make other contributions. One member of the group, for example, may be an imaginative person who comes up rapidly with many stimulating and original ideas. Others, such as the general counsel or the head of research, may make the group do a rigorous job of sifting ideas. In this way, the different contributions required for a competent job of thinking and decision-making are introduced.

In addition, these people become experienced in effective group functioning. They know what leadership involves. If the president grows absorbed in some detail and fails to keep the group focused on the topic for discussion, the members will help by performing appropriate leadership functions, such as asking, 'Where are we? What have we decided so far? Why don't we summarize?' (These functions are discussed in Chapter 11.)

There are other advantages to this sort of group action. The motivation is high to communicate accurately all relevant and important information. If any one of these men holds back important facts affecting the company so that he can take it to the president later, the president is likely to ask him why he withheld the information and request him to report it to the group at the next session. The group also is apt to be hard on any member who withholds important information from them. Moreover, the group can get ideas across to the boss that no subordinate dares tell him. As a consequence, there is better communication, which brings a better awareness of problems, and better decision-making than with the man-to-man system.

Another important advantage of effective group action is the high degree of motivation on the part of each member to do his best to implement decisions and to achieve the group goals. Since the goals of the group are arrived at through group decisions, each individual group member tends to have a high level of ego identification with the goals because of his involvement in the decisions.

Finally, there are indications that an organization operating in this way can be staffed for less than peak loads at each point. When one man is overburdened, some of his colleagues can pick up part of the load temporarily. This is possible with group methods of supervision because the struggle for power and status is less. Everybody recognizes his broad area of responsibility and is not alarmed by occasional shifts in one direction or the other. Moreover, he knows that his chances for promotion depend not upon the width of his responsibility, but upon his total performance, of which his work in the group is an important part. The group, including the president, comes to know the strengths and weaknesses of each member well as a result of working closely with him.

A few years ago a department of fifteen people in a medium-sized company shifted from a man-to-man pattern of supervision to the group pattern. Each operation under the man-to-man system was staffed to carry adequately the peak loads encountered, but these peaks virtually never occurred for all jobs at the same time. In shifting to group supervision, the department studied how the work was being done. They concluded that seven persons instead of fifteen could carry the load except in emergencies. Gradually, over several months, the persons not needed transferred to other departments and the income of those doing the work was increased 50 per cent. The work is being done well, peak loads are handled, those doing it have more favorable attitudes, and there is less absence and turnover than under the man-to-man system.

Responsibility and situational requirements

In every organization there are many basic facts of life which cannot be ignored if the organization is to achieve its objectives. For example, there are often deadlines or minimum financial conditions as to earnings and reserves to be met. These hard, objective realities are the *situational requirements* which impose limitations on the decision-making processes.

The supervisor of every work group must be fully aware of the situational requirements which apply to the operation of his group. In making decisions, he and his group should never lose sight of them. If the group is so divided in opinion that there is not time to reach decisions by consensus which adequately meet these requirements, the superior has the responsibility of making a decision which does meet them. In this event, the superior may be wise to accept the solution preferred by the individuals in the group who will have the major responsibility for implementing the decision, provided, of course, the superior himself feels that the solution is reasonably sound.

Sometimes the differences of opinion exist not between members of the work group, but between the superior and his subordinates. In this event, the superior should participate fully in the discussion and present clearly the evidence which makes him hold another point of view. If, after further discussion, the group still prefers a course of action different from that which the chief favors, the superior faces a tough decision. He can overrule the group and take the action he favors. This is likely to affect adversely group loyalties and the capacity of his work group to function well as a group. Or he can go along with the group and accept the decision they prefer. If he overrules the group, the superior usually reduces the amount of work-group loyalty which he has 'in the bank'. If the costs of a mistake are not too great, he may prefer to accept the group's decision in order to strengthen the group as a group and to provide an opportunity for his group to learn from its mistakes. If the costs of a mistake are likely to be excessive, the superior may feel that he has no choice but to do what his own experience indicates is best. But whatever course of action is taken, *he is responsible and must accept full responsibility for what occurs.*

The 'linking-pin' function

Figure 3 and the preceding discussion have been concerned with the group pattern of organization at the very top of a company. Our theoretical derivation indicates, however, that this pattern is equally applicable at all levels of an organization. If an organization is to apply this system effectively at all organizational levels, an important linking function must be performed.

The concept of the 'linking pin' is shown by the arrows in Figure 4. The research pointing to the importance of upward

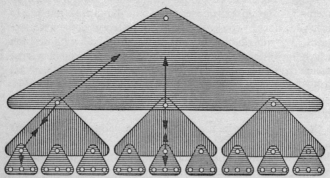

Figure 4 The linking pin

influence in an organization has already been described in Chapter 7. The study by Pelz (1951, 1952) showed that there was only a slight relationship between some fifty different measures of supervisory practices and points of view, as reported by the supervisors, and the attitudes and morale of the subordinates. Pelz found that an important variable was responsible for the absence of more marked relationships. This variable proved to be the amount of influence which a supervisor felt he had with his own superior. To function effectively, a supervisor must have sufficient influence with his own superior to be able to affect the superior's decisions. Subordinates expect their supervisors to be able to exercise an influence upward in dealing with problems on the job and in handling problems which affect them and their well-being. As Pelz's analysis shows, when a supervisor cannot exert sufficient influence upward in the hierarchy to handle these problems constructively, an unfavorable reaction to the supervisor and to the organization is likely to occur.

Other research confirms the importance of Pelz's findings and also indicates that the ability to exert an influence upward affects not only morale and motivation but also productivity and performance variables (Katz *et al.*, 1950; Likert and Willits, 1940). Ronken and Lawrence (1952) summarize their findings on this matter as follows:

An additional complication for the foreman was the necessity of learning how to work with new supervisors and a new group of subordinates. When the foreman experienced difficulty in communicating with his superior, he was not able to understand his subordinates' problems or to gain their spontaneous cooperation, and the work suffered. When he felt more confident of his relations upward, he administered his own group with greater skill. During such periods his operators showed considerable initiative in their work, contributed more useful suggestions, and raced with themselves and each other to increase output.

These results demonstrate that *the capacity to exert influence upward is essential if a supervisor (or manager) is to perform his supervisory functions successfully*. To be effective in leading his own work group, a superior must be able to influence his own boss; that is, he needs to be skilled both as a supervisor and as a subordinate. In terms of group functioning, he must be skilled in both leadership and membership functions and roles.

Effective groups with high group loyalty are characterized by efficient and full communication and by the fact that their members respect each other, welcome attempts by the other members to influence them, and are influenced in their thinking and behavior when they believe that the evidence submitted by the other members warrants it. The linking-pin function, consequently, will be performed well in an organization when each work group at all the different hierarchical levels above the nonsupervisory level is functioning effectively as a group and when every member of each group is performing his functions and roles well. Whenever an individual member of one of these groups fails in his leadership and membership roles (see Chapter 11), the group or groups under him will not be linked into the organization effectively and will fail in the performance of their tasks. When an entire work group ceases to function effectively as a group, the activities and performance of all the work groups below such a group will be correspondingly adversely affected.

The linking-pin function requires effective group processes and points to the following:

1. An organization will not derive the full benefit from its highly effective groups unless they are linked to the total organization by means of equally effective overlapping groups such as those illustrated in Figures 1 and 4. The use of highly effective groups in only one part or in scattered portions of an organization will fail, therefore, to achieve the full potential value of such groups.

2. The potential power of the overlapping group form of organization will not be approached until all the groups in the organization are functioning reasonably well. The failure of any group will adversely affect the performance of the total organization.

3. The higher an ineffective group is in the hierarchy, the greater is the adverse effect of its failure on the performance of the organization. The linking process is more important at high levels in an organization than at low because the policies and problems dealt with are more important to the total organization and affect more people.

4. To help maintain an effective organization, it is desirable for superiors not only to hold group meetings of their own subordinates, but also to have occasional meetings over two hierarchical levels. This enables the superior to observe any breakdown in the linking-pin process as performed by the subordinates reporting to him. If in such meetings the subordinates under one of his subordinates are reluctant to talk, never question any procedure or policy, or give other evidence of fear, the superior can conclude that he has a coaching job to do with his own subordinate, who is failing both as a leader and in his performance of the linking-pin function. This subordinate needs help in learning how to build his own subordinates into a work group with high group loyalty and with confidence and trust in their supervisor (see Chapters 9 and 11).

5. An organization takes a serious risk when it relies on a single linking pin or single linking process to tie the organization together.

As will be discussed further in subsequent chapters, an organization is strengthened by having staff groups and *ad hoc* committees provide multiple overlapping groups through which linking functions are performed and the organization bound together.

Organizational objectives and goals of units

The ability of a superior to behave in a supportive manner is circumscribed by the degree of compatibility between the objectives of the organization and the needs of the individuals comprising it. If the objectives of the organization are in basic conflict with the needs and desires of the individual members, it is virtually impossible for the superior to be supportive to subordinates and at the same time serve the objectives of the organization. The principle of supportive relationships, consequently, points to the necessity for an adequate degree of harmony between organizational objectives and the needs and desires of its individual members.

This conclusion is applicable to every kind of organization: industrial, governmental, or voluntary. A business organization, if it is to function well, needs to have objectives which represent a satisfactory integration of the needs and desires of all the major segments involved: its share owners, its suppliers, its consumers, its employees (including all levels of supervisory and nonsupervisory personnel) and its union(s). If governmental agencies are to function effectively, their objectives similarly must be a satisfactory integration of the needs and desires of all the different segments involved in their activities: employees, citizens and legislators.

Neither the needs and desires of individuals nor the objectives of organizations are stable and unchanging. The desires of individuals grow and change as people interact with other people. Similarly, the objectives of organizations must change continuously to meet the requirements of changed technologies, changed conditions, and the changes in needs and desires of those involved in the organization or served by it. The interaction process of the organization must be capable of dealing effectively with these requirements for continuous change.

In every healthy organization there is, consequently, an unending process of examining and modifying individual goals and organizational objectives as well as consideration of the methods for achieving them. The newer theory specifies that:

1. The objectives of the entire organization and of its component parts must be in satisfactory harmony with the relevant needs and desires of the great majority, if not all, of the members of the organization and of the persons served by it.

2. The goals and assignments of each member of the organization must be established in such a way that he is highly motivated to achieve them. The methods and procedures used by the organization and its subunits to achieve the agreed-upon objectives must be developed and adopted in such a way that the members are highly motivated to use these methods to their maximum potentiality.

3. The members of the organization and the persons related to it must feel that the reward system of the organization – salaries, wages, bonuses, dividends, interest payments – yields them equitable compensation for their efforts and contributions.

The overlapping group form of organization offers a structure which, in conjunction with a high level of group interactional skills, is particularly effective in performing the processes necessary to meet these requirements.

Constructive use of conflict

An organization operating under the newer theory is not free from conflict. Conflict and differences of opinion always exist in a healthy, virile organization, for it is usually from such differences that new and better objectives and methods emerge. Differences are essential to progress, but bitter, unresolved differences can immobilize an organization. The central problem, consequently, becomes not how to reduce or eliminate conflict, but how to deal constructively with it. Effective organizations have extraordinary capacity to handle conflict. Their success is due to three very important characteristics:

1. They possess the machinery to deal constructively with conflict. They have an organizational structure which facilitates constructive interaction between individuals and between work groups.

2. The personnel of the organization is skilled in the processes of effective interaction and mutual influence. (Skills in group leadership and membership roles and in group building and maintenance functions are discussed in Chapter 11.)

3. There is high confidence and trust among the members of the organization in each other, high loyalty to the work group and to the organization, and high motivation to achieve the organization's objectives. Confidence, loyalty and cooperative motivation produce earnest, sincere and determined efforts to find solutions to conflict. There is greater motivation to find a constructive solution than to maintain an irreconcilable conflict. The solutions reached are often highly creative and represent a far better solution than any initially proposed by the conflicting interests (Metcalf and Urwick, 1940).

The discussion in this chapter has deliberately focused on and emphasized the group aspects of organization and management. This has been done to make clear some of the major differences between the classical and the newer theories of management. It should also sharpen the awareness of the kind of changes needed to start applying the newer theory.

Any organization which bases its operation on this theory will necessarily make use of individual counseling and coaching by superiors of subordinates. There is need in every situation for a balanced use of both procedures, individual and group. Here, as with other aspects of supervision, the balance which will be most appropriate and work best will depend upon the experience, expectations and skills of the people involved.

Tests of the newer theory

The validity of the newer theory of management and of its derivations can be tested in two ways. Tests can be applied experimentally in pilot plants to see whether the newer system significantly improves all aspects of performance: productivity, quality, costs, employee satisfaction, etc. Although it will take several years to know the results, this kind of test is now under way.

The second kind of test is an examination of the extent to which the methods and procedures called for by the theory, or by the derivations based on the theory, are associated with above-average performance in the current operations of companies. The results of this kind of test do not require waiting for the outcome of an experimental application of the theory, but can be examined now. Several tests of this latter kind have recently been made.

These were based on data which have been collected during the past few years. The results indicate, as we shall see in Chapter 9, that the newer theory, skilfully used, will produce an organization with impressive performance characteristics.

References

ARGYRIS, C. (1957), *Personality and Organisation*, Harper & Row.

CARTWRIGHT, D., and ZANDER, A. (eds.) (1960), *Group Dynamics: research and theory*, 2nd edn., Ron Peterson.

KATZ, D., and KAHN, R. L. (1951), 'Human organization and worker motivation', in L. Reed Tripp (ed.), *Industrial Productivity*, Industrial Relations Research Association, pp. 146–71.

KATZ, D., *et al.* (1951), *Productivity, Supervision and Morale in an Office Situation*, Institute for Social Research.

KRULEE, G. K. (1955), 'The Scanlon plan: co-operation through participation', *Journal of Business*, no. 28 (2), pp. 100–113.

LIKERT, R., and WILLITS, J. M. (1940), *Morale and Agency Management*, Life Insurance Agency Management Association.

MARCH, J. G., and SIMON, H. A. (1958), *Organizations*, Wiley.

METCALF, H. C., and URWICK, L. (eds.) (1940), *Dynamic Administration: the collected works of Mary Parker Follett*, Harper & Row.

PELZ, D. C. (1951), *The Influence of the Supervisor Within his Department as a Conditioner of the way Supervisory Practices Affect Employee Attitudes*, unpublished doctoral dissertation, University of Michigan.

PELZ, D. C. (1952), 'Influence: a key to effective leadership in the first-line supervisor', *Personnel*, November, pp. 3–11.

ROGERS, C. R. (1942), *Counseling and Psychotherapy*, Houghton Mifflin.

RONKEN, H. O., and LAWRENCE, P. R. (1952), *Administering Changes*, Harvard Graduate School of Business Administration.

VITELES, M. S. (1953), *Motivation and Morale in Industry*, Norton.

16 D. McGregor

Theory X and Theory Y

D. McGregor, 'Theory X: the traditional view of direction and control', and 'Theory Y: the integration of individual and organizational goals', *The Human Side of Enterprise*, McGraw-Hill, 1960, chapters 3 and 4, pp. 33–57.

Theory X: the traditional view of direction and control

Behind every managerial decision or action are assumptions about human nature and human behavior. A few of these are remarkably pervasive. They are implicit in most of the literature of organization and in much current managerial policy and practice.

1. *The average human being has an inherent dislike of work and will avoid it if he can.* This assumption has deep roots. The punishment of Adam and Eve for eating the fruit of the Tree of Knowledge was to be banished from Eden into a world where they had to work for a living. The stress that management places on productivity, on the concept of 'a fair day's work', on the evils of featherbedding and restriction of output, on rewards for performance – while it has a logic in terms of the objectives of enterprise – reflects an underlying belief that management must counteract an inherent human tendency to avoid work. The evidence for the correctness of this assumption would seem to most managers to be incontrovertible.

2. *Because of this human characteristic of dislike of work, most people must be coerced, controlled, directed, threatened with punishment to get them to put forth adequate effort toward the achievement of organizational objectives.* The dislike of work is so strong that even the promise of rewards is not generally enough to overcome it. People will accept the rewards and demand continually higher ones, but these alone will not produce the necessary effort. Only the threat of punishment will do the trick.

The current wave of criticism of 'human relations', the derogatory comments about 'permissiveness' and 'democracy' in industry, the trends in some companies toward recentralization after the postwar wave of decentralization – all these are assertions of the underlying assumption that people will only work under external coercion and control. The recession of 1957–8 ended a decade of experimentation with the 'soft' managerial approach, and this assumption (which never really was abandoned) is being openly espoused once more.

3. *The average human being prefers to be directed, wishes to avoid responsibility, has relatively little ambition, wants security above all.* This assumption of the 'mediocrity of the masses' is rarely expressed so bluntly. In fact, a good deal of lip service is given to the ideal of the worth of the average human being. Our political and social values demand such public expressions. Nevertheless, a great many managers will give private support to this assumption, and it is easy to see it reflected in policy and practice. Paternalism has become a nasty word, but it is by no means a defunct managerial philosophy.

I have suggested elsewhere the name Theory X for this set of assumptions. In later chapters of this book I will attempt to show that Theory X is not a straw man for purposes of demolition, but is in fact a theory which materially influences managerial strategy in a wide sector of American industry today. Moreover, the principles of organization which comprise the bulk of the literature of management *could only have been derived from assumptions such as those of Theory X.* Other beliefs about human nature would have led inevitably to quite different organizational principles.

Theory X provides an explanation of some human behavior in industry. These assumptions would not have persisted if there were not a considerable body of evidence to support them. Nevertheless, there are many readily observable phenomena in industry and elsewhere which are not consistent with this view of human nature.

Such a state of affairs is not uncommon. The history of science provides many examples of theoretical explanations which persist over long periods despite the fact that they are only partially adequate. Newton's laws of motion are a case in point. It was not until development of the theory of relativity during the present century that important inconsistencies and inadequacies in Newtonian theory could be understood and corrected.

The growth of knowledge in the social sciences during the past quarter century has made it possible to reformulate some assumptions about human nature and human behavior in the organizational setting which resolve certain of the inconsistencies inherent in Theory X. While this reformulation is, of course, tentative, it provides an improved basis for prediction and control of human behavior in industry.

Some assumptions about motivation

At the core of any theory of the management of human resources are assumptions about human motivation. This has been a confusing subject because there have been so many conflicting points of view even among social scientists. In recent years, however, there has been a convergence of research findings and a growing acceptance of a few rather basic ideas about motivation. These ideas appear to have considerable power. They help to explain the inadequacies of Theory X as well as the limited sense in which it is correct. In addition, they provide the basis for an entirely different theory of management.

The following generalizations about motivation are somewhat oversimplified. If all of the qualifications which would be required by a truly adequate treatment were introduced, the gross essentials which are particularly significant for management would be obscured. These generalizations do not misrepresent the facts, but they do ignore some complexities of human behavior which are relatively unimportant for our purposes.

Man is a wanting animal – as soon as one of his needs is satisfied, another appears in its place. This process is unending. It continues from birth to death. Man continuously puts forth effort – works, if you please – to satisfy his needs.

Human needs are organized in a series of levels – a hierarchy of importance. At the lowest level, but pre-eminent in importance when they are thwarted, are the physiological needs. Man lives by bread alone, when there is no bread. Unless the circumstances are unusual, his needs for love, for status, for recognition are inoperative when his stomach has been empty for a while. But when he eats regularly and adequately, hunger ceases to be an important need. The sated man has hunger only in the sense that a full bottle has emptiness. The same is true of the other physiological needs of man – for rest, exercise, shelter, protection from the elements.

A satisfied need is not a motivator of behavior! This is a fact of profound significance. It is a fact which is unrecognized in Theory X and is, therefore, ignored in the conventional approach to the management of people. I shall return to it later. For the moment, an example will make the point. Consider your own need for air. Except as you are deprived of it, it has no appreciable motivating effect upon your behavior.

When the physiological needs are reasonably satisfied, needs at the next higher level begin to dominate man's behavior – to motivate him. These are the safety needs, for protection against danger, threat, deprivation. Some people mistakenly refer to these as needs for security. However, unless man is in a dependent relationship where he fears arbitrary deprivation, he does not demand security. The need is for the 'fairest possible break'. When he is confident of this, he is more than willing to take risks. But when he feels threatened or dependent, his greatest need is for protection, for security.

The fact needs little emphasis that since every industrial employee is in at least a partially dependent relationship, safety needs may assume considerable importance. Arbitrary management actions, behavior which arouses uncertainty with respect to continued employment or which reflects favoritism or discrimination, unpredictable administration of policy – these can be powerful motivators of the safety needs in the employment relationship at every level from worker to vice president. In addition, the safety needs of managers are often aroused by their dependence downward or laterally. This is a major reason for emphasis on management prerogatives and clear assignments of authority.

When man's physiological needs are satisfied and he is no longer fearful about his physical welfare, his social needs become important motivators of his behavior. These are such needs as those for belonging, for association, for acceptance by one's fellows, for giving and receiving friendship and love.

Management knows today of the existence of these needs, but it is often assumed quite wrongly that they represent a threat to the organization. Many studies have demonstrated that the tightly knit, cohesive work group may, under proper conditions, be far more effective than an equal number of separate individuals in achieving organizational goals. Yet management, fearing group hostility to its own objectives, often goes to considerable lengths to control and direct human efforts in ways that are inimical to the natural 'groupiness' of human beings. When man's social needs – and perhaps his safety needs, too – are thus thwarted, he behaves in ways which tend to defeat organizational objectives. He becomes resistant, antagonistic, uncooperative. But this behavior is a consequence, not a cause.

Above the social needs – in the sense that they do not usually become motivators until lower needs are reasonably satisfied – are the needs of greatest significance to management and to man himself. They are the egoistic needs, and they are of two kinds:

1. Those that relate to one's self-esteem: needs for self-respect and self-confidence, for autonomy, for achievement, for competence, for knowledge.

2. Those that relate to one's reputation: needs for status, for recognition, for appreciation, for the deserved respect of one's fellows.

Unlike the lower needs, these are rarely satisfied; man seeks indefinitely for more satisfaction of these needs once they have become important to him. However, they do not usually appear in any significant way until physiological, safety and social needs are reasonably satisfied. Exceptions to this generalization are to be observed, particularly under circumstance where, in addition to severe deprivation of physiological needs, human dignity is trampled upon. Political revolutions often grow out of thwarted social and ego, as well as physiological, needs.

The typical industrial organization offers only limited opportunities for the satisfaction of egoistic needs to people at lower levels in the hierarchy. The conventional methods of organizing work, particularly in mass production industries, give little heed to these aspects of human motivation. If the practices of 'scientific management' were deliberately calculated to thwart these needs – which, of course, they are not – they could hardly accomplish this purpose better than they do.

Finally – a capstone, as it were, on the hierarchy – there are the needs for self-fulfillment. These are the needs for realizing one's own potentialities, for continued self-development, for being creative in the broadest sense of that term.

The conditions of modern industrial life give only limited opportunity for these relatively dormant human needs to find expression. The deprivation most people experience with respect to other lower-level needs diverts their energies into the struggle to satisfy *those* needs, and the needs for self-fulfillment remain below the level of consciousness.

Now, briefly, a few general comments about motivation:

We recognize readily enough that a man suffering from a severe dietary deficiency is sick. The deprivation of physiological needs has behavioral consequences. The same is true, although less well recognized, of the deprivation of higher-level needs. The man whose needs for safety, association, independence, or status are thwarted is sick, just as surely as is he who has rickets. And his sickness will have behavioral consequences. We will be mistaken if we attribute his resultant passivity, or his hostility, or his refusal to accept responsibility to his inherent 'human nature'. These forms of behavior are *symptoms* of illness – of deprivation of his social and egoistic needs.

The man whose lower-level needs are satisfied is not motivated to satisfy *those* needs. For practical purposes they exist no longer. (Remember my point about your need for air.) Management often asks, 'Why aren't people more productive? We pay good wages, provide good working conditions, have excellent fringe benefits and steady employment. Yet people do not seem to be willing to put forth more than minimum effort.' It is unnecessary to look far for the reasons.

Consideration of the rewards typically provided the worker for satisfying his needs through his employment leads to the interesting conclusion that most of these rewards can be used for satisfying his needs *only when he leaves the job*. Wages, for example, cannot be spent at work. The only contribution they can make to his satisfaction on the job is in terms of status differences resulting from wage differentials. (This, incidentally, is one of the reasons why small and apparently unimportant differences in wage rates can be the subject of so much heated dispute. The issue is not the pennies involved, but the fact that the status differences which they reflect are one of the few ways in which wages can result in need satisfaction in the job situation itself.)

Most fringe benefits – overtime pay, shift differentials, vacations, health and medical benefits, annuities and the proceeds from stock purchase plans or profit-sharing plans – yield needed satisfaction only when the individual leaves the job. Yet these, along with wages, are among the major rewards provided by management for effort. It is not surprising, therefore, that for many wage earners *work is perceived as a form of punishment* which is the price to be paid for various kinds of satisfaction away from the job. To the extent that this is their perception, we would hardly expect them to undergo more of this punishment than is necessary.

Under today's conditions management has provided relatively well for the satisfaction of physiological and safety needs. The standard of living in our country is high; people do not suffer major deprivation of their physiological needs except during periods of severe unemployment. Even then, the social legislation developed since the thirties cushions the shock.

But the fact that management has provided for these physiological and safety needs has shifted the motivational emphasis to the social and the egoistic needs. Unless there are opportunities *at work* to satisfy these higher-level needs, people will be deprived; and their behavior will reflect this deprivation. Under such conditions, if management continues to focus its attention on physiological needs, the mere provision of rewards is bound to be ineffective, and reliance on the threat of punishment will be inevitable. Thus one of the assumptions of Theory X will appear to be validated, but only because we have mistaken effects for causes.

People *will* make insistent demands for more money under these conditions. It becomes more important than ever to buy the material goods and services which can provide limited satisfaction of the thwarted needs. Although money has only limited value in satisfying many higher-level needs, it can become the focus of interest if it is the only means available.

The 'carrot and stick' theory of motivation which goes along with Theory X works reasonably well under certain circumstances. The *means* for satisfying man's physiological and (within limits) safety needs can be provided or withheld by management. Employment itself is such a means, and so are wages, working conditions, and benefits. By these means the individual can be controlled so long as he is struggling for subsistence. Man tends to live for bread alone when there is little bread.

But the 'carrot and stick' theory does not work at all once man has reached an adequate subsistence level and is motivated primarily by higher needs. Management cannot provide a man with self-respect, or with the respect of his fellows, or with the satisfaction of needs for self-fulfillment. We can create conditions such that he is encouraged and enabled to seek such satisfactions for himself, or we can thwart him by failing to create those conditions.

But this creation of conditions is not 'control' in the usual sense; it does not seem to be a particularly good device for directing behavior. And so management finds itself in an odd position. The high standard of living created by our modern technological know-how provides quite adequately for the satisfaction of physiological and safety needs. The only significant exception is where management practices have not created confidence in a 'fair break' – and thus where safety needs are thwarted. But by making possible the satisfaction of lower-level needs, management has deprived itself of the ability to use the control devices on which the conventional assumptions of Theory X has taught it to rely: rewards, promises, incentives, or threats and other coercive devices.

The philosophy of management by direction and control – *regardless of whether it is hard or soft* – is inadequate to motivate because the human needs on which this approach relies are relatively unimportant motivators of behavior in our society today. Direction and control are of limited value in motivating people whose important needs are social and egoistic.

People, deprived of opportunities to satisfy at work the needs which are now important to them, behave exactly as we might predict – with indolence, passivity, unwillingness to accept responsibility, resistance to change, willingness to follow the demagogue, unreasonable demands for economic benefits. It would seem that we may be caught in a web of our own weaving.

Theory X explains the *consequences* of a particular managerial strategy; it neither explains nor describes human nature although it purports to. Because its assumptions are so unnecessarily limiting, it prevents our seeing the possibilities inherent in other managerial strategies. What sometimes appear to be new strategies – decentralization, management by objectives, consultative supervision, 'democratic' leadership – are usually but old wine in new bottles because the procedures developed to implement them are derived from the same inadequate assumptions about human nature. Management is constantly becoming disillusioned with widely touted and expertly merchandized 'new approaches' to the human side of enterprise. The real difficulty is that these new approaches are no more than different tactics – programs, procedures, gadgets – within an unchanged strategy based on Theory X.

In child rearing, it is recognized that parental strategies of control must be progressively modified to adapt to the changed capabilities and characteristics of the human individual as he develops from infancy to adulthood. To some extent industrial management recognizes that the human *adult* possesses capabilities for continued learning and growth. Witness the many current activities in the fields of training and management development. In its *basic* conceptions of managing human resources, however, management appears to have concluded that the average human being is permanently arrested in his development in early adolescence. Theory X is built on the least common human denominator: the factory 'hand' of the past. As Chris Argyris has shown dramatically in his *Personality and Organization,* conventional managerial strategies for the organization, direction, and control of the human resources of enterprise are admirably suited to the capacities and characteristics of the child rather than the adult.

In one limited area – that of research administration – there has been some recent recognition of the need for selective adaptation in managerial strategy. This, however, has been perceived as a unique problem, and its broader implications have not been recognized. As pointed out in this and the previous chapter, changes in the population at large – in educational level, attitudes and values, motivation, degree of dependence – have created both the opportunity and the need for other forms of selective adaptation. However, so long as the assumptions of Theory X continue to influence managerial strategy, we will fail to discover, let alone utilize, the potentialities of the average human being.

Theory Y: the integration of individual and organizational goals

To some, the preceding analysis will appear harsh. Have we not made major modifications in the management of the human resources of industry during the past quarter century? Have we not recognized the importance of people and made vitally significant changes in managerial strategy as a consequence? Do the developments since the twenties in personnel administration and labor relations add up to nothing?

There is no question that important progress has been made in the past two or three decades. During this period the human side of enterprise has become a major preoccupation of management. A tremendous number of policies, programs and practices which were virtually unknown thirty years ago have become commonplace. The lot of the industrial employee – be he worker, professional, or executive – has improved to a degree which could hardly have been imagined by his counterpart of the nineteen twenties. Management has adopted generally a far more humanitarian set of values; it has successfully striven to give more equitable and more generous treatment to its employees. It has significantly reduced economic hardships, eliminated the more extreme forms of industrial warfare, provided a generally safe and pleasant working environment, *but it has done all these things without changing its fundamental theory of management*. There are exceptions here and there, and they are important; nevertheless, the assumptions of Theory X remain predominant throughout our economy.

Management was subjected to severe pressures during the Great Depression of the thirties. The wave of public antagonism, the open warfare accompanying the unionization of the mass production industries, the general reaction against authoritarianism, the legislation of the New Deal, produced a wide 'pendulum swing'. However, the changes in policy and practice which took place during that and the next decade were primarily adjustments to the increased power of organized labor and to the pressures of public opinion.

Some of the movement was away from 'hard' and toward 'soft' management, but it was short-lived, and for good reasons. It has become clear that many of the initial strategic interpretations accompanying the 'human relations approach' were as naïve as those which characterized the early stages of progressive education. We have now discovered that there is no answer in the simple removal of control – that abdication is not a workable alternative to authoritarianism. We have learned that there is no direct correlation between employee satisfaction and productivity. We recognize that 'industrial democracy' cannot consist in permitting everyone to decide everything, that industrial health does not flow automatically from the elimination of dissatisfaction, disagreement, or even open conflict. Peace is not synonymous with organizational health; socially responsible management is not co-extensive with permissive management.

Now that management has regained its earlier prestige and power, it has become obvious that the trend toward 'soft' management was a temporary and relatively superficial reaction rather than a general modification of fundamental assumptions or basic strategy. Moreover, while the progress we have made in the past quarter century is substantial, it has reached the point of diminishing returns. The tactical possibilities within conventional managerial strategies have been pretty completely exploited, and significant new developments will be unlikely without major modifications in theory.

The assumptions of Theory Y

There have been few dramatic break-throughs in social science theory like those which have occurred in the physical sciences during the past half century. Nevertheless, the accumulation of knowledge about human behavior in many specialized fields has made possible the formulation of a number of generalizations which provide a modest beginning for new theory with respect to the management of human resources. Some of these assumptions were outlined in the discussion of motivation in Chapter 3. Some others, which will hereafter be referred to as Theory Y, are as follows:

1. *The expenditure of physical and mental effort in work is as natural as play or rest.* The average human being does not inherently dislike work. Depending upon controllable conditions, work may be a source of satisfaction (and will be voluntarily performed) or a source of punishment (and will be avoided if possible).

2. *External control and the threat of punishment are not the only means for bringing about effort toward organizational objectives. Man will exercise self-direction and self-control in the service of objectives to which he is committed.*

3. *Commitment to objectives is a function of the rewards associated*

with their achievement. The most significant of such rewards, e.g., the satisfaction of ego and self-actualization needs, can be direct products of effort directed toward organizational objectives.

4. *The average human being learns, under proper conditions, not only to accept but to seek responsibility.* Avoidance of responsibility, lack of ambition and emphasis on security are generally consequences of experience, not inherent human characteristics.

5. *The capacity to exercise a relatively high degree of imagination, ingenuity and creativity in the solution of organizational problems is widely, not narrowly, distributed in the population.*

6. *Under the conditions of modern industrial life, the intellectual potentialities of the average human being are only partially utilized.*

These assumptions involve sharply different implications for managerial strategy than do those of Theory X. They are dynamic rather than static: They indicate the possibility of human growth, and development ; they stress the necessity for selective adaptation rather than for a single absolute form of control. They are not framed in terms of the least common denominator of the factory hand, but in terms of a resource which has substantial potentialities.

Above all, the assumptions of Theory Y point up the fact that the limits on human collaboration in the organizational setting are not limits of human nature but of management's ingenuity in discovering how to realize the potential represented by its human resources. Theory X offers management an easy rationalization for ineffective organizational performance: It is due to the nature of the human resources with which we must work. Theory Y, on the other hand, places the problems squarely in the lap of management. If employees are lazy, indifferent, unwilling to take responsibility, intransigent, uncreative, uncooperative, Theory Y implies that the causes lie in management's methods of organization and control.

The assumptions of Theory Y are not finally validated. Nevertheless, they are far more consistent with existing knowledge in the social sciences than are the assumptions of Theory X. They will undoubtedly be refined, elaborated, modified as further research accumulates, but they are unlikely to be completely contradicted.

On the surface, these assumptions may not seem particularly difficult to accept. Carrying their implications into practice, however, is not easy. They challenge a number of deeply ingrained managerial habits of thought and action.

The principle of integration

The central principle of organization which derives from Theory X is that of direction and control through the exercise of authority – what has been called 'the scalar principle'. The central principle which derives from Theory Y is that of integration: the creation of conditions such that the members of the organization can achieve their own goals *best* by directing their efforts toward the success of the enterprise. These two principles have profoundly different implications with respect to the task of managing human resources, but the scalar principle is so firmly built into managerial attitudes that the implications of the principle of integration are not easy to perceive.

Someone once said that fish discover water last. The 'psychological environment' of industrial management – like water for fish – is so much a part of organizational life that we are unaware of it. Certain characteristics of our society, and of organizational life within it, are so completely established, so pervasive, that we cannot conceive of their being otherwise. As a result, a great many policies and practices and decisions and relationships could only be – it seems – what they are.

Among these pervasive characteristics of organizational life in the United States today is a managerial attitude (stemming from Theory X) toward membership in the industrial organization. It is assumed almost without question that organizational requirements take precedence over the needs of individual members. Basically, the employment agreement is that in return for the rewards which are offered, the individual will accept external direction and control. The very idea of integration and self-control is foreign to our way of thinking about the employment relationship. The tendency, therefore, is either to reject it out of hand (as socialistic, or anarchistic, or inconsistent with human nature) or to twist it unconsciously until it fits existing conceptions.

The concept of integration and self-control carries the implication that the organization will be more effective in achieving its economic objectives if adjustments are made, in significant ways, to the needs and goals of its members.

A district manager in a large, geographically decentralized company is notified that he is being promoted to a policy-level position at headquarters. It is a big promotion with a large salary increase. His role in the organization will be a much more powerful one, and he will be associated with the major executives of the firm.

The headquarters group who selected him for this position have carefully considered a number of possible candidates. This man stands out among them in a way which makes him the natural choice. His performance has been under observation for some time, and there is little question that he possesses the necessary qualifications, not only for this opening but for an even higher position. There is genuine satisfaction that such an outstanding candidate is available.

The man is appalled. He doesn't want the job. His goal, as he expresses it, is to be the 'best damned district manager in the company'. He enjoys his direct associations with operating people in the field, and he doesn't want a policy-level job. He and his wife enjoy the kind of life they have created in a small city, and they dislike actively both the living conditions and the social obligations of the headquarters city.

He expresses his feelings as strongly as he can, but his objections are brushed aside. The organization's needs are such that his refusal to accept the promotion would be unthinkable. His superiors say to themselves that of course when he has settled into the new job, he will recognize that it was the right thing. And so he makes the move.

Two years later he is in an even higher position in the company's headquarters organization, and there is talk that he will probably be the executive vice-president before long. Privately he expresses considerable unhappiness and dissatisfaction. He (and his wife) would 'give anything' to be back in the situation he left two years ago.

Within the context of the pervasive assumptions of Theory X, promotions and transfers in large numbers are made by unilateral decision. The requirements of the organization are given priority automatically and almost without question. If the individual's personal goals are considered at all, it is assumed that the rewards of salary and position will satisfy him. Should an individual actually refuse such a move without reason, such as health or a severe family crisis, he would be considered to have jeopardized his future because of this 'selfish' attitude. It is rare indeed for management to give the individual the opportunity to be a genuine and active partner in such a decision, even though it may affect his most important personal goals. Yet the implications following from Theory Y are that the organization is likely to suffer if it ignores these personal needs and goals. In making unilateral decisions with respect to promotion, management is failing to utilize its human resources in the most effective way.

The principle of integration demands that both the organization's and the individual's needs be recognized. Of course, when there is a sincere joint effort to find it, an integrative solution which meets the needs of the individual *and* the organization is a frequent outcome. But not always – and this is the point at which Theory Y begins to appear unrealistic. It collides head on with pervasive attitudes associated with management by direction and control.

The assumptions of Theory Y imply that unless integration is achieved *the organization will suffer*. The objectives of the organization are *not* achieved best by the unilateral administration of promotions, because this form of management by direction and control will not create the commitment which would make available the full resources of those affected. The lesser motivation, the lesser resulting degree of self-direction and self-control are costs which, when added up for many instances over time, will more than offset the gains obtained by unilateral decisions 'for the good of the organization'.

One other example will perhaps clarify further the sharply different implications of Theory X and Theory Y.

It could be argued that management is already giving a great deal of attention to the principle of integration through its efforts in the field of economic education. Many millions of dollars and much ingenuity have been expended in attempts to persuade employees that their welfare is intimately connected with the success of the free enterprise system and of their own companies. The idea that they can achieve their own goals best by directing their effort toward the objectives of the organization has been explored and developed and communicated in every possible way. Is this not evidence that management is already committed to the principle of integration?

The answer is a definite no. These managerial efforts, with rare exceptions, reflect clearly the influence of the assumptions of Theory X. The central message is an exhortation to the industrial employee to work hard and follow orders in order to protect his job and his standard of living. Much has been achieved, it says, by our established way of running industry, and much more could be achieved if employees would adapt themselves *to management's definition* of what is required. Behind these exhortations lies the expectation that of course the requirements of the organization and its economic success must have priority over the needs of the individual.

Naturally, integration means working together for the success of the enterprise so we all may share in the resulting rewards. But management's implicit assumption is that working together means adjusting to the requirements of the organization *as management perceives them*. In terms of existing views, it seems inconceivable that individuals, seeking their own goals, would further the ends of the enterprise. On the contrary, this would lead to anarchy, chaos, irreconcilable conflicts of self-interest, lack of responsibility, inability to make decisions and failure to carry out those that were made.

All these consequences, and other worse ones, *would* be inevitable unless conditions could be created such that the members of the organization perceived that they could achieve their own goals *best* by directing their efforts toward the success of the enterprise. If the assumptions of Theory Y are valid, the practical question is whether, and to what extent, such conditions can be created. To that question the balance of this volume is addressed.

The application of Theory Y

In the physical sciences there are many theoretical phenomena which cannot be achieved in practice. Absolute zero and a perfect vacuum are examples. Others, such as nuclear power, jet aircraft and human space flight, are recognized theoretically to be possible long before they become feasible. This fact does not make theory less useful. If it were not for our theoretical convictions, we would not even be attempting to develop the means for human flight into space today. In fact, were it not for the development of physical science theory during the past century and a half, we would still be depending upon the horse and buggy and the sailing vessel for transportation. Virtually all significant technological developments wait on the formulation of relevant theory.

Similarly, in the management of the human resources of industry, the assumptions and theories about human nature at any given time limit innovation. Possibilities are not recognized, innovating efforts are not undertaken, until theoretical conceptions lay a groundwork for them. Assumptions like those of Theory X permit us to conceive of certain possible ways of organizing and directing human effort, *but not others*. Assumptions like those of Theory Y open up a range of possibilities for new managerial policies and practices. As in the case of the development of new physical science theory, some of these possibilities are not immediately feasible, and others may forever remain unattainable. They may be too costly, or it may be that we simply cannot discover how to create the necessary 'hardware'.

There is substantial evidence for the statement that the potentialities of the average human being are far above those which we typically realize in industry today. If our assumptions are like those of Theory X, we will not even recognize the existence of these potentialities and there will be no reason to devote time, effort, or money to discovering how to realize them. If, however, we accept assumptions like those of Theory Y, we will be challenged to innovate, to discover new ways of organizing and directing human effort, even though we recognize that the perfect organization, like the perfect vacuum, is practically out of reach.

We need not be overwhelmed by the dimensions of the managerial task implied by Theory Y. To be sure, a large mass-production operation in which the workers have been organized by a militant and hostile union faces management with problems which appear at present to be insurmountable with respect to the application of the principle of integration. It may be decades before sufficient knowledge will have accumulated to make such an application feasible. Applications of Theory Y will have to be tested initially in more limited ways and under more favorable circumstances. However, a number of applications of Theory Y *in managing managers and professional people* are possible today. Within the managerial hierarchy, the assumptions can be tested and refined, techniques can be invented and skill acquired in their use. As knowledge accumulates, some of the problems of application at the worker level in large organizations may appear less baffling than they do at present.

Perfect integration of organizational requirements and individual goals and needs is, of course, not a realistic objective. In adopting this principle, we seek that degree of integration in which the individual can achieve his goals *best* by directing his efforts toward the success of the organization. 'Best' means that this alternative will be more attractive than the many others available to him: indifference, irresponsibility, minimal compliance, hostility, sabotage. It means that he will continuously be encouraged to develop and utilize voluntarily his capacities, his knowledge, his skill, his ingenuity in ways which contribute to the success of the enterprise.[1]

Acceptance of Theory Y does not imply abdication, or 'soft' management, or 'permissiveness'. As was indicated above, such notions stem from the acceptance of authority as the *single* means of managerial control, and from attempts to minimize its negative consequences. Theory Y assumes that people will exercise self-direction and self-control in the achievement of organizational objectives *to the degree that they are committed to those objectives*. If that commitment is small, only a slight degree of self-direction and self-control will be likely, and a substantial amount of external influence will be necessary. If it is large, many conventional external controls will be relatively superfluous, and to some extent self-defeating. Managerial policies and practices materially affect this degree of commitment.

Authority is an inappropriate means for obtaining commitment to objectives. Other forms of influence – help in achieving integration, for example – are required for this purpose. Theory Y points to the possibility of lessening the emphasis on external forms of control to the degree that commitment to organizational objectives can be achieved. Its underlying assumptions emphasize the capacity of human beings for self-control, and the consequent possibility of greater managerial reliance on other means of influence. Nevertheless, it is clear that authority *is* an appropriate means for control under certain circumstances – particularly where genuine

1. A recent, highly significant study of the sources of job satisfaction and dissatisfaction among managerial and professional people suggests that these opportunities for 'self-actualization' are the essential requirements of both job satisfaction and high performance. The researchers find that 'the wants of employees divide into two groups. One group revolves around the need to develop in one's occupation as a source of personal growth. The second group operates as an essential base to the first and is associated with fair treatment in compensation, supervision, working conditions, and administrative practices. *The fulfillment of the needs of the second group does not motivate the individual to high levels of job satisfaction and . . . to extra performance on the job.* All we can expect from satisfying [this second group of needs] is the prevention of dissatisfaction and poor job performance.' Herzberg, Mausner and Snyderman (1959), pp. 114–15. (Italics mine.)

commitment to objectives cannot be achieved. The assumptions of Theory Y do not deny the appropriateness of authority, but they do deny that it is appropriate for all purposes and under all circumstances.

Many statements have been made to the effect that we have acquired today the know-how to cope with virtually any technological problems which may arise, and that the major industrial advances of the next half century will occur on the human side of enterprise. Such advances, however, are improbable so long as management continues to organize and direct and control its human resources on the basis of assumptions – tacit or explicit – like those of Theory X. Genuine innovation, in contrast to a refurbishing and patching of present managerial strategies, requires first the acceptance of less limiting assumptions about the nature of the human resources we seek to control, and second the readiness to adapt selectively to the implications contained in those new assumptions. Theory Y is an invitation to innovation.

Reference

HERZBERG, F., MAUSNER, B., and SNYDERMAN, B. B. (1959), *The Motivation to Work*, Wiley.

17 F. Herzberg

The Motivation–Hygiene Theory

F. Herzberg, 'The motivation–hygiene theory', *Work and the Nature of Man*, World Publishing Co., 1966, chapter 6, pp. 71–91.

With the duality of man's nature in mind, it is well to return to the significance of these essays to industry by reviewing the motivation-hygiene concept of job attitudes as it was reported in Herzberg, Mausner and Snyderman (1959). This study was designed to test the concept that man has two sets of needs: his need as an animal to avoid pain and his need as a human to grow psychologically.

For those who have not read *The Motivation to Work* (Herzberg, Mausner and Snyderman, 1959), I will summarize the highlights of that study. Two hundred engineers and accountants, who represented a cross-section of Pittsburgh industry, were interviewed. They were asked about events they had experienced at work which either had resulted in a marked improvement in their job satisfaction or had led to a marked reduction in job satisfaction.

The interviewers began by asking the engineers and accountants to recall a time when they had felt exceptionally good about their jobs. Keeping in mind the time that had brought about the good feelings, the interviewers proceeded to probe for the reasons why the engineers and accountants felt as they did. The workers were asked also if the feelings of satisfaction in regard to their work had affected their performance, their personal relationships and their well-being.

Finally, the nature of the sequence of events that served to return the workers' attitudes to 'normal' was elicited. Following the narration of a sequence of events, the interview was repeated, but this time the subjects were asked to describe a sequence of events that resulted in negative feelings about their jobs. As many sequences as the respondents were able to give were recorded within the criteria of an acceptable sequence. These were the criteria:

First, the sequence must revolve around an event or series of events; that is, there must be some objective happening. The report cannot be concerned entirely with the respondent's psychological reactions or feelings.

Second, the sequence of events must be bound by time; it should have a beginning that can be identified, a middle and, unless the events are still in process, some sort of identifiable ending (although the cessation of events does not have to be dramatic or abrupt).

Third, the sequence of events must have taken place during a period in which feelings about the job were either exceptionally good or exceptionally bad.

Fourth, the story must be centered on a period in the respondent's life when he held a position that fell within the limits of our sample. However, there were a few exceptions. Stories involving aspirations to professional work or transitions from subprofessional to professional levels were included.

Fifth, the story must be about a situation in which the respondent's feelings about his job were directly affected, not about a sequence of events unrelated to the job that caused high or low spirits.

Figure 1, reproduced from *The Motivation to Work*, shows the major findings of this study. The factors listed are a kind of shorthand for summarizing the 'objective' events that each respondent described. The length of each box represents the frequency with which the factor appeared in the events presented. The width of the box indicates the period in which the good or bad job attitude lasted, in terms of a classification of short duration and long duration. A short duration of attitude change did not last longer than two weeks, while a long duration of attitude change may have lasted for years.

Five factors stand out as strong determiners of job satisfaction – *achievement, recognition, work itself, responsibility* and *advancement* – the last three being of greater importance for lasting change of attitudes. These five factors appeared very infrequently when the respondents described events that paralleled job dissatisfaction feelings. A further word on *recognition:* when it appeared in a 'high' sequence of events, it referred to recognition for achievement rather than to recognition as a human-relations tool divorced from any accomplishment. The latter type of recognition does not serve as a 'satisfier'.

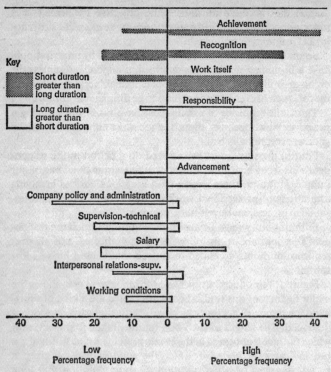

Figure 1 Comparison of satisfiers and dissatisfiers (reproduced from Herzberg, Mausner and Snyderman, *The Motivation to Work,* Wiley, 1959, by permission of the publishers)

When the factors involved in the job dissatisfaction events were coded, an entirely different set of factors evolved. These factors were similar to the satisfiers in their unidimensional effect. This time, however, they served only to bring about job dissatisfaction and were rarely involved in events that led to positive job attitudes. Also, unlike the 'satisfiers', the 'dissatisfiers' consistently produced short-term changes in job attitudes. The major dissatisfiers were *company policy and administration, supervision, salary, interpersonal relations* and *working conditions.*

What is the explanation of such results? Do the two sets of

factors have two separate themes? It appears so, for the factors on the right of Figure 1 all seem to describe man's relationship to what he does: his job content, achievement on a task, recognition for task achievement, the nature of the task, responsibility for a task and professional advancement or growth in task capability.

What is the central theme for the dissatisfiers? Restating the factors as the kind of administration and supervision received in doing the job, the nature of interpersonal relationships and working conditions that surround the job and the effect of salary suggest the distinction from the 'satisfier' factors. Rather than describe man's relationship to what he does, the 'dissatisfier' factors describe his relationship to the context or environment in which he does his job. One cluster of factors relates to what the person does and the other to the situation in which he does it.

Since the dissatisfier factors essentially describe the environment and serve primarily to prevent job dissatisfaction, while having little effect on positive job attitudes, they have been named the *hygiene* factors. This is an analogy to the medical use of the term meaning 'preventative and environmental'. Another term for these factors in current use is *maintenance* factors. I am indebted to Dr Robert Ford of the American Telephone and Telegraph Company for this excellent synonym. The 'satisfier' factors were named the *motivators*, since other findings of the study suggest that they are effective in motivating the individual to superior performance and effort.

So far, I have described that part of the interview that was restricted to determining the actual objective events as reported by the respondents (first level of analysis). They were also asked to interpret the events, to tell why the particular event led to a change in their feelings about their jobs (second level of analysis). The principal result of the analysis of this data was to suggest that the hygiene or maintenance events led to job dissatisfaction because of a need to *avoid* unpleasantness; the motivator events led to job satisfaction because of a need for growth or self-actualization. At the psychological level, the two dimensions of job attitudes reflected a two-dimensional need structure: one need system for the avoidance of unpleasantness and a parallel need system for personal growth.

The discussion so far has paved the way for the explanation of the duality of job-attitude results. Why do the hygiene factors serve as dissatisfiers? They represent the environment to which man the animal is constantly trying to adjust, for the environment is the source of Adam's suffering. The hygiene factors listed are the major environmental aspects of work.

Why do the motivators affect motivation in the positive direction? An analogy drawn from a familiar example of psychological growth in children may be useful. When a child learns to ride a bicycle, he is becoming more competent, increasing the repertory of his behavior, expanding his skills – psychologically growing. In the process of the child's learning to master a bicycle, the parents can love him with all the zeal and compassion of the most devoted mother and father. They can safeguard the child from injury by providing the safest and most hygienic area in which to practice; they can offer all kinds of incentives and rewards, and they can provide the most expert instructions. But the child will never, never learn to ride the bicycle – unless he is given a bicycle! The hygiene factors are not a valid contributor to psychological growth. The substance of a task is required to achieve growth goals. Similarly, you cannot love an engineer into creativity, although by this approach you can avoid his dissatisfactions with the way you treat him. Creativity will require a potentially creative task to do.

In summary, two essential findings were derived from this study. First, the factors involved in producing job satisfaction were *separate* and *distinct* from the factors that led to job dissatisfaction. Since separate factors needed to be considered, depending on whether job satisfaction or job dissatisfaction was involved, it followed that these two feelings were not the obverse of each other. Thus, the opposite of job satisfaction would not be job dissatisfaction, but rather *no* job satisfaction; similarly, the opposite of job dissatisfaction is *no* job dissatisfaction, not satisfaction with one's job. The fact that job satisfaction is made up of two unipolar traits is not unique, but it remains a difficult concept to grasp.

Perhaps another analogy will help explain this new way of thinking about job attitudes. Let us characterize job satisfaction as vision and job dissatisfaction as hearing. It is readily seen that we are talking about two separate dimensions, since the stimulus for vision is light, and increasing and decreasing light will have no effect on man's hearing. The stimulus for audition is sound, and, in a similar fashion, increasing or decreasing loudness will have no effect on vision.

Man's basic needs can be diagrammed as two parallel arrows pointing in opposite directions. One arrow depicts his Animal-Adam nature, which is concerned with avoidance of pain stemming from the environment, and for man the psychological environment is the major source of this pain. The other arrow represents man's Human-Abraham nature, which is concerned with approaching self-fulfillment or psychological growth through the accomplishment of tasks.

Animal-Adam – avoidance of pain from environment

$\longleftarrow$ ─────────────────────────────────

Human-Abraham – seeking growth from tasks

───────────────────────────────── $\longrightarrow$

The problem of establishing a zero point in psychology, with the procedural necessity of using instead a bench mark (e.g., the mean of a population) from which to start our measurement, has led to the conception that psychological traits are bipolar. Recent empirical investigations, however, have cast some shadows on the assumptions of bipolarity for many psychological attributes, in addition to job attitudes, as shown in *The Motivation to Work*.

Thus, the hypothesis with which the study of motivation began appears to be verified. The factors on the right of Figure 1 that led to satisfaction (*achievement, recognition, work itself, responsibility* and *advancement*) are mainly unipolar; that is, they contribute very little to job dissatisfaction. Conversely, the dissatisfiers (*company policy and administration, supervision, interpersonal relations, working conditions* and *salary*) contribute very little to job satisfaction.

Sixteen separate job-attitude factors were investigated in the original study dealing with accountants and engineers. Only those motivators and hygiene factors that were found to differentiate statistically between positive and negative job attitudes were presented. However, the other factors have similarly been shown to fall into one category or the other in the follow-up studies to be described in subsequent chapters. These factors are *possibility of growth*, a task-centered motivator, and the hygiene factors, *salary, status, job security* and *effect on personal life*.

In Chapter 2, I indicated a desire to define a human being and in the following sections I have attempted to organize man's needs to reach such a definition. Since man is capable of such a variety of behavior and still can survive, it is little wonder that so many ways of acting can be declared normal, dependent on their cultural acceptance. In this sense, a prominent difference between cultures lies in the kinds of pathology that are declared normal. At this point, the theory of job motivation will be expanded to a general concept of mental health, and this in turn will allow for a culture-free definition of mental illness.

Just as there are two sets of needs at work – hygiene needs and motivator needs – and two continua to represent them, so we may speak of two continua in mental health: a mental-illness continuum and a mental-health continuum. We have seen that a conceptual shift in viewpoint regarding job attitudes has been made in order to incorporate the two-dimensional motivation-hygiene theory. Essentially the same shift might well lead to an equally important change in theory and research on mental health.

The argument for this generalization has been presented in two papers by Dr Roy Hamlin of the Veterans Administration and myself. The implications for mental health are best introduced by recalling the subjective reactions of the employees as to why the various factors affected them as they did. For the job-dissatisfied situation the subjects reported that they were made unhappy mostly because they felt they were being treated unfairly or that they found the situation unpleasant or painful. On the other hand, the common denominator for the reasons for positive job attitudes seemed to be variations on the theme of feelings of psychological growth, the fulfillment of self-actualizing needs. There was an approach-avoidance dichotomy with respect to job adjustment. A need to avoid unpleasant job environments led to job dissatisfaction; the need for self-realization led to job satisfaction when the opportunity for self-realization was afforded.

A 'hygienic' environment prevents discontent with a job, but such an environment cannot lead the individual beyond a minimal adjustment consisting of the absence of dissatisfaction. A positive 'happiness' seems to require some attainment of psychological growth.

It is clear why the hygiene factors fail to provide for positive satisfactions: they do not possess the characteristics necessary for giving an individual a sense of growth. To feel that one has grown depends on achievement in tasks that have meaning to the individual, and since the hygiene factors do not relate to the task, they are powerless to give such meaning to the individual. Growth is dependent on some achievements, but achievement requires a task. The motivators are task factors and thus are necessary for growth; they provide the psychological stimulation by which the individual can be activated toward his self-realization needs.

To generalize from job attitudes to mental attitudes, we can think of two types of adjustment for mental equilibrium. First, an adjustment to the environment, which is mainly an avoidance adjustment; second, an adjustment to oneself, which is dependent on the successful striving for psychological growth, self-actualization, self-realization or, most simply, being psychologically more than one has been in the past.

Traditionally, mental health has been regarded as the obverse of mental illness. Mental health, in this sense, is the mere *absence* of mental illness. At one time, the psychiatrist anticipated that mental health would be automatically *released* when the conflicts of mental illness were resolved. And, currently, the biochemist hopes that mental health will bloom once neuroenzymes are properly balanced and optimally distributed in the brain.

In essence, this traditional view ignores *mental health*. In general, the focus has been on mental illness – on anxiety, anxiety-reducing mechanisms, past frustrations, childhood trauma, distressing interpersonal relations, disturbing ideas and worries, current patterns of inefficiency and stressful present environment. Except for sporadic lip service, positive attitudes and experiences have been considered chiefly in an atmosphere of alleviating distress and dependency.

The factors that determine mental illness are *not the obverse* of the mental health factors. Rather, the mental illness factors belong to the category of hygiene factors, which describe the environment of man and serve to cause illness when they are deficient but effect little positive increase in mental health. They are factors that cause avoidance behavior; yet, as will be explained, only in the 'sick' individual is there an attempt to activate approach behavior.

The implications of the conceptual shift for job satisfaction have been discussed. Traditional research on job attitudes has focused almost exclusively on only one set of factors, on the hygiene or job-context factors. The motivating factors, the positive or self-actualizing factors, have been largely neglected. The thesis holds that a very similar neglect has characterized traditional research on mental health.

Specifically, the resolution of conflicts, the correction of bio-chemical imbalance and the modification of psychic defenses might all be assigned to the attempts to modify the hygiene or avoidance needs of the individual. The positive motivating factors – self-actualization and personal growth – have received treatment of two sorts. Either they have been neglected or dismissed as irre-levant, or they have been regarded as so individually sacred and vague as to defy research analysis. At best, the mental health factors have been looked upon as important *forces* that might be released by the removal of mental illness factors.

The motivation-hygiene concept stresses three points regarding mental adjustment. The first is the proposition that mental illness and mental health are not of the same dimension. Contrary to classical psychiatric belief, there are degrees of sickness and there are degrees of health. The degree of sickness reflects an individual's reaction to the hygiene factors, while the degree of mental health represents his reaction to the motivator factors.

Second, the motivator-mental-health aspect of personal adjust-ment has been sadly neglected in theory, in research and in application. The positive side of personal adjustment has been considered to be a dividend or consequence of successful attention to the 'negative-maladjustment' side.

The third point is a new definition or idea of mental illness. The new definition derives from the first proposition that mental illness is not the opposite of mental health, as is suggested by some of the data on job satisfaction.

While the incidents in which job satisfaction were reported almost always contained the factors that related to the job task – the motivators – there were some individuals who reported receiv-ing job satisfaction solely from hygiene factors, that is, from some aspect of the job environment. Commenting on this reversal, the authors of *The Motivation to Work* suggest that 'there may be individuals who because of their training and because of the things that have happened to them have learned to react positively to the factors associated with the *context* of their jobs.' The hygiene seekers are primarily attracted to things that usually serve only to prevent dissatisfaction, not to be a source of positive feelings. The hygiene seekers have not reached a stage of personality development at which self-actualizing needs are active. From this point of view, they are fixated at a less mature level of personal adjustment.

Implied in *The Motivation to Work* is the admonition to industry that the lack of 'motivators' in jobs will increase the sensitivity of employees to real or imagined bad job hygiene, and consequently the amount and quality of hygiene given to employees must be constantly improved. There is also the reported finding that the relief from job dissatisfaction by hygiene factors has only a temporary effect and therefore adds to the necessity for more frequent attention to the job environment. The graphs shown in Figure 1 indicate that the hygiene factors stem from short-range events, as contrasted with the longer range of motivator events. It will be recalled in Chapter 4, on the basic needs of man, that animal or hygiene drives, being cyclical, are only temporarily satisfied. The cyclical nature of these drives is necessary in order to sustain life. The hygiene factors on the job partake of the quality of briefly acting analgesics for meaningless work; the individual becomes unhappy without them, but is relieved only temporarily with them, for their effects soon wear off and the hygiene seeker is left chronically dissatisfied.

A hygiene seeker is not merely a victim of circumstances, but is *motivated* in the direction of temporary satisfaction. It is not that his job offers little opportunity for self-actualization; rather, it is that his needs lie predominantly in another direction, that of satisfying avoidance needs. He is seeking positive happiness via the route of avoidance behavior, and thus his resultant chronic dissatisfaction is an illness of motivation. Chronic unhappiness, a motivation pattern that insures continual dissatisfaction, a failure to grow or to want to grow – these characteristics add up to a neurotic personality.

So it appears that the neurotic is an individual with a lifetime pattern of hygiene seeking and that the definition of a neurotic, in terms of defenses against anxiety arising from early psychological conflicts, represents at best the *origin* of his hygiene seeking. The motivation-hygiene view of a neurotic adjustment is free of substantial ties with any theory of etiology, and therefore the thesis is independent of conceptualizations regarding the traditional dynamics of personality development and adjustment. The neurotic motivation pattern of hygiene seeking is mostly a learned process that arises from the value systems endemic in society.

Since total adaptation depends on the gratification of two separate types of needs, a rough operational categorization of adjustment can be made by examining the sources of a person's satisfactions.

A first category is characterized by positive mental health. Persons in this category show a preponderance of lifetime contentment stemming from situations in which the motivator factors are paramount. These factors are necessary in providing them with a sense of personal growth. They can be identified as directly involving the individual in some task, project or activity in which achievement or the consequences of achievement are possible. Those factors found meaningful for industrial job satisfaction may not be complete or may not be sufficiently descriptive to encompass the total life picture of an individual.

Other factors may be necessary to describe the motivators in this larger sense. Whatever they may be, the criteria for their selection must include activity on the part of the individual – some task, episode, adventure or activity in which the individual achieves a growth experience and without which the individual *will not* feel unhappy, dissatisfied or uncomfortable. In addition, to belong to this positive category the individual must have frequent opportunity for the gratification of these motivator needs. How frequent and how challenging the growth opportunities must be will depend on the level of ability (both genetic and learned) of the individual and, secondly, on his tolerance for delayed success. This tolerance, too, may be constitutional, learned or governed by dynamic conflicts; the source does not really matter to the argument.

The motivation-hygiene concept may seem to involve certain paradoxes. For example, is all achievement work and no play? Is the individual of limited ability doomed to be a nonachiever, and therefore a hygiene seeker?

In regard to work and play, achievements include all personal growth experiences. While it is true that *The Motivation to Work* focuses on industrial production, as demanded by society or company policy, the satisfying sequences reported are rich in examples of creativity and individual initiative. Artistic and scholarly interests, receptive openness to new insights, true relaxation and regrouping of growth potentials (as contrasted with plain laziness) are all achievement or elements in achievement. Nowhere is the balanced work-play growth element in achievement more apparent than in the mentally healthy individual.

In regard to limitations resulting from meager ability, the motivating history of achievement depends to an important degree on a realistic attitude. The individual who concerns himself largely with vague aspirations, completely unrelated to his abilities and to the actual situation, is simply one kind of hygiene seeker. He does not seek satisfaction in the job itself, but rather in those surrounding conditions that include such cultural noises as 'any American boy can be president' or 'every young man should have a college degree'. The quotation by Carl Jung bears repetition: 'The supreme goal of man is to fulfil himself as a creative, *unique* individual according to his own *innate potentialities* and within the *limits of reality*.' (Italics supplied.)

A final condition for membership in this mentally healthy group would be a good life environment or the successful avoidance of poor hygiene factors. Again, those conditions mentioned previously for the work situation may not suffice for all the environments of the individual.

Three conditions, then, will serve to define a mentally healthy individual: seeking life satisfaction through personal growth experiences (experiences defined as containing the motivator factors); sufficient success, commensurate with ability and tolerance for delay, to give direct evidence of growth, and, finally, successful avoidance of discomfort from poor hygiene.

If the hygiene is poor, the mental health is not affected, but obviously the individual becomes unhappy. This second category of adjustment – self-fulfillment, accompanied by dissatisfaction with the rewards of life, perhaps characterizes that large segment of the population that continues to do a good job despite reason for complaint. There is research evidence to support the idea that a motivator seeker who is effective in his performance will be listed among the gripers in a company. This is not surprising, for he feels justified in his criticisms because he earns his right to complain and is perhaps bright enough to see reasons for his ill temper.

A third category consists of individuals characterized by symptom-free adjustment. Individuals grouped in this category would also have sought and obtained their satisfactions primarily from the motivator factors. However, their growth needs will be much less reinforced during their life because of lack of opportunity. Such individuals will not have achieved a complete sense of accomplishment because of circumstances extrinsic to their motivation. Routine jobs and routine life-experiences attenuate the growth of these individuals, not their motivation. Because their motivation is healthy, we do not place these persons on the sick continuum. In addition, those in this category must have sufficient satisfactions of their hygiene needs.

It is not unusual, though it is infrequent, to find that a respondent in the job-attitude investigations will stress one or more of the motivator factors as contributing to his job dissatisfaction. In other words, a satisfier acts as a dissatisfier. This occurrence most frequently includes the factors of failure of advancement, lack of recognition, lack of responsibility and uninteresting work. Closer inspection of these incidents reveals that many are insincere protestations covering a more latent hygiene desire. For example, the respondent who declares that his unhappiest time on the job occurred when his boss did not recognize his work is often saying that he misses the comfort and security of an accepting supervisor. His hygiene needs are simply wrapped in motivator clothing.

However, there are some highly growth-oriented persons who so desire the motivators and seek so very much a positive aspect for their lives that deprivation in this area may be interpreted by them as pain. In this case, their inversion of a motivator for a dissatisfaction episode is legitimate, but it represents a misinterpretation of their feelings. Their lack of happiness is felt as unhappiness, although it is qualitatively quite different from the unhappiness they experience because of the lack of the 'hygiene' factors. Often these people summarize their job-attitude feelings by saying, 'I really can't complain, but I sure don't like what I am doing,' or, 'As a job goes, this isn't bad, but I'm not getting anywhere.'

The fourth category of essentially health-oriented people includes those who, paradoxically, are miserable. These are the motivator seekers who are denied any psychological growth opportunities and, in addition, find themselves with their hygiene needs simultaneously deprived. However miserable they might be, they are differentiated from the next three categories by their reluctance to adopt neurotic or psychotic defense mechanisms to allay their dual pain.

The next category represents a qualitative jump from the mental health dimension to the mental illness dimension. This category may be called the *maladjusted*. The basic characteristic of persons in this group is that they have sought positive satisfaction from the hygiene factors. There is an inversion of motivation away from the approach behavior of growth to the avoidance behavior of comfortable environments. Members of this group are the hygiene seekers, whose maladjustment is defined by the direction of their motivation and is evidenced by the environmental source of their satisfactions.

Many in this category will have had a significant number of personal achievements that result in no growth experience. It has been noted that hygiene satisfactions are short-lived and partake of the characteristics of opiates. The environmental satisfactions for persons whom we call maladjusted must be rather frequent and of substantial quality. It is the satisfactions of their hygiene needs that differentiate the maladjusted from the next category in our system – the mentally ill.

The mentally ill are lifetime hygiene seekers with poor hygiene satisfactions (as perceived by the individual). This poor hygiene may be realistic or it may reflect mostly the accentuated sensitivity to hygiene deprivation because of the inversion of motivation.

One of the extremes to which the 'hygiene or maintenance' seeker resorts is to deny his hygiene needs altogether. This is termed the 'monastic' defense. Seemingly, this line of reasoning asserts that the denial of man's animal nature will reward the individual with happiness, because the proponents of the 'monastic' view of man's nature have discovered that no amount of hygiene rewards lead to human happiness. This sometime revered approach to the human dilemma now emerges as the blatant *non sequitur* that it is. How can psychological growth be achieved by denying hygiene realities? The illness is at two levels. The primary sickness is the denial of man's animal nature. Second, psychological growth and happiness depend on two separate factors, and no denial of irrelevant factors will serve man in his pursuit of happiness.

The motivation-hygiene concept holds that mental health depends on the individual's history or past experience. The history of the healthy individual shows success in growth achievements. In contrast, mental illness depends on a different pattern of past experience. The unhealthy individual has concerned himself with surrounding conditions. His search for satisfaction has focused on the limitations imposed by objective reality and by other individuals, including society and culture.

In the usual job situation these limitations consist of company policy, supervision, interpersonal relations and the like. In broader life adjustments the surrounding conditions include cultural taboos, social demands for material production and limited native ability. The hygiene seeker devotes his energies to concern with the surrounding limitations, to 'defenses' in the Freudian sense. He seeks satisfaction, or mental health, in a policy of 'defense'. No personal growth occurs and his search for health is fruitless, for it leads to ever more intricate maneuvers of defense or hygiene seeking. Mental illness is an inversion – the attempt to accentuate or deny one set of needs in the hope of obtaining the other set.

To reiterate, mankind has two sets of needs. Think about man twice: once about events that cause him pain and, secondly, about events that make him happy. Those who seek only to gratify the needs of their animal natures are doomed to live in dreadful anticipation of pain and suffering. This is the fate of those human beings who want to satisfy only their biological needs. But some men have become aware of the advantage humans have over their animal brothers. In addition to the compulsion to avoid pain, the human being has been blessed with the potentiality to achieve happiness. And, as I hope I have demonstrated, man can be happy only by seeking to satisfy both his animal need to avoid pain and his human need to grow psychologically.

The seven classifications of adjustment continua are shown in Figure 2, using the motivation-hygiene theory frame of reference

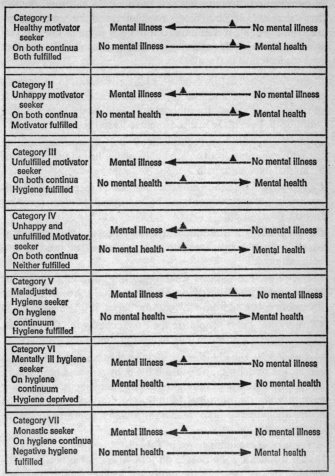

Figure 2

of parallel and diverging arrows. Within each category, the top arrow depicts the mental illness continuum and the bottom arrow the mental health continuum. The triangle signifies the scale on which the individual is operating and the degree of his gratification with the factors of that scale.

Category I: The healthy motivator seeker is shown to be on both the mental illness and the mental health continua, and he is successful in achieving the motivator (mental health) needs and in avoiding the pain of the hygiene (mental illness) needs.

Category II: The unhappy motivator seeker is depicted as obtaining human significance from his job but receiving little amelioration of his animal-avoidance pains.

Category III: This shows the motivator seeker searching for gratification of both sets of needs but being successful only in avoiding hygiene deprivation.

Category IV: The miserable motivator seeker is illustrated as basically healthy but, unfortunately, with neither need system being serviced.

Category V: The hygiene seeker who is motivated only by his hygiene needs is indicated here. He is successful at avoiding mental illness but debarred from achieving mental health.

Category VI: These people are the true mentally ill. They are the hygiene seekers who fail in their hygiene gratification.

Category VII: Finally, there is that interesting form of hygiene seeker, the 'monastic', who also is living by only one need system and is fulfilling his hygiene requirements by denying them. Familiar examples are the no-talent beatnik, the sacrificing mother, the severe disciplinarian in the military world and, less often today, his counterpart in industry.

These types are summarized in Table 1.

Can we identify the people on jobs who are the healthy individuals, that is, who are the motivator seekers, as distinguished from the hygiene seekers? What are the consequences to companies that select and reinforce hygiene seekers? These questions will be examined in the final chapter, but at this point a brief description of hygiene seekers and of the consequences to the company hiring them will be useful.

Table 1 Types of Adjustments

Classification	Orientation	Motivator satisfaction	Hygiene satisfaction
Mental Health	Motivator	Yes	Yes
Unhappy	Motivator	Yes	No
Unfulfilled	Motivator	No	Yes
Unhappy and unfulfilled	Motivator	No	No
Maladjusted	Hygiene	Not pertinent	Yes
Mental illness	Hygiene	Not pertinent	No
Monastic	Hygiene	Not pertinent	Denied

The hygiene seeker, as opposed to the motivator seeker, is motivated by the nature of the environment of his job rather than by his tasks. He suffers from a chronic and heightened dissatisfaction with his job hygiene. Why? Because he lives by it. He has an overreaction to improvement in hygiene factors. You give him a salary raise and you become the most wonderful boss in the world; he is in the most wonderful company in the world – he protests too much. In other words, you have given him a shot in the arm. But the satisfactions of hygiene factors are of short duration – and the short action applies as well to the motivator seeker, because this is the nature of the beast.

The hygiene seeker realizes little satisfaction from accomplishments and consequently shows little interest in the kind and quality of the work he does. Why? Since he is basically an avoidance-oriented organism, how can he have a positive outlook on life? He does not profit professionally from experience. The only profit he desires is a more comfortable environment. 'What did you learn?' 'Nothing, it was a complete waste of time.' Obviously, there was no definite reward. In other words, even though you can stimulate him for a temporary action, he does not have his own generator. And I think, also, that many companies feel they have to keep doing his stimulating.

The hygiene seeker is ultraliberal or ultraconservative. He parrots management's philosophy. As a means of reducing ambiguity he acts more like top management than top management does. The question arises whether he may be successful on the job because of talent. The question is then legitimately asked: If a man does well on the job because of hygiene satisfactions, what difference does it make?

The answer is twofold. I believe that hygiene seekers will let the company down when their talents are most needed. They are motivated only for short times and only when there is an external reward to be obtained. It is just when an emergency situation arises, and when the organization cannot be bothered with hygiene, that these key men may fail to do their jobs. In the Army, they are known as 'barracks soldiers'.

The second answer I suggest, and one that I believe to be of more serious import, is that hygiene seekers offer their own motivational characteristics as the pattern to be instilled in their subordinates. They become the template from which the new recruit to industry learns his motivational pattern. Hygiene seekers in key positions set the extrinsic reward atmosphere for the units of the company that they control. Because of the talent they possess, their influence on conditioning the atmosphere is generally out of proportion to their long-term effectiveness to the company.

Table 2 Characteristics of Hygiene and Motivation Seekers

Hygiene seeker	*Motivation seeker*
1. Motivated by nature of the environment	Motivated by nature of the task
2. Chronic and heightened dissatisfaction with various aspects of his job context, e.g., salary, supervision, working conditions, status, job security, company policy and administration, fellow employees	Higher tolerance for poor hygiene factors
3. Overreaction with satisfaction to improvement in hygiene factors	Less reaction to improvement in hygiene factors
4. Short duration of satisfaction when the hygiene factors are improved	Similar

Hygiene seeker	Motivation seeker
5. Overreaction with dissatisfaction when hygiene factors are not improved	Milder discontent when hygiene factors need improvement
6. Realizes little satisfactions from accomplishments	Realizes great satisfaction from accomplishments
7. Shows little interest in the kind and quality of the work he does	Shows capacity to enjoy the kind of work he does
8. Cynicism regarding positive virtues of work and life in general	Has positive feelings toward work and life in general
9. Does not profit professionally from experience	Profits professionally from experience
10. Prone to cultural noises (a) Ultraliberal, ultraconservative (b) Parrots management philosophy (c) Acts more like top management than top management does	Belief systems sincere and considered
11. May be successful on the job because of talent	May be an overachiever

If we accept the notion that one of the most important functions of a manager is the development of future managers, the teaching of hygiene motivations becomes a serious defect to the company. This, I believe, is one of the major implications that the motivation-hygiene theory has for modern personnel practices. Previous research knowledge has strongly indicated that the effectiveness of management development is attuned to its congruence with the company atmosphere, as it is manifested in the superior's beliefs and behavior. The superior who is a hygiene seeker cannot but have an adverse effect on management development, which is aimed at the personal growth and actualization of subordinates.

Table 2 summarizes the characteristics of the hygiene seeker and the motivator seeker as manifested at work. Further explorations of their characteristics will be made in the final chapter.

In this chapter, we have given a brief summary of the motivation-hygiene theory, which began with a study of job attitudes of engineers and accountants in Pittsburgh. In the next two chapters, the subsequent investigations that document this theory will be reviewed.

Reference

HERZBERG, F., MAUSNER, B., and SNYDERMAN, B. B. (1959), *The Motivation to Work*, Wiley.

18 E. A. Trist and K.W. Bamforth

Some Social and Psychological Consequences of the Longwall Method of Coal-Getting

From E. L. Trist and K. W. Bamforth, 'Some social and psychological consequences of the longwall method of coal-getting', *Human Relations*, vol. 4, 1951, no. 1, pp. 6–24 and 37–8.

The character of the pre-mechanized equilibrium and the nature of its disturbance

Hand-got systems and the responsible autonomy of the pair-based work group

The outstanding feature of the social pattern with which the pre-mechanized equilibrium was associated is its emphasis on small group organization at the coal-face. The groups themselves were interdependent working pairs to whom one or two extra individuals might be attached. It was common practice for two colliers – a hewer and his mate – to make their own contract with the colliery management and to work their own small face with the assistance of a boy 'trammer'. This working unit could function equally well in a variety of engineering layouts both of the advance and retreat type, whether step-wise or direct. Sometimes it extended its numbers to seven or eight, when three or four colliers, and their attendant trammers, would work together.[1]

A primary work-organization of this type has the advantage of placing responsibility for the complete coal-getting task squarely on the shoulders of a single, small, face-to-face group which experiences the entire cycle of operations within the compass of its membership. For each participant the task has total significance and dynamic closure. Though the contract may have been in the name of the hewer, it was regarded as a joint undertaking. Leadership and 'supervision' were internal to the group, which had a

---

1. Hand-got methods contained a number of variants, but discussion of these is beyond present scope.

quality of *responsible autonomy*. The capacity of these groups for self-regulation was a function of the wholeness of their work task, this connection being represented in their contractual status. A whole has power as an independent detachment, but a part requires external control.

Within these pair-based units was contained the full range of coal-face skills; each collier being an all-round workman, usually able to substitute for his mate. Though his equipment was simple, his tasks were multiple. The 'underground skill' on which their efficient and safe execution depended was almost entirely person-carried. He had craft pride and artisan independence. These qualities obviated status difficulties and contributed to responsible autonomy.

Choice of workmates posed a crucial question. These choices were made by the men themselves, sociometrically, under full pressure of the reality situation and with long-standing knowledge of each other. Stable relationships tended to result, which frequently endured over many years. In circumstances where a man was injured or killed, it was not uncommon for his mate to care for his family. These work relationships were often reinforced by kinship ties, the contract system and the small group autonomy allowing a close but spontaneous connection to be maintained between family and occupation, which avoided tying the one to the other. In segregated mining communities the link between kinship and occupation can be oppressive as well as supportive; against this danger, 'exogamous' choice was a safeguard. But against too emotional a relationship, more likely to develop between non-kin associates, kinship barriers were in turn a safeguard.

The wholeness of the work task, the multiplicity of the skills of the individual, and the self-selection of the group were congruent attributes of a pattern of responsible autonomy that characterized the pair-based face teams of hand-got mining.

The adaptability of the small group to the underground situation

Being able to work their own short faces continuously, these pair, or near pair, groups could stop at whatever point may have been reached by the end of a shift. The flexibility in work pace so allowed had special advantages in the underground situation; for when bad conditions were encountered, the extraction process in a series of stalls could proceed unevenly in correspondence with the uneven distribution of these bad conditions, which tend to occur now in one and now in another section along a seam. Even under good conditions, groups of this kind were free to set their own targets, so that aspirations levels with respect to production could be adjusted to the age and stamina of the individuals concerned.

In the underground situation external dangers must be faced in darkness. Darkness also awakens internal dangers. The need to share with others anxieties aroused by this double threat may be taken as self-evident. In view of the restricted range of effective communication, these others have to be immediately present. Their number therefore is limited. These conditions point to the strong need in the underground worker for a role in a small primary group.

A second characteristic of the underground situation is the wide dispersal of particular activities, in view of the large area over which operations generally are extended. The small groups of the hand-got systems tended to become isolated from each other even when working in the same series of stalls; the isolation of the group, as of the individual, being intensified by the darkness. Under these conditions there is no possibility of continuous supervision, in the factory sense, from any individual external to the primary work group.

The small group, capable of responsible autonomy, and able to vary its work pace in correspondence with changing conditions, would appear to be the type of social structure ideally adapted to the underground situation. It is instructive that the traditional work systems, evolved from the experience of successive generations, should have been founded on a group with these attributes.

But to earn a living under hand-got conditions often entailed physical effort of a formidable order, and possession of exceptional skill was required to extract a bare existence from a hard seam with a bad roof. To tram tubs was 'horse-work'. Trammers were commonly identified by scabs, called 'buttons', on the bone joints of their backs, caused by catching the roof while pushing and holding tubs on and off 'the gates'. Hand-got conditions still obtain, for by no means all faces are serviced by conveyors and coal-cutters. In some circumstances this equipment is unsuitable.

But hardness of work is a separate consideration from the quality of the group.

The counter balance of the large undifferentiated collectivity

The psychological disadvantages of a work system, the small group organization of which is based on pair relationships, raises issues of a far-reaching kind only recently submitted to study in group dynamics (Bion, 1949). It would appear that the self-enclosed character of the relationship makes it difficult for groups of this kind to combine effectively in differentiated structures of a somewhat larger social magnitude, though this inability does not seem to hold in respect of much larger collectivities of a simpler mass character. But in premechanized mining there was no technological necessity for intermediate structures, equivalent to factory departments, to make their appearance between the small pair-based primary units and the larger collectivities called into action by situations of crisis and common danger. To meet situations requiring the mobilization of the large mass group, mining communities have developed traditions generally recognized as above the norm commonly attained by occupational groups in our society. This supra-normative quality was present also in the traditions of the small pair-based organizations. But between these extremes there was little experience.

Sociologically, this situation is not atypical of industries which, though large-scale, have experienced delay in undergoing mechanization. The pair-based face teams corresponded to the technological simplicity of the hand-got methods, with their short faces, autonomously worked and loosely coordinated on a district basis. The mass collectivities reflected the large-scale size of the pit as an overall industrial unit. Absent were structures at the level of the factory department, whose process-linked, fractionated role-systems, dependent on external supervision, were antithetical alike to the pattern of small group autonomy and to the artisan outlook of the collier.

In the pre-mechanized pattern, the pair-based primaries and the large relatively undifferentiated collectivities composed a dynamically interrelated system that permitted an enduring social balance. The intense reciprocities of the former, with their personal and family significance, and the diffuse identifications of the latter, with their community and class connectedness, were mutually supportive. The face teams could bear the responsibility of their autonomy through the security of their dependence on the united collectivity of the pit.

Difficulties arose largely from rivalries and conflicts between the various pairs and small teams. A common form of 'graft' was to bribe the deputy in order to secure a good 'benk', i.e. a 'length' with a 'rack roof', under which the coal was notoriously soft and easy to work. Trammers were encouraged to resort to sharp practices to obtain adequate supplies of tubs. As supplies were often short, the amount of coal a working pair could send up depended not a little on the prowess of their trammer. Going early to work, he would turn two or three tubs on their sides in his 'gate', maintaining he had taken only one. Ensuing disputes caused frequent fights both underground and in the community. In the common saying, it was he who could lie, cheat, or bully the most who made the best trammer. All this was accepted as part of the system.

Inter-team conflict provided a channel for aggression that preserved intact the loyalties on which the small group depended. In the large group aggression received structured expression in trade-union resistance. If the struggle was harsh, it was at least direct and understandable. It was not the insidious kind that knocked the bottom out of life, leaving those concerned without a sense of a scheme in things – the 'anomic' described by Halliday (1949) after the transition to the longwall. The system as a whole contained its bad in a way that did not destroy its good. The balance persisted, albeit that work was of the hardest, rewards often meagre, and the social climate rough at times and even violent.

Mechanization and the problem of intermediate organization

With the advent of coal-cutters and mechanical conveyors, the degree of technological complexity of the coal-getting task was raised to a different level. Mechanization made possible the working of a single long face in place of a series of short faces. In thin seams short faces increase costs, since a large number of 'gates' (see Figure 1) have to be 'ripped' up several feet above the height of the seam to create haulage and travelling facilities. In British coal, seams less than 4 ft in thickness are common, so that there was a tendency to make full use of the possibility of working optimally long rather than optimally short faces. For this reason, and for others also, discussion of which is beyond present scope, the longwall method came into being. Applicable to thick as well as to thin seams, it became the general method of coal-getting in the British industry, enabling the average type of pit, which may contain three or four seams of different thickness, to work its entire coal economically, and to develop its layout and organize its production in terms of a single, self-consistent plan. In America, where thick seams are the rule, mechanization has developed in terms of shorter faces and room-and-pillar techniques.

The associated characteristics of mechanized complexity, and of largeness as regards the scale of the primary production unit, created a situation in which it was impossible for the method to develop as a technological system without bringing into existence a work relationship structure radically different from that associated with hand-got procedures. The artisan type of pair, composed of the skilled man and his mate, assisted by one or more labourers, was out of keeping as a model for the type of work group required. Need arose for a unit more of the size and differentiated complexity of a small factory department. A structure of intermediate social magnitude began therefore to emerge. The basic pattern round which the work relationships of the longwall production unit were organized became the cycle group of 40–50 men, their shot-firer and shift 'deputies', who were responsible to the pit management for the working as a whole. Only in relation to this total cycle group could various smaller sub-groups secure function and acquire social form.

This centring of the new system on a differentiated structure of intermediate social magnitude disturbed the simple balance that had existed between the very small and very large traditional groups, and impaired the quality of responsible autonomy. The psychological and sociological problems posed by the technological needs of the longwall system were those with respect to which experience in the industry was least, and towards which its traditions were antithetical. The consequences of this conflict between the demands of the new situation and the resources available from past experience will be taken up in the light of the detailed account, which will now be presented, of the longwall system itself.

The lack of recognition of the nature of the difficulties

No new equilibrium came into being. As was mentioned in the introduction, disturbances associated with industrial struggle and economic depression have tended to mask those associated with the coal-getting method. Though perception of these latter has begun to clarify since nationalization, shortcomings such as those in the haulage system, more readily appreciated in engineering terms, continue to attract the wider attention. It is only since the morale changes accompanying recent face-work innovations have begun actually to be experienced in working groups that the nature of longwall troubles is becoming manifest. That they require understanding in social and psychological terms is something that still remains largely unrecognized. Accounts so far appearing have presented recent changes almost exclusively in engineering terms.

Anyone who has listened to the talk of older miners who have experienced in their own work-lives the change-over to the longwall cannot fail to be impressed by the confused mourning for the past that still goes on in them together with a dismay over the present coloured by despair and indignation. To the clinical worker the quality of these talks has at times a ring that is familiar. Those with rehabilitation experience will recognize it as similar to the quality of feeling expressed by rehabilitees when ventilating the aftermath in themselves of an impairment accepted as irreversible.

Expectation was widespread that something magical would happen as a result of nationalization. But as one filler put it: 'My coals don't wear any new look since Investment Day. They give me a look as black as before.' When some of these same men take on a new lease of life, perhaps exaggeratedly, after experiencing one of the new group methods and refuse to return to a conventional working having found a new spirit in themselves and their workmates, strong clues are already to hand regarding the character of longwall deficiencies. But what has been intuitively grasped has still to become articulate. So close is the relationship between the various aspects that the social and the psychological can be understood only in terms of the detailed engineering facts and of the way the technological system as a whole behaves in the environment of the underground situation. These points will be taken up in the next two Sections.

Features and difficulties of the longwall production unit as a whole[2]

The scale and spatio-temporal structure of the three-shift cycle

In the longwall method, a direct advance is made into the coal on a continuous front; faces of 180–200 yds being typical, though longer faces are not uncommon. The work is broken down into a standard series of component operations that follow each other in rigid succession over three shifts of seven and a half hours each, so that a total coal-getting cycle may be completed once in each twenty-four hours of the working week. The shift spread of the forty workmen on an average face is: ten each to the first ('cutting') and second ('ripping') shifts; twenty to the third ('filling') shift. The amount of coal scheduled for extraction varies under different conditions but is commonly in the neighbourhood of 200 tons per cycle. A medium-size pit with three seams would have 12–15 longwall faces in operation simultaneously.

These faces are laid out in districts as shown in Figure 1. Since the longwall method is specially applicable to thin seams, Figure 1 has been set up in terms of a 3-ft working. The face, extending 90

2. The procedure followed both in the text and in Figures 1 and 2 and Table 1 has been to build up a model of the system in terms of the experience of a group of faces similarly run and well known at first hand. What follows is therefore an account of one version of the system, though the version is a common one. Faces exist that are twice as long as that given. In thick seams these may require 40–50 fillers alone (even more), apart altogether from other personnel. In thin seams with high gates more than twice the number of rippers given may be employed, eight or more on the main gate and some 6–4 on the side gates respectively. On shorter faces there may be only one borer and at least one gummer. Under some conditions packing and drawing-off are separated from belt-work, and loading-point personnel are included as face workers. There are differences in nomenclature in different areas, e.g. 'dinters' for 'rippers'. Variations arise partly from differences in natural conditions (thickness of seam, hardness of coal, type of roof and floor, etc.), partly from preferences in the matter of lay-out, and partly from the amount and character of the equipment available or judged necessary. Though conveyor serviced, quite a long face may be hand-got if the coal is soft; alternatively, two cutting units may be employed if it is hard and the face exceptionally long. Belts are of several varieties ('floor', 'plate', 'top', etc.). Where the seam is thick enough to eliminate ripping an approximation may be made to a two-shift system. Productivity varies widely in accordance with these differences, as does smoothness of functioning and the degree of stress experienced. Nevertheless, all are versions of one method. The basic pattern is the same.

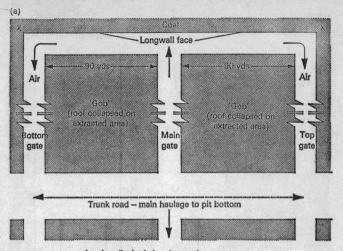

(a)

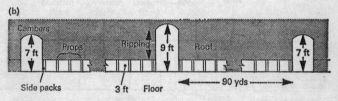

(b)

Figure 1 Layout of a district, longwall method. (a) Horizontal section. (b) Vertical section (at point X in (a))

yds on either side of the main gate is within average limits for a seam of this thickness. The height of the face area – that of the 3-ft seam itself – may be contrasted with the 9 ft and 7 ft to which the main and side gates have been ripped and built up as permanent structures with cambers and side-packs. By regulation, props must be placed every 3 ft, and the line of props shown in Figure 1b is that placed immediately against a coal-face waiting to be filled off. The area marked 'Gob' (to use a term common in mining vernacular) indicates the expanse from which the coal has already been extracted. On this area the roof is left to collapse. Only the tunnels

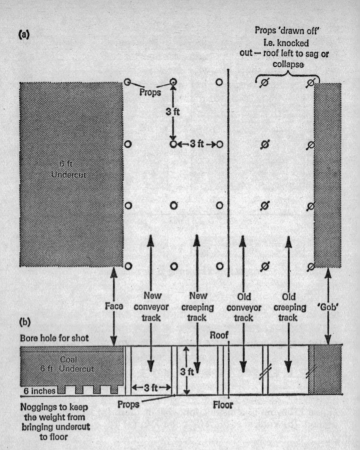

Figure 2 Coal face as set for filling shift. (a) Horizontal section.
(b) Vertical section — side elevation

made by the main and side gates, which are used for ventilation and
for haulage and travelling, are kept open. These tunnels may sometimes extend for distances of two miles, and even more, before the
coal face itself is reached from the trunk road leading from the pit
bottom.

In each coal-getting cycle the advance made into the coal is equal
to the depth of the undercut. A cut of 6 ft represents typical prac-

tice in a thin seam with a good roof. All equipment has to be moved forward as each cycle contributes to the advance. The detail in the face area is represented in Figure 2, where the coal is shown cut and waiting for the shot-firer, whose task is the last to be performed before the fillers come on. The combined width of the lanes marked 'New Creeping Track' and 'New Conveyor Track' equal the depth of 6 ft, from which the coal has been removed by the fillers on the last shift of the previous cycle. As part of the preparation work of the current cycle (before the fillers can come on again), the conveyor has to be moved from its previous position in the 'Old Conveyor Track' to its present position, shown in Figure 2, in the 'New Conveyor Track', against the face. At the same time the two lines of props on either side of the 'Old Creeping Track' are withdrawn (allowing the roof to sag or collapse) and thrown over beside the conveyor for the fillers to use in propping up their roof as they get into the next 6 ft of coal. The term 'creeping track' refers to the single, propped, 3-ft lane, adjacent to that occupied by the conveyor but on the side away from the coal. It allows free passage up and down the face, and is called a creeping track since in thin seams the low roof makes it necessary for all locomotion to take the form of 'creeping', i.e. crawling on the hands and knees.

The mass-production character of the longwall operation necessitates a large-scale, mobile layout of the type described. But the spatio-temporal structure imposed by the long face and the shift sequence makes a difficult habitat when considered as a theatre in which effective communication and good working relationships must be maintained between forty men, their shot-firer and shift deputies. On the one hand, the group is spread over 200 yds in a tunnel 2 yds wide and 1 yd high, cross-cut only by the main and side gates; on the other, it is spread over twenty-four hours and divided up in three successive shifts. The production engineer might write a simple equation: 200 tons equals forty men over 200 yds over twenty-four hours. But there are no solutions of equivalent simplicity to the psychological and social difficulties raised. For psychological and social difficulties of a new order appear when the scale of a task transcends the limits of simple spatio-temporal structure. By this is meant conditions under which those concerned can complete a job in one place at one time, i.e., the situation of the face-to-face, or singular group.

E. A. Trist and K. W. Bamforth 355

Once a job is too big for a singular group, a multiple group comes into existence, composed of a number of sub-groups of the singular type. In these differentiated organizations of intermediate social magnitude, problems of inter-group relationships are super-imposed on, and inter-act with, the intra-group tensions of the primary components. In the longwall production unit, the scale of the task introduces the contradiction of spatio-temporal disintegration as a condition of multiple group integration.

The differentiation and interdependence of tasks

Occupational roles express the relationship between a production process and the social organization of the group. In one direction, they are related to tasks, which are related to each other; in the other, to people, who are also related to each other. At workman level, there are seven of these roles in the longwall system – borer, cutter, gummer, belt-breaker, belt-builder, ripper and filler – which are linked to the component tasks of the production process. In Table 1 the functions of these seven categories in the interrelated technological and social structures are described in detail in a comprehensive table. For analytical purposes, however, it is neces-sary to treat separately these two different aspects of occupational roles; and, in this section, consideration will be given to the inter-dependence of component tasks in the production process, and to occupational roles so far as they are related to this. These tasks fall into four groups, concerned with (1) the preparation of the coal-face for shot-firing, (2) shifting the conveyor, (3) ripping and build-ing up the main and side gates and (4) moving the shot coal on to the conveyor.

The face preparation tasks are all performed on the first shift. They include boring holes for the shot-firer, with pneumatic or electrically operated drills, near the roof of the seam through to the depth of the undercut, at short distances (within each filler's 'length') along the entire expanse of face; driving the coal-cutter so that the blade or 'jib' makes an even undercut into the coal some six inches from the floor to whatever depth has been assigned, again along the entire expanse of face; taking out the six inches of coal (called the 'gummings') left in the undercut, so that the main weight of coal can drop and break freely when the shots are fired; placing supporting 'noggings' underneath it so that this weight does not cause it to sag down to the floor while the 'cut' is standing during the next shift. These tasks are performed in the order given. Three of the seven work roles are associated with their execution, two men being fully occupied boring the holes, a further two in managing the coal-cutter, and four in clearing out the undercut.

The success of the shots fired at the end of the second shift to make the coal finally ready for the filler depends on the efficiency with which each of these interdependent preparation tasks has been carried out. Bad execution of any one of them diminishes, and may even cancel out, the effect of the shots, with consequent havoc in the lengths of the particular fillers where such breakdowns have occurred. Holes bored too low leave a quantity of coal, difficult to extract, clinging to the roof after the shots have been fired. If the roof is sticky, this gives rise to 'sticky tops'. Holes not bored through to the full depth of the undercut create the condition of 'hard backs', the shots having no effect on this part of the coal. The coal-cutter only too frequently has a tendency to leave the floor and 'get up into the coal', producing an uneven cut. This means less working height for the filler, and also less wages, since his tonnage is reduced. When the 'gummings' are left in, the shot is wasted; the coal has nowhere to drop and the powder blows out of the hole (usually up the 'cutting break' in the roof) so that the mass to be extracted is left solid. Failure to insert noggings, which leads to the cut sagging down, also renders useless the services of the shot-firer.

The group of operations concerned with the conveyor involves – since forward movement is blocked by props which must be left standing – breaking up the sections of belt in the old conveyor track and building them up in the new. Each of these tasks requires two men: the belt-breakers and belt-builders. The dismantling part is done on the first shift in the wake of the cutting operation. The reasons include the necessity of shifting belt-engines and tension-ends out of the gate areas (where they are positioned when the conveyor is working) in order to allow the ripping operation to proceed. The reassembly of the conveyor is the only task performed in the face area during the second shift. Unless the conveyor is properly jointed, set close to the new face, and accurately sighted in a straight line, a further crop of difficulties arise, and frequent stoppages may interfere with filling. The most modern types of belt, e.g., floor belts, avoid the labour of breaking up and re-assembling plates. Belt-engines and tension-ends are cumbersome equipment, but they must nevertheless be shifted every day. Similarly, the last two lines of props have to be taken down and thrown forward.

The third group of tasks comprises those that entail ripping up the roof of the main and side gates to the depth of the undercut, and building them up with a stable roof and firmly packed sides so that haulage- and air-ways can advance with the face. Unless this work is expertly done, the danger of roof falls is acute, with the likelihood both of men and equipment being blocked in the face. This work is carried out by a team of 7–8 rippers.

Only when all these operations have been completed, can the shots be fired and the fillers come on. For the filling operation, the entire face is divided up into equal lengths – except that the corner positions are somewhat shorter in view of difficulties created by the proximity of belt-engines and tension-ends. In a 3-ft seam, lengths would be 8–10 yds, and some twenty fillers would be required, ten in each half-face of 90–100 yds. Each filler is required to extract the entire coal from his length, going back to the depth of the 6 ft undercut. When he has thrown his last load on to the conveyor he has 'filled off', i.e., finished his 'length' or 'stint'. As he progresses into his coal, he has the additional task of propping up his roof every 3 ft. As well as a handpick and shovel, his tool kit includes an air pick, used for dealing with some of the difficulties created by bad preparation, or in any case when his coal is hard.

At a later point there will be a discussion of the differential distribution of bad conditions among the lengths of a face. Here it may be noted that the face is not 'filled off' until each and every length has been cleared, and that until this has been done, the new cycle cannot begin. Disorganization on the filling shift disorganizes the subsequent shifts, and its own disorganization is often produced by the bad preparation left by these teams. Every time the cycle is stopped, some two hundred tons of coal are lost.

So close is the task interdependence that the system becomes vulnerable from its need for one hundred per cent performance at each step. The most sensitive interaction is between the face-preparation activities and filling, but it is in relation to this that social organization is weakest. This point will be taken up in later sections.

With respect to the way in which the work roles have been institutionalized as regards the persons and groups concerned, a basic segregation of the various categories of workers from each other follows from the fact that it has been the traditional practice for a face-worker to be trained in only one of the seven roles, and to spend all or most of his underground life in this one occupation. This basic segregation of roles is intensified by the five different methods of payment described in Table 1, and by the exaggeration of status differences, despite the common background of 'underground skill' and the equivalence of earnings (apart from the rather lower rate received by the gummers).

It is still further reinforced by the segregation of shifts. As will be seen from the shift time-tables, the three shifts never meet. Moreover, the two preparation groups alternate on the so-called 'back shifts' while the fillers alternate on 'days' and 'afternoons', so that a far-reaching community, as well as work, split is effected between the fillers and the others. The 'back shift' men are either going to or coming from work in the evening, so that they are cut off from normal community activities during the week. Even at weekends they are down the pit either on Saturday afternoon or Sunday evening.

As regards the primary work groups in which those performing the various roles participate, there are four radically different patterns: the series of interdependent pairs – borers, belt-builders and belt-breakers; the extended pair organization of the cutters and gummers; the self-sufficient group of eight rippers; and the aggregate of twenty fillers spread out over the 200-yd face. The uneven social quality of these different types of primary group will be discussed in sections V–VII [not included], both with respect to intra- and inter-group relations. This unevenness, taken together with the role and shift segregation, works against the social integration of the cycle group as a whole. Yet, in view of the close interdependence of tasks, the social integration of the total work group is a first essential of the system.

It is submitted that the non-existence of the cycle group as a social whole in face of the interdependence of the component tasks is one of the major contradictions present in the longwall method. The social organization is a simple reflection of the 'job break-

Table 1 Occupational Structure in the Longwall System

Shift sequence	Occupational roles of men	No. of men	Methods of payment	Group organization	Tasks	Skills	Status differences and ranking
First (usually called 'cutting' shift). Either night, 8 p.m.–3.30 a.m., or afternoon, 12 noon–7.30 p.m. (borers start an hour earlier). Though alternating between night and afternoon, personnel on the cutting shift are never on days.	Borer	2	Per hole	Inter-dependent pair on same note.	Boring holes for shot-firer in each stint to depth of undercut.	Management of electric or pneumatic drills, placing of holes, judgement of roof, hardness of coal, etc.	4–5, equal in pair.
	Cutter	2	Per yard	Inter-dependent pair on same note, front man and back man.	Operating coal-cutter to achieve even cut at assigned depth the entire length of the face; knocking out (front man) re-setting (back man) props as cutter passes. Back man inserts noggings.	Requires rather more 'engineering' skill than other coal-face tasks. Mining skills in keeping cut even under changing conditions, watching roof control.	1, front man senior and responsible for cut; back man assists; cutting is the key preparation task.
	Gummer	4	Day wage	Loose group attached to cutters, though front man without supervisory authority.	Cleaning out undercut, so that clear space for coal to drop and level floor for filler. The coal between undercut and floor is called "the gummings".	Unskilled, heavy manual task, which unless conscientiously done creates difficulties for filler, for when gummings left in, the shot simply blows out and coal is left solid.	7, equal in group; some chance of promotion to cutter eventually.
	Belt-breaker	2	Per yard	Inter-dependent pair on same note.	Shifting belt-engine and tension-end into face clear of rippers; breaking up conveyor in old track, placing plates, etc., ready in new track, drawing off props in old creeping track; some packing as required.	Belt-breaking is a relatively simple engineering task; engine shifting is awkward and heavy; drawing off and packing involve responsibility for roof control and require solid underground experience.	4–5, equal in pair.

Role	No.	Payment	Relationships	Task	Skill and responsibilities	Status/earnings
Belt-builder	2	Per yard	Interdependent pair on same note.	Reassembling conveyor in new track; positioning belt-engine and tension-end in line with this; testing running of reassembled conveyor; placing chocks; packing as required.	As with breaking, the level of engineering skill is relatively simple; inconvenience caused to fillers if belt out of position. The roof control responsibilities demand solid underground experience.	4-5, equal in pair.
Ripper	8	Cubic measure	Cohesive functionally inter-related group on same note.	To 'rip', 'dirt' out of main and side gates to assigned heights; place cambers and build up roof into a solid, safe and durable structure; pack-up the sides. The ripping team carries out all operations necessary to their task, doing their own boring. The task is a complete job in itself, seen through by the group within the compass of one shift.	This work requires the highest degree of building skill among coal face tasks. Some very heavy labour is entailed. Since the work is relatively permanent there is much price of craft. On the ripper depends the safety of all gates and main ways.	2, the status of the 'main ripper' is next to that of the front man or the cutter, but he is not separately paid. The group usually contains all degrees of experience and is egalitarian.
Filler	20	Weight-tonnage on conveyors	Aggregate of individuals with equal 'stints'; all on same note; fractionated relationships and much isolation.	The length of the 'stint' is determined by the depth of the cut and the thickness of the seam. Using hand or air pick and shovel, the filler 'throws' the 'shot' coal on to the conveyor until he has cleared his length, i.e. 'filled off'. He props up every 2 ft 6 in as he works in.	The filler remains in one work place while conditions change. Considerable underground experience is required to cope with bad conditions. Each man is responsible for his own section of roof. Bad work on other shifts makes the task harder. It is heavy in any case and varies in different parts of the wall.	4-5, equal throughout the group; 'corner' men are envied, reputation of being good or bad workman is important.
40 men	5 methods	4 types		The common background of 'underground' skill is more important than the task differences.		Differences in status and weekly earnings are small, apart from the case of the gunmers.
7 roles						
3 shifts						

Second (usually called the 'ripping' shift). Either *night* or *afternoon* alternating with cutting shift. Rippers may start rather later than builders. None of these personnel go on *day* shift proper.

Third (usually called 'filling' shift). Either *day*, 6 a.m.–1.30 p.m., or *afternoon*, 2 p.m.–9.30 p.m. Never *night*.

down'. Because this latter is reintegrated into a technological whole by the task sequence it does not follow that the differentiated role-groups concerned are also and thereby reintegrated into a social whole. Differentiation gives rise to the need for social as well as technological integration. No attempt seems to have been made in the longwall method to achieve any living social integration of the primary and shift groups into which the cycle aggregate has been differentiated. This, of course, is a common omission in mass-production systems.

The stress of mass production in the underground situation
The interaction of bad conditions and bad work

Differentiated, rigidly sequenced work systems, organized on mass-production lines to deal with large quantities of material on a multi-shift cycle, are a basic feature of the factory pattern. Even in the factory situation, their maintenance at a level which allows full and continuous realization of their technological potentialities creates a difficult problem of industrial management. In the under-ground situation these difficulties are of a higher order, it being virtually impossible to establish the kind of constant background to the task that is taken for granted in the factory. A very large variety of unfavourable and changing environmental conditions is encountered at the coal-face, many of which are impossible to predict. Others, though predictable, are impossible to alter.

The factory and underground situations are different with respect to the 'figure-ground' relationship of the production process to its environmental background. In the factory a comparatively high degree of control can be exercised over the complex and moving 'figure' of a production sequence, since it is possible to maintain the 'ground' in a comparatively passive and constant state. But at the coal face, there is always present the threat of some untoward activity in the 'ground'. The internal organization of the task 'figure' is therefore much more liable to disorganization. The instability of the 'ground' limits the applicability in the under-ground situation of methods derived from the factory.

Unfavourable natural conditions, as distinct from 'bad work' – which is the result of human shortcomings – are referred to as 'bad conditions'. Some of the most dreaded, such as wet, heat, or dust, are permanent features of the working environment of certain faces.

But others, less known outside the industry, may also make the production tasks of the face-worker both difficult and dangerous, even though the seam in which he is working is well ventilated, cool, and dry without being dusty. Rolls or faults may appear in the seam. Control may be lost over the roof for considerable periods. Especially in the middle of a long face, certain types of roof are apt to sag down. Changes may occur in the floor; the condition known as 'rising floor' being not uncommon. Since some of these conditions [descriptions not included in this reading] reduce working height, their appearance is particularly troublesome in thin seams. If the difference between working in 5 ft 6 in and 5 ft may be of small account, that between working in 3 ft and 2 ft 6 in may often produce intolerable conditions. Loss of roof-control is serious, whatever the working height. In general, bad conditions mean not only additional danger but additional labour. The need to insert packs to support a loose roof is a common example.

Special tasks of any kind, over and above the specific production operation for which a given category of face-worker receives his basic pay, are known as 'bye-work'. Though many bye-work tasks have gained the status of specially remunerated activities, the rates are such that the overall wage received at the end of a week during which a good deal of bye-work has been necessary is less than that which would have been received had the whole of the five shifts been available for production work. From the face-worker's point of view, bad conditions mean not only more danger and harder work but less pay; and they may also compel overtime. To stay behind an hour or sometimes three hours longer under bad conditions may involve a degree of hardship beyond the capacity of many face-workers to endure, especially if they are older, and if overtime demands are repeated in close succession.

'Bad conditions' tend to instigate 'bad work'. When they occur, the smooth sequence of tasks in the production cycle is more likely to be disturbed by faulty performance. Bad work can, and does, arise when conditions are good, from personal shortcomings and social tensions, in themselves independent of bad conditions; but difficulties arising from human failings are more readily – and conveniently – expressed when the additional difficulty, and excuse, of bad conditions is also present. The result is a tendency for circular causal processes of a disruptive character to be touched off. Unless rapidly checked by special measures, often of an emergency character, these, once started, threaten to culminate in the fillers not filling off, and the cycle being stopped. The system is therefore always to some extent working against the threat of its own break-down, so that tension and anxiety are created.

The magnification of local disturbances

Under these conditions, the closeness of the functional inter-dependence of tasks tends to rebound on itself. Mistakes and diffi-culties made or encountered at one stage are carried forward, producing yet other difficulties in the next. The inflexible character of the succession gives no scope for proceeding with later tasks when hold-ups have occurred earlier, and the temporal extension of the cycle increases the likelihood of interference from unpre-dictable events, which are provided with twenty-four hours in which to occur. The aspects of mass-production engineering methods (rigid sequence, functional interdependence and spatio-temporal extension), which create vulnerability in the underground situation, all stem from the large-scale character of the longwall cycle. For it is the magnitude of the cycle, produced by the long expanse of face scheduled for clearance, that leads to the segre-gated treatment of the component tasks – in view of the large amount of work required on each – and thence to their fixed, extended succession. In an organization of this scale, local disturb-ances at specific points – resulting from the interaction of bad conditions and bad work – resonate through a relatively large social space, becoming magnified for this reason.

Stricter field-theory formulation may assist the more dynamic description of this situation. The size of the bounded region in which the system exists as a whole, together with the high degree of differentiation in its unidirectional internal connectedness, first increases the number of points at which small disturbances may occur, and thereafter enlarges the scope of their effects to a scale proportional to the magnitude of the whole. Since these effects must be contained within a closed system, single events are, as the result of induction which takes place from the power field of the whole, endowed with the potentiality of disrupting the cycle. No matter that this potentiality is realized only in the extreme case;

disturbance is always experienced to some extent under pressure of this potentiality. Stress arising from this pressure itself produces fresh disturbances. Measures necessary to prevent these from still further spreading absorb a correspondingly greater amount of the available concern and energy.

Variations in the level of functioning

It has been mentioned that a characteristic of bad conditions and bad work is their uneven distribution – not only between different faces, but also over different sections and among different tasks within the same face. The consequence is an uneven level of functional efficiency, more generally lowered also by the magnified resonances and induced pressures described above. The atmosphere of uncertainty thus created arouses the expectation in the individual that bad work done by someone else will increase his own difficulties, or that some untoward event will occur to keep him down at the end of his shift. The resulting attitudes and suspicions are ingrained in the culture of the longwall work group and adversely affect the entire pattern of relationships at the coal-face.

No systematic survey of the incidence of cycle stoppages was possible within the limits of the present study. But on one of the best faces known at first hand by the writers it was a matter of self-congratulation that the fillers had failed to fill off only three times during the past year. Experienced informants gave once in two months, or five or six times during the course of a year, as a more usual frequency, with instances of many more stoppages in 'bad faces' in 'bad pits'. If one week's work is commonly lost in this way during a year, the overall loss in production would amount to some 2 per cent. This relatively low figure expresses the extent of the efforts made to check disturbances short of the point where the cycle is stopped.

The strain of cycle control

The main burden of keeping down the number of cycle stoppages falls on the deputy, who is the only person in the face area with cycle, as distinct from task, responsibility. Discussion with groups of deputies readily yields evidence of the strain involved. A common and reality-based complaint is that the authority of the deputy is incommensurate with responsibility of this order. The background to this complaint is the fact, noted in the discussion of the hand-got systems, that, in view of the darkness and the spread out character of the work, there is no possibility of close supervision. Responsibility for seeing to it that bad work is not done, however bad the conditions, rests with the face-workers themselves. But the responsible autonomy of some, especially, of the occupational sub-groups has been impaired in the longwall method. This problem will be taken up in succeeding sections.

As a result, management complain of lack of support from the men, who are accused of being concerned only with their own fractional tasks and unwilling to take broader cycle responsibility. The parallel complaint of the workers is of being driven and tricked by management, who are resented as outsiders – intermittent visitors and 'stick' men, who interfere without sharing the hard, physical work and in-group life of the face. On occasions, for example, the deputy is reduced to bargaining with the men as to whether they will agree to carry out essential bye-work. The complaint of the men is that deputies' promises are rarely kept, and that they have gone unpaid too often to be again easily persuaded. The deputy's answer is that the under-manager or manager has refused to uphold his case. Whether he presented it, how he presented it, or what reasons may have dictated the managerial view are a type of issue on which effective communication back to the man breaks down. The deputy has equally little chance of increasing the insight of the workmen into their own tendency to drive sharp bargains.

The strain of cycle control tends to produce a group 'culture' of angry and suspicious bargaining over which both management and men are in collusion. There is displacement both upwards and downwards of the tensions generated. The 'hell' that breaks loose in the under-manager's office when news comes in that the fillers are unlikely to fill off in one or more faces resounds through the pit.

The norm of low productivity

In all work at the coal-face two distinct tasks are simultaneously present; those that belong to the production cycle being always to some extent carried out on the background of a second activity arising from the need to contend with interferences, actual or threatened, emanating from the underground situation. The activity of the 'ground' has always to be dealt with, and ability to contend with this second or background task comprises the common fund of underground skill shared alike by all experienced face-workers. This common skill is of a higher order than that required simply to carry out, as such, any of the operations belonging to the production cycle. For these, initial training is short, and may be measured in months; it is longest for those, such as cutting, where the engineering component is largest. But the specifically mining skill of contending with underground conditions, and of maintaining a high level of performance when difficulties arise, is developed only as the result of several years of experience at the face. A work-system basically appropriate to the underground situation requires to have built into its organization the findings of this experience. Unless this has been done, it will not only fail to engage the face-worker to the limit of his capabilities, but will restrict him to a level of performance below his potentiality.

The evidence suggests that the longwall method acts in this way. The crises of cycle stoppages and the stress of the deputy's role are but symptoms of a wider situation characterized by the establishment of a norm of low productivity, as the only adaptive method of handling, in the contingencies of the underground situation, a complicated, rigid, and large-scale work system, borrowed with too little modification from an engineering culture appropriate to the radically different situation of the factory. At the time the long-wall method developed, there were no precedents for the adaptive underground application of a machine technology. In the absence of relevant experience in the mining tradition itself it was almost inevitable that heavy culture-borrowing of this kind should have taken place. There was also no psychological or sociological knowledge in existence at that time which might have assisted in lessening the difficulties.

[...]

Conclusions

The fact that the desperate economic incentives of the between-war period no longer operate means a greater intolerance of unsatisfying or difficult working conditions, or systems of organization, among miners, even though they may not always be clear as to the exact nature of the resentment or hostility which they often appear to feel. The persistence of socially ineffective structures at the coal-face is likely to be a major factor in preventing a rise of morale, in discouraging recruitment, and in increasing labour turnover.

The innovations in social organization of face-work groups, which have begun to appear, and the success of some of these developments, suggest that the organizational changes brought about by nationalization provide a not inappropriate opportunity for the experimental working through of problems of the types which have been indicated. It can certainly be said with some confidence that within the industry there exist the necessary resources and creativity to allow widespread constructive developments to take place.

As regards the longwall system, the first need is for systematic study and evaluation of the changes so far tried.[3] It seems to the present writers, however, that a qualitative change will have to be effected in the general character of the method, so that a social as well as a technological whole can come into existence. Only if this is achieved can the relationships of the cycle work-group be successfully integrated and a new social balance be created.

The immediate problems are to develop formal small-group organization on the filling shift and to work out an acceptable solution to the authority questions in the cutting team. But it is difficult to see how these problems can be solved effectively without restoring responsible autonomy to primary groups throughout the system and ensuring that each of these groups has a satisfying sub-whole as its work task, and some scope for flexibility in work-pace. Only if this is done will the stress of the deputy's role be reduced and his task of maintaining the cycle receive spontaneous support from the primary work groups.

It is likely that any attempts in this direction would require to take advantage of the recent trend of training face-workers for more than one role, so that interchangeability of tasks would be possible within work teams. Moreover, the problem of shift segregation will not be overcome until the situation is altered in which one large group is permanently organized round the day shift and the others round the back shifts. Some interchange

3. One of the most interesting of these is W. V. Sheppard, 'An Experiment in Continuous Longwall Mining at Bolsover Colliery', The Institution of Mining Engineers, Annual General Meeting, Jan. 1951.

between roles in preparation and filling tasks would seem worth consideration. Once preparation workers and fillers could experience each other's situations, mutual understanding and tolerance would be likely to increase.

It is to be borne in mind that developments in room-and-pillar methods appear to be stressing the value of the strongly-knit primary work-group and that the most recent advances in mechanization, such as power loaders or strippers, both require work teams of this kind.

References

BION, W. R. (1949), 'Experiences in groups, III', *Human Relations*, vol. 2, no. 1, pp. 13–22.

HALLIDAY, J. L. (1949), *Psychosocial Medicine: A Study of the Sick Society*, Heinemann.

Further Reading

General

J. G. March (ed.), *Handbook of Organizations*, Rand McNally, 1965.
D. S. Pugh, 'Modern organization theory', *Psychological Bulletin*,
vol. 66, 1966, no. 4, pp. 235–51.

The Structure of Organization

T. Burns and G. M. Stalker, *The Management of Innovation*,
2nd edn, Tavistock, 1968.
D. Cartwright and A. Zander (eds.), *Group Dynamics: Research
and Theory*, 3rd edn, Tavistock, 1968.
H. H. Gerth and C. W. Mills (eds.), *From Max Weber: Essays in
Sociology*, Routledge, 1947.
J. G. March and H. A. Simon, *Organizations*, Wiley, 1958.
W. H. Starbuck (ed.), *Organizational Growth and Development*,
Penguin, 1971.
M. Weber, *Theory of Social and Economic Organization*, Free
Press, 1947.
J. Woodward, *Industrial Organization: Theory and Practice*, Oxford
University Press, 1965.
J. Woodward (ed.), *Industrial Organization: Behaviour and Control*,
Oxford University Press, 1970.

The Management of Organizations

H. I. Ansoff (ed.), *Business Strategy*, Penguin, 1969.
C. I. Barnard, *The Functions of The Executive*, Harvard University
Press, 1938.
C. I. Barnard, *Organization and Management*, Harvard University
Press, 1948.
M. B. Brodie, *Fayol on Administration*, Lyon, Grant and
Green, 1967.
A. D. Chandler, *Strategy and Structure*, MIT Press, 1962.
R. M. Cyert and J. G. March, *A Behavioral Theory of the Firm*,
Prentice-Hall, 1963.
H. Fayol, *General and Industrial Management*, Pitman, 1949.
G. Friedmann, *Industrial Society*, Free Press, 1955.
M. P. Follett, *Dynamic Administration*, Longman, 1941.

H. A. Simon, *Administrative Behavior*, 2nd edn, Macmillan Co., 1960.

H. A. Simon, *The New Science of Management Decision*, Harper & Row, 1960.

H. A. Simon, *The Shape of Automation*, Harper & Row, 1965.

A. P. Sloan, *My Years with General Motors*, Pan, 1967.

F. W. Taylor, *Scientific Management*, Harper & Row, 1947.

Behaviour in Organizations

L. A. Allen, *Management and Organization*, McGraw-Hill, 1958.

C. Argyris, *Understanding Organizational Behaviour*, Dorsey, 1960.

C. Argyris, *Organization and Innovation*, Irwin, 1965.

R. Bendix, *Work and Authority in Industry*, Wiley, 1956.

A. Brown, *Organization of Industry*, Prentice-Hall, 1947.

J. A. C. Brown, *The Social Psychology of Industry*, Penguin, 1954.

R. J. Cordiner, *New Frontiers for Professional Managers*, McGraw-Hill, 1956.

R. Dubin, *The World of Work: Industrial Society and Human Relations*, Prentice-Hall, 1958.

F. E. Emery (ed.), *Systems Thinking*, Penguin, 1969.

H. Fayol, *General and Industrial Administration*, Pitman, 1949.

G. Friedmann, *Industrial Society: The Emergence of the Human Problems of Automation*, Free Press, 1955.

F. Herzberg, *Work and the Nature of Man*, World Publishing Co., 1966.

F. Herzberg, 'One more time: How do you motivate employees?', *Harvard Business Review*, January–February 1968, pp. 53–62.

F. Herzberg, B. Mausner and B. B. Snyderman, *The Motivation to Work*, Wiley, 1959.

A. W. Gouldner, *Patterns of Industrial Bureaucracy*, Free Press, 1954.

H. Koontz and C. O'Donnell, *Principles of Management*, McGraw-Hill, 1955.

D. Krech and R. S. Crutchfield, *Theory and Problems of Social Psychology*, McGraw-Hill, 1948.

H. J. Leavitt, *Managerial Psychology*, University of Chicago Press, 1958.

K. Lewin, *Resolving Social Conflict: selected papers on Group Dynamics*, Harper, 1948.

K. Lewin, *Field Theory in Social Science*, Harper & Row, 1951.

R. Likert, *New Patterns of Management*, McGraw-Hill, 1961.

R. Likert, *The Human Organization: its Management and Value*, McGraw-Hill, 1967.

D. McGregor, *The Human Side of Enterprise*, McGraw-Hill, 1960.

D. McGregor, *The Professional Manager*, McGraw-Hill, 1967.

R. N. McMurry, 'The case for benevolent autocracy', *Harvard Business Review*, vol. 36, 1958, no. 1, January–February.

A. H. Maslow, *Motivation and Personality*, Harper & Row, 1954.

E. Mayo, *The Human Problems of an Industrial Civilisation*, Macmillan, 1933.

E. Mayo, *The Social Problems of an Industrial Civilisation*, Routledge, 1949.

A. K. Rice, *Productivity and Social Organizations: The Ahmedabad Experiment*, Tavistock, 1958.

F. J. Roethlisberger and W. J. Dickson, *Management and the Worker*, Harvard University Press, 1949.

R. Stagner, *The Psychology of Industrial Conflict*, Wiley, 1956.

E. L. Trist and K. W. Bamforth, 'Some social and psychological consequences of the longwall method of coal-getting', *Human Relations*, 1951, no. 4, pp. 3–38.

E. L. Trist *et al.*, *Organizational Choice*, Tavistock, 1963.

L. Urwick, *The Elements of Administration*, Harper & Row, 1944.

V. H. Vroom and E. L. Deci (eds.), *Management and Motivation*, Penguin, 1970.

C. R. Walker, *Toward the Automatic Factory*, Yale University Press, 1957.

W. F. Whyte, *Money and Motivation*, Harper & Row, 1955.

A. Zaleznik, C. R. Christensen and F. J. Roethlisberger, *The Motivation, Productivity, and Satisfaction of Workers: A Prediction Study*, Division of Research, The Graduate School of Business Administration, Harvard University, 1958.

Acknowledgements

Permission to reprint the Readings in this volume is
acknowledged to the following sources:

1 Free Press
2 John Wiley & Sons, Inc.
3 Tom Burns
4 Her Majesty's Stationery Office
5 American Psychological Association, and H. J. Leavitt
6 Pitman & Sons, Ltd
7 Harper & Row Publishers, Inc.
8 Pitman & Sons Ltd and Harper & Row Publishers, Inc.
9 Harvard University Press
10 Doubleday & Co. Inc., and Sidgwick & Jackson, Ltd
11 Harper & Row Publishers, Inc.
12 Routledge & Kegan Paul Ltd and Division of Research, Harvard
   University Graduate School of Business Administration
13 Journal Press, and R. Lippitt and R. K. White
14 Tavistock Publications Ltd, and C. Argyris
15 McGraw-Hill Book Co.
16 McGraw-Hill Book Co.
17 World Publishing Co. and MacGibbon & Kee Ltd
18 Plenum Publishing Co.

Author Index

Subject Index

Aggression, 230–59
  and cultural environment, 256, 257
  field theoretic approach to, 256
  and leadership style, 230–59
  and rigidity of group structure, 254, 255
  and tension, 252
Authority
  and bureaucracy, 15–29
  charismatic, 15, 16
  delegation, 35
  depersonalization of, 154, 155, 156
  levels of, and technology, 65
  and liberty, 159, 160
  and order giving, 147–59
  origins of, 15 *et seq.*
  as principle of management, 101, 103
  rational–legal, 15, 17–22
  and responsibility, 103, 209
  the scalar principle of, 18, 115–17
  traditional, 15, 16
  visibility of, 39
Authoritarian leadership, 153, 154, 230–59
  and aggression, 230–59
  and aggression against objects, 249
  and apathy, 250
  and frustration, 243
  and group climate, 238–42
  and hostility, 236
  and scapegoating, 237–8
Automation, 197–212
  and authority, 209

and decision making, 197–212
and division of labour, 199–202
and job satisfaction, 200
and motivation, 208
and organizational design, 202–12
rate of introduction, 198
and unemployment, 198

Bonus payments, 110
Bureaucracy, 15–29
  and capitalism, 26
  and the Catholic Church, 22
  and communications, 27
  conflict among subunits of, 36
  and decision making, 33
  and delegation of authority, 35
  development of industrial society, 44–6
  dysfunctions of, 30–41, 47
  and formalism, 28
  general model of, 31
  ideal type of, 15, 16
  and individual personality, 31, 32, 33
  legal basis of, 15–29
  and legitimate authority, 15–29
  monocratic, 25
  need for, 25
  and official secrets, 27
  patrimonial, 23
  principle of hierarchy, 18
  and revolution, 26
  rules and norms of, 18, 19
  sphere of competence, 18
  the 'spirit' of, 28
  social consequences of, 28
  and socialism, 27